**For Reference**

Not to be taken from this room

# *The* PHASES *of* JEWISH HISTORY

*Philip Ginsbury* • *Raphael Cutler*

DEVORA PUBLISHING

**THE PHASES OF JEWISH HISTORY**

Published by DEVORA PUBLISHING COMPANY

Text Copyright © 2005 by Philip Ginsbury and Raphael Cutler
Editor: Toby Weissman
Cover and Book Design: Benjie Herskowitz

Hard Cover ISBN: 1-932687-48-3
Soft Cover   ISBN: 1-932687-49-1

Email: sales@devorapublishing.com
Web Site: www.devorapublishing.com

Printed in Israel

To Allegra Cutler

# Acknowledgments

The authors would like to thank Yaacov Peterseil of Devora Publishing Company for his constant encouragement and faith in our project.

To Eva Cohen for her splendid rendition of the charts and maps in this book. To Toby Weissman for her meticulous attention to detail and her careful review of every aspect of this work.

And to Benjie Herskowitz, who designed this book with an eye towards making it reader-friendly and visually pleasing.

# Contents

*continued on next page*

# FOREWORD
# by Sir Martin Gilbert

Philip Ginsbury, and my cousin Raphael Cutler, have done a great service. All Jews, and many non-Jews, will be grateful to them for their unusual, thought-provoking perspective on Jewish history. Many writers and historians, including the author of this Foreword, have laboured in the extra-oridinarily fertile vineyard of Jewish history, seeking to write within a single volume a concise history of the Jewish people and their faith. Others, like Heinrich Graetz, Simon Dubnow and Salo Baron, have produced multi-volume works of millions of words.

We Jews are known as "The People of the Book", that book being the Biblical narrative with all its richness. That book, the authors write, is the source of both the faith and precepts that have always accompanied and defined the Jewish people, "and which spans time." We are also a people who love to write books, just as our ancestors created a wealth of commentaries on the original, holy text.

It is good that the authors of this book followed their inclination, and persevered to the end. Their approach strikes me as a sound, and indeed a profound one: the recurring phenomenon – they trace eight phases in almost four millennia – of near destruction and miraculous renewal. The first seven phases take us to 1500, the final phase from 1500 to the year 2000. How the pattern of threat and survival came about: the personalities involved, and the meaning behind the drama, are the theme and attraction of the book.

It is on the personalities, many of them great rabbis and sages, that the authors throw particular light, convinced – as all readers will be after reading this book – that "individuals can shape history no less than movements and economic and social factors". There is much to be learned about those individuals in these pages: of perseverance, of courage, and of faith. This is not only history with a human face, but with a deep understanding of the religious imperatives that sustained a people in exile and enabled them to survive enemies and pressures that brought many other ancient peoples to the dust. It is the story of the triumph of the spirit, as sustained by men of integrity and vision.

# Preface

It is commonly observed that civilizations, no less than plants and animals, pass through the stages of birth, growth and decline. The moon also waxes and wanes, except that its cycles are endless, for which reason it has long served as a paradigm of Jewish history. The Jews, at certain critical periods in their past, have been separated from destruction by the narrowest of margins, yet have always miraculously survived to renew the process of national rebirth and rejuvenation. It is possible, in almost four millennia of Jewish history, to trace eight such phases. Each of the eight chapters of this book is devoted to one epoch.

Maimonides (Laws of Idolatry, chapter one) alludes to the phenomenon of decay and rebirth, in the spiritual sense, when he writes that the monotheistic ideal had all but disappeared when Abraham reintroduced it to mankind. It had all but disappeared a second time, centuries later, when it was reintroduced by Moses. David revived national fortunes at a later critical period, and the Talmud takes up the theme by stating that the Torah was in danger of being forgotten in successive epochs, until first Ezra and later Hillel came from Babylon to restore it (Sukkah 20b).

In round figures, the time span between Abraham and the end of the biblical period totalled 1500 years, divided into three main periods and delineated by the lives of Abraham, Moses, David and Ezra. The approximate 500 year time spans continued in post-Biblical history, with Hillel active around the beginning of the Common Era, and the compilation of the Talmud in about 500 C.E., associated mainly with Rav Ashi, which preserved national unity as the Jews became a people of the Diaspora.

Jewish fortunes were at a particularly low ebb around the year 1000 C.E., with the decline of the Babylonian center and the effective end of its great academies. Yet conforming to the pattern of decline and rebirth, a new center arose in Northern Europe to take its place, headed by Rashi. Around 1500 C.E., the Jews were expelled from the Iberian peninsula, bringing to an end another major center of Jewish culture and another epoch. Among other places of refuge, some of the exiles eventually reached Safed in Galilee, including R. Joseph Karo. The spiritual light he and other famous contemporaries created there reached Eastern Europe, where it sustained Jewish life until that center was destroyed during the atrocities of World War II. Immediately after the war, the land of Israel again became the scene of national regeneration.

The centrality of the land of Israel and the exposition of Judaism by its leading scholars are the two themes that run like golden threads through every epoch of Jewish history, providing continuity from the very beginning to the present day. The Bible, Midrash, Mishnah, Jerusalem Talmud, liturgical compositions, Masorah and the Shulchan Aruch were all compiled in the Holy Land. Abraham, Ezra, Hillel and Joseph Karo all made it their eventual destination. Moses led the Exodus from Egypt to journey there, and David made Jerusalem its eternal capital and established its borders. Although Rav Ashi and Rashi did not live in the Holy Land, their great works of achievement were based on its scholarship.

It is not surprising therefore that the moments of national rebirth traced in this book coincide largely with the account of new phases in Jewish scholarship inaugurated in, or influenced by the ancient Jewish homeland. For without their religion, and a knowledge of its requirements, the Jews could never have outlived the empires that so often persecuted them. Yet it should be stressed that although there are periods of rejuvenation, as far as Jewish scholarship is concerned, there is an overall diminution in authority. Thus the scholars of any given period are considered less authoritative than those of the preceding one, but more so than those that follow. This is based on the principle that those who lived closer in time to the source of Jewish tradition, namely to the period of Moses, Sinai and the prophets, are considered more knowledgeable and possessed of greater understanding than their successors.

In addition to time, place and circumstances are also determining factors in tracing the chain of tradition. The prophets of the first Temple period are considered second only to Moses, because they lived when the Jews were an independent nation in their own land, and conditions were conducive to prophecy. Less sublime than the era of prophecy was the period brought to a close by the compilation of the Mishnah. Although the sages still lived in the Holy Land, conditions were invariably influenced by the successive empires of Persia, Greece and Rome from without, and by the Hellenisers, Sadducees and Hasmonean kings from within.

As the center of scholarship passed from the Holy Land to Babylon, the compilation of the Talmud and the period of the Geonim marked further distinctive stages, when scholars of the later periods deferred to those who preceded. The pattern was continued in the periods of the earlier and later Authorities, as the number of diaspora centers increased even further. Although many were brought to a tragic end in the Holocaust, they live on in name and influence in present-day Israel.

Subsequently even present-day scholars of Jewish law are in effect the latest link in a chain of tradition that stretches back thousands of years in time, to Moses the lawgiver himself, preserving Jewish knowledge and Judaism's very existence until the Messianic Era.

Decline, as stated at the beginning of this introduction, is an inevitable law of nature, whether for plants, animals or civilizations. But whereas for so many other peoples decline has been a prelude to national extinction, for the Jews it has merely been a prelude to rebirth and rejuvenation. This is one of the unique features of Jewish existence.

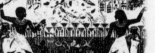

## 2000 B.C.E.

### ABRAHAM
**THE PATRIARCHS**

Teachers of Monotheism

**HAMMURABI'S LAWS**

Hittite & Egyptian Empires

**DECLINE OF EGYPTIAN POWER**

**1**

## 1500 B.C.E.

### MOSES
JUDGES

Earlier Prophets

BEGINNING OF PHILISTINE SETTLEMENTS

Spread of Mediterranean Civilization

**2**

## 1000 B.C.E.

### DAVID
KINGS

Later Prophets

RISE OF PHOENICIAN TRADE

Mesopotamian Empires

END OF BIBLICAL PERIOD

**3**

## 500 B.C.E.

### EZRA
ZUGOTH

Joint leaders of the Sanhedrin and the rule of the Wise

BEGINNING OF ROMAN REPUBLIC

Spread of Hellenism

END OF ROMAN REPUBLIC

**4**

## 0

### HILLEL
TALMUDIC PERIOD

Compilation of the Oral Law

BEGINNING OF ROMAN EMPIRE

Spread of Christianity

END OF ROMAN EMPIRE

**5**

## 500 C.E.

### RAV ASHI
THE GEONIM

Heads of the Babylonian Academies

BEGINNING OF MIDDLE AGES

Spread of Islam

DECLINE OF BAGHDAD CALIPHATE

**6**

## 1000 C.E.

### RASHI
THE RISHONIM

Earlier Authorities: Commentators & Codifiers of Talmudic Law

HOLY ROMAN EMPIRE

Crusades

END OF MIDDLE AGES

**7**

## 1500 C.E.

### JOSEPH KARO
THE ACHARONIM

Later Authorities: Commentators & Compilers of the Halacha

RENAISSANCE & REFORMATION

Spread of Western Civilization

END OF OTTOMAN EMPIRE RETURN TO ZION

**8**

## 2000 C.E.

**2000 B.C.E.**
*Abraham*

**290 years**

Abraham re-stated the teaching of monotheism when it was in danger of disappearing. He thereby became the spiritual ancestor of all those who believe in a single God, and the ancestor of the Jewish people in particular, through his descendants Isaac and Jacob.

Abraham left his birth place in Ur of the Chaldees for the Land of Canaan, which was subsequently promised to him in a covenant. The covenant was renewed with Isaac and Jacob and bound them and their descendants in all generations to a single God and a Promised Land.

In addition to the covenant, which is a unique feature of Jewish history, each of the Patriarchs made formal acts of acquisition, to give legal sanction to their ownership of the Land.

Possession of the fertile valley between the rivers Tigris and Euphrates from where Abraham emigrated was always a source of rivalry in the ancient world. Hamurabi, who may have been a contemporary of Abraham, issued a code of laws that made the area one of the best administered.

*Jacob and his family enter Egypt*

The period of bondage in Egypt began after the death of Jacob and his twelve sons. Pharoah's persecution of their descendants is the first recorded attempt of genocide.

Forced by famine to temporarily leave the Land, Abraham's descendents found refuge in Egypt, and while there developed into a people.

The Pharoahs who welcomed the Israelites into Egypt are identified by some historians with the Hyksos, who were also a Semitic people.

**210 years**

The influence of Egyptian idolatry led to a spiritual decline until the monotheistic ideal was in danger of disappearing once again.

Their expulsion by native Egyptians would then correspond to the beginning of Israelite enslavement, and the "New King who knew not Joseph" would be the founder of the 18th dynasty.

*Moses and the Exodus*

It was revived by Moses at the time of the Exodus, 500 years after the birth of Abraham.

**1500 B.C.E.**

*Chapter One*

# The Period of the Patriarchs

From Abraham to Moses (c. 2000 – 1500 B.C.E.)
Introduction – Land, People and Faith

"Now as to these matters, every one of my readers may think as he pleases, but I am under a necessity of relating this history as it is described in the Sacred Books."

Josephus, the famous first century Jewish historian, made this qualifying statement when describing biblical events for a mainly Roman audience. Books of Josephus' time were in fact scrolls, like the Torah Scrolls read regularly in Synagogues from antiquity to the present day. Scrolls of the Law, as they are also called, describe the origins of the Jews and of Judaism, creating a symbiosis between the people and their religion, strengthened by a biblical precept to recount certain historical events.

Because the scrolls are Judaism's most sacred possession, the religious (and not only Jews) treat biblical history with a reverence lacking among secularists. Thus in 1917, many Gentiles welcomed the Balfour Declaration, in that it acknowledged the right of the Jews to their ancient biblical homeland. Balfour, who was a keen student of the Bible, was opposed in the main by those who were not, including Jewish assimilationists, who often feel they must give up something to be accepted, whether it is religious practice or territory.

Jewish claim to an independent homeland is based on the biblical premise that Jews are simultaneously members of a divinely-ordained nation and religion. Once a distinction is made between these two concepts, it may be claimed that Jews do not need their own country, since they do not constitute a nation. Conversely, arguing that Jews are primarily members of a race and not of a religion leads to the type of secularism that totally rejects the existence of a divine mission to the Jewish people.

Perhaps the only conclusion common to all viewpoints, is that neither the Jews or their history are subjects for dispassionate study, not least because any conclusions drawn may have far-reaching, practical consequences. And as most people begin with some degree of preconceived opinion, Josephus was surely justified in inviting his readers to think as they pleased, while he himself relied on "the Sacred Books." The authors of this work reiterate his words, in the belief that the intervening two millennia offer additional evidence that Jewish survival depends on the three-fold connection of people, faith and land. Each of these factors has its origin with Abraham in the land of Canaan.

### Abraham's Journey to Canaan

Unlike individuals who are mortal, successive generations can achieve eternity if they span recorded time, and whereas the story of an individual is called biography, the story of successive generations constitutes history. (The Hebrew word *Toldot* means both generations and history.) For this reason Jewish history begins with Abraham, because he realised that only successive generations of descendants could keep his message of monotheism alive for all time. Thus a key passage states: "For I know him, that he will command his children and his household after him, and they shall keep the ways of the Lord, to do righteousness and justice" (Gen. 19:18).

Abraham was born in Mesopotamia, so called from a Greek word meaning "between rivers," referring to the Tigris and Euphrates in western Asia, corresponding to modern Iraq. But biblical history is very selective, and little is known about the first part of his life in Mesopotamia, just as little is known of the preceding generations; and it is only when God commanded him to leave his homeland and settle in Canaan (estimated at 1948 BCE) that Abraham's story, and that of the land, truly begin.

Abraham's journey to Canaan followed the Fertile Crescent, which is formed by the Tigris and Euphrates in the east, and by Canaan and Egypt, bordering on the Mediterranean Sea, in the west. In the city of Haran, situated at the crescent's apex, Abraham's father Terach died, and so he completed the journey to Canaan accompanied by his wife Sarah, his nephew Lot and members of his household. Entering the country from the north, the party continued travelling southward along the high central ridge that serves as a main route.

Avoiding the more populated coastal plain, Abraham's two major regions of encampment were centered around the city of Hebron and in the arid Negev in the

**Abraham's route from Ur to Canaan, following the Fertile Crescent**

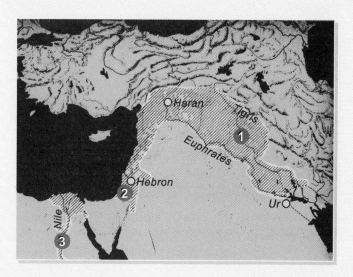

**1 Mesopotamia,** where Abraham began his journey, is known as the melting pot of the ancient world. From approximately 2000 B.C.E. until the end of the Biblical period, it was ruled by the Amorites, Hittites, Assyrians, Chaldeans and Persians. In modern times, it corresponds approximately to Iraq.

**2 Canaan,** was inhabited in Abraham's time by no less than ten different peoples. Possession of the future homeland of the Jewish people has always been strongly contested, due to its strategic importance at the hub of three sub continents: Europe, Africa and Asia.

**3 Egypt,** generally represented a stable and unified society. As in Mesopotamia, where civilization developed between the banks of the Tigris and Euphrates, Egyptian civilization developed along the banks of the Nile.

south. But wherever he went, Abraham's dual intention was always to possess the Land as an inheritance for his descendants, and to spread the message of monotheism.

## Polytheism

According to the biblical account, monotheism preceded Abraham, but in the course of time became corrupted with the worship of material objects, until it all but disappeared. Contrary to popular misconception, therefore, instead of polytheism evolving into monotheism, monotheism became degraded by stages into polytheism, and Abraham's life marks a watershed, in that henceforth an entire people would dedicate itself to upholding belief in a single God.

Two examples illustrate the idolatrous influence prevalent in Abraham's time. The first is provided by his ancestors, including his own father, as Joshua, a future leader of the people testified: "Your fathers dwelt on the other side of the river... Terach, the father of Abraham... and they served other gods" (Josh. 24:2). The second example is provided by Hammurabi, the enlightened Mesopotamian king, who may have been Abraham's contemporary. At the top of his famous Code of Law, exhibited in the Paris Louvre, there is a depiction of the sun god, just as at the summit of the ziggurats, built about the same time, there were idolatrous shrines.

By ascribing supernatural powers to inanimate objects in human or animal form, idolatry, was in the first place, an intellectual aberration. But even more objectionable was its association with immorality, in the form of fertility rites, temple maidens and the gods themselves, who set neither for themselves nor their worshippers, moral or ethical standards. In Abraham's own time, idolatrous Sodom was so corrupt that its name would become synonymous with depravity, and even the aesthetically sophisticated Greeks, in a later period, believed in anthropomorphic gods on Mt. Olympus, who squabbled amongst themselves. To a certain extent, the Romans identified Greek deities with their own.

## Monotheism

So it came about that the ancestors of the Jews proclaimed an idea too sublime even for the combined genius of Greece and Rome to grasp, namely, that there was only one God, Who requires consideration for everyone, but especially for the less fortunate, as part of His service. This consideration expressed itself, in the biblical account of Abraham's life, in the way he provided hospitality for complete strangers, attending to them himself, and then by interceding on behalf of Sodom and Gemorrah, the cities of the plain, even though he opposed everything they stood for.

There have always been converts to monotheism, who are called by the psalmist: "The people of the God of Abraham" (Ps. 47:10), because he is their spiritual ancestor. The Aramaic translation to Genesis 12:5, specifically mentions Abraham making converts, even before he entered Canaan. This universal connotation is contained in his name (originally it was Avram), which was changed to mean "the father of a multitude of nations" (Gen. 17:5), and which today includes Christians and Moslems, who inherit from him their belief in God.

For the Jews, Abraham has a dual role as founder of both race and religion, and Canaan was to be the homeland for his descendants. From there his monotheistic message could be best transmitted, as Isaiah would later put it: "For out of Zion shall go forth the Law and the word of the Lord from Jerusalem" (Is. 2:3). The country's strategic position makes it ideal for disseminating universal ideals, because it forms a bridge between the land-masses of Africa, Asia and Europe, and therefore holds a central position on important land and sea routes. Ezekiel, another prophet, stressed the country's key location when speaking of its capital city: "This is Jerusalem, I have set it in the midst of the nations, and countries are round about" (Ezek. 5:5).

## *The Promised Land*

The strip of territory between the eastern Mediterranean shoreline and the Jordan River has been given different names throughout history. Between 50 and 110 kilometres (30 – 70 miles) wide, and some 225 kilometres (140 miles) long, prior to the conquest under Joshua the country was known as Canaan, one of several tribes inhabiting the region. The Promised Land refers to the covenant (*Brith Bein Habetarim*) whereby it was promised to Abraham and his descendants. By Christians and Moslems as well as by Jews, it is also referred to as the Holy Land.

The Philistines, who lived along the southern coastline and with whom Abraham came into contact, were not the same people as the Philistines in the time of the Judges, after whom the Romans renamed the country Palestine. Rome's intention was to remind the Jews of their traditional adversary and separate them from their homeland, giving the word Palestine a derogatory connotation. For this reason it is generally avoided throughout this book.

Many of Abraham's movements after he arrived in Canaan show concern for the future welfare of his descendants, in addition to providing for more immediate needs. He established residence by digging wells and planting. In more recent times, on the basis of the verse "Abraham planted a tamarisk in Beer Sheva" (Gen. 21:23), there have been mass plantings of tamarisks in the area, because, where rainfall is scarce, it is one of the few trees to flourish. Wells from the period of Abraham have also been discovered, with clear waters once cleaned of sand. Whether in ancient or modern times, trees to bind the top soil and a permanent water supply are essential for present cultivation and future settlement.

The opportunity for Abraham to redeem land from foreign rule came after his nephew Lot chose to live in Sodom and possess the lush pastures of the Jordan Valley for his flocks. Sodom was part of a coalition of five city states, ruled by a stronger alliance of four Mesopotamian kings. After being dominated for twelve years, the five kings rebelled, inviting a successful punitive expedition, in which Lot was taken captive.

In order to rescue his nephew, Abraham led another coalition that pursued the victors to the north of the country, where he compensated for inferior numbers by utilising the cover of night. The surprise tactics worked, and Abraham's prestige reached new heights. By freeing part of the country from alien rule, he was recognised as a liberator.

### The Cave of Machpelah

On three occasions, ancestors of the Jewish people acquired sites in the Holy Land through purchase, the first of which was the cave of Machpelah, bought by Abraham. (The second acquisition was made by Jacob at Shechem and the third by David, who acquired the Temple Mount. Ironically, nowhere today is a Jewish presence more vigorously contested than in these places.)

Abraham requested the cave as a sepulchre after his wife Sarah's death, and eventually three generations of patriarchs and their wives (except for Rachel) would be buried there. Hebron, where the cave is situated, is one of the oldest cities in the world, and together with Jerusalem, Safed and Tiberias, is one of the four cities holy to the Jewish people. In the days of the Temple, the first light that silhouetted Hebron's skyline was a sign to begin the daily service (Mishna Yoma 3:1).

When Abraham died, his two sons, Isaac and Ishmael, buried him in the family sepulchre.

### Isaac

Isaac was the only son that Abraham shared with Sarah, and although he had other children from other wives, Isaac alone was to be his true heir. The closest rival was an older half-brother, called Ishmael, whose Egyptian mother Hagar had been Sarah's handmaid. After Sarah realised that she was barren, she persuaded Abraham to take Hagar as a surrogate wife. But when Hagar became pregnant, she looked on her mistress with contempt, temporarily fled, and then returned to give birth to Ishmael. When Abraham was circumcised together with the members of his household, as a sign of the covenant, Ishmael was thirteen years old.

Isaac was born to Sarah in her old age, and when he was weaned, she persuaded

Abraham (with divine approval) to expel both Hagar and Ishmael, looking upon the latter as unworthy to inherit with her son. Fraternal rivalry, whether provoked by jealousy, inheritance or religious matters, is a recurring theme throughout the Bible, particularly in the book of Genesis. It is invariably the younger son who triumphs, just as Abraham bequeathed the greater part of his possessions to Isaac.

Ishmael is mainly remembered as the traditional ancestor of the Arabs. Like the Jews, therefore, they also look to Abraham as their ancestor, but regard Hagar, not Sarah, as his true wife, and Ishmael, not Isaac, as his true heir. Following Ishmael's example, Moslems also practice circumcision.

Although Isaac lived longer than the other two patriarchs, he is the subject of least biographical detail. Often when he is mentioned, his role is passive, either as the son of Abraham, or the father of Jacob. Thus his wife Rebekah was chosen for him by Eliezer, Abraham's servant, who brought her from Mesopotamia, and during the most dramatic experience of his life, when he was bound on the altar to be offered as a sacrifice, his father who held the knife is the center of attention. In some illustrations of the event, Isaac is portrayed as a youth, despite the fact that at the time he was a mature adult.

Most significant in the incident of the binding of Isaac is the counter commandment, not to sacrifice him. Thereby the sanctity of life was confirmed, as well as the ultimate degree of obedience by both father and son to God's word. The rejection of human sacrifice, common in different parts of the world up to modern times, as well as the ideal description of divine will, would later be expressed by Micah in the following words: "Shall I give my first born for my transgression…? He has told you, O man, what is good, and what does the Lord require of you, but to do justly, to love mercy, and to walk humbly with your God" (Micah 6:7-8).

### *Isaac follows Abraham's footsteps*

Unlike Abraham or Jacob, Isaac's name was never changed nor did he ever leave the Promised Land, even during a famine. In similar circumstances, Abraham had sought refuge in Egypt, telling the Egyptians that Sarah was his sister. On this assumption she was taken to Pharaoh's palace, but once the truth became known, both were obliged to leave the country. The same scenario was re-enacted in a Philistine city called Gerar, whose king was called Avimelech. Avimelech was a title, just as the kings of Egypt were called Pharaoh, which explains why there was also an Avimelech in the time of Isaac. When faced with famine, Isaac stayed in Gerar instead of leaving the country, and following his father's example also referred to his wife as a sister.

On each occasion, the husband of a beautiful wife faced greater danger than the brother of a beautiful sister. An all-powerful ruler could kill the husband to take his wife, but would allow a brother to live, as Abraham put it: "There is no fear of God in this place, and they will kill me on account of my wife" (Gen. 20:11). Better for both husband and wife to resort to a temporary subterfuge in order to stay alive and provide mutual help, rather than separately face death or dishonor.

The Avimelech in the time of Abraham had allowed him to settle wherever he wished, unlike the one in the time of Isaac, who became jealous and expelled him from his land. A covenant that the Philistines made with Abraham was meant to last for three generations, but with Isaac's expulsion, was prematurely annulled. The animosity towards Isaac was due in no small measure to his success, whether in large numbers of cattle and flocks or by reaping a hundred fold of what he sowed. Isaac is the only patriarch specifically described as tilling the soil.

The Philistines expressed their hostility by filling in the wells Abraham had dug, and when Isaac dug them again and cleaned them, he was careful to call them by their former names, thereby stressing continuity and that they were his by inheritance. Isaac also dug new wells and made a new treaty with the Philistines, implying a mutual desire to live in peace, and recognition of his rights in the land. Abraham is described as proclaiming God's name in Beer Sheva, which means that he proclaimed the message of monotheism. Isaac followed his example, after he built an altar there.

### Jacob and Esau

Each patriarch had a primary wife who remained childless for a long period. Isaac alone took but one wife, and she was barren for twenty years before giving birth to two sons. Although Jacob and Esau were twins, they were in no way identical. The former was described as "a simple man, dwelling in tents" (Gen. 25:27) whereas his brother was ruddy in complexion and a hunter. He was also the favorite of Isaac, just as, by the same attraction of opposites, the "simple" Jacob was the favorite of Rebekah, who came from a more worldly background. Conforming to the general biblical pattern of fraternal rivalry, Jacob purchased from Esau the rights of the first-born. Whatever the rights entailed, they were held in contempt by Esau, who exchanged them for a pottage of lentils.

Towards the end of Isaac's life, when he intended to bless Esau, Rebekah exploited his poor eyesight and devised a plan whereby the blessing went instead to Jacob, who impersonated his older brother. The consequence for Rebekah was that she never saw her favorite son again, because after Esau swore vengeance, Jacob was forced to flee to Mesopotamia, where he stayed for twenty years. Isaac's last recorded act was to bless Jacob prior to his leaving, and this time, fully aware of his identity, told him: "May God give you the blessing of Abraham... that you may inherit the land" (Gen. 28:4).

Jacob, who had played a reluctant part in deceiving his father, was himself deceived after arriving in Mesopotamia. Laban, Rebekah's brother, tricked him into marrying Leah, his elder daughter, before Rachel, whom alone he loved. As part of the marriage agreement, Jacob tended his father-in-law's flocks for fourteen years, after which he stayed for another six, providing the opportunity to build up his own stock.

## Jacob-Israel

While Leah gave birth to six sons and one daughter, Rachel remained childless. The names of Leah's children sometimes expressed her bitterness. Reuben, the first-born, means in Hebrew: "The Lord has looked on my affliction" (Gen. 29:32) while Shimon signifies "The Lord has heard that I was hated" (Gen. 29:33). When Rachel eventually gave birth, she named the child Joseph, which expresses a wish that God give her another son, later fulfilled through Benjamin. Jacob also had two sons each from Bilhah and Zilpah, his wives' handmaids, making him a patriarchal figure, with a large family and flocks, by the time he returned to Canaan.

On the eve of crossing the Jordan, Jacob wrestled until dawn with a mysterious stranger, who changed his name to Israel, which means: "You have contended with God and man, and have prevailed" (Gen. 32:19). Once a people (until the Babylonian exile), Jacob's descendants would be known as the Children of Israel, and in an even later period, the Land of Israel would designate their country. The latest use of the name is the State of Israel, whose citizens are Israelis.

Jacob called the place where the struggle occurred Penuel. Altogether there were three sites to which he gave names on the eastern side of the Jordan, where he also built a home for himself and shelter for his flocks. These activities indicate ownership, and later some tribes settled in the area. (In 1921 the League of Nations included the eastern side of the Jordan in the Jewish National Home.)

Jacob's first meeting with Esau in twenty years resulted in reconciliation, after which he continued to acquire territory on the Jordan's western side. He bought land for encampment close to the city of Shechem, and where Rachel died near Bethlehem he erected a memorial that has long been a site of pilgrimage. The present structure is one of the most visited sepulchres in the world.

## Joseph and Exile

Fraternal rivalry in previous generations between Isaac and Ishmael, Jacob and Esau, was continued among Jacob's sons by Joseph and his brothers. The situation was exacerbated by Jacob, who showed favoritism towards his younger son, and by Joseph himself, when he related dreams of self importance.

Motivated by fear of being spiritually disinherited, as had happened to Ishmael and Esau, the brothers sold Joseph into Egypt, where he reached a position of authority in the household of Potiphar, a senior Egyptian official. Falsely accused by Potiphar's wife, Joseph was sent to prison, but even there was appointed supervisor. His reputation as an interpreter of dreams brought him before Pharaoh, who was troubled by a vision of fat and thin cows, followed by a second one of fat and thin stalks of grain. Joseph interpreted the dreams as years of plenty followed by famine, and advised Pharaoh how to plan accordingly. With a combination of charisma and administrative skill, he became responsible for the Egyptian economy, second in authority only to the throne.

Referring to the period under discussion, scientists speak of a cataclysmic eruption on an island off southern Greece. It was strong enough to cause famine by detrimentally changing the climate and Canaan was in the fallout area. Whatever the cause, Jacob sent his sons to Egypt to buy grain and, although Joseph recognised them, they did not recognise him. The eventual denouement and reconciliation led to Jacob and his family settling in the Land of Goshen, on Egypt's eastern border. The area lay open to marauders attracted by the fertile Nile Valley, thus it was in Pharaoh's interest to have it serve as a security zone. The Israelites, related to Egypt's most senior administrator, constituted a friendly population and, as the Egyptians disdained shepherds, they were allowed to tend their flocks there unhindered.

### A new Pharaoh

The last seventeen years of Jacob's life were spent in Egypt, where just before his death he bestowed upon Joseph the double share of the first-born, signifying that when Canaan would later be divided among twelve tribes, Joseph would receive a double portion through his two sons, Ephraim and Manasseh. Joseph and his brothers fulfilled their father's last wish and buried him in Hebron, after which they returned to Egypt and prospered under tolerant rulers, identified by many historians with the Hyksos. The Hyksos were a Semitic people sympathetic to the Israelites but not accepted by the general population, and after about a century (c.1640-1540 B.C.E), their rule came to an end.

It is assumed that the Hyksos were expelled by the founder of the eighteenth dynasty, which would then cast him in the role of "the new king who knew not Joseph" (Ex. 1:8). Representing a new generation, this new king openly doubted the loyalty of the Israelites, whose exceptionally high birth rate turned them into a nation within a nation. Suspected of being a potential fifth column ready to side with any intruder, they were treated as such and persecuted.

The Pharaoh of the oppression was a great builder, who saw in the Israelites a free source of slave labor. To this end he turned them into a stateless minority, and then deprived them of their rights. One of the store cities built by the Israelites was Rameses, on the eastern delta, possibly named after Rameses II, who left monuments to himself all over Egypt. The Israelites submitted to their fate of servitude enforced through a series of vicious decrees.

Yet even greater then the threat to their physical existence, was their spiritual plight as they forsook the monotheism Abraham had pledged to pass on to his descendants. Two biblical passages refer to this backsliding. The first, in the Book of Joshua, states: "Put away the gods your fathers served in Egypt" (Josh. 24:14). In the second passage, Ezekiel says: "Neither did they forsake the idols of Egypt" (Ezek. 20:8).

The tribe of Levi alone remained free of idolatrous influence, and one couple from that tribe, Amram and Jochebed, realised that the best way to avert national extinction was to create life. Of their three children, the youngest, Moses, would become the deliverer of his people.

### The end of the period

If the period between Abraham and the subjugation in Egypt could be illustrated by a line on a graph, it would show a steady decline. Abraham himself was recognised by his contemporaries as "A prince of God" (Gen. 23:6) and a Philistine king told him: "My land is before you; dwell where it pleases you" (20:15). However in the next generation, the Philistines succumbed to jealousy by expelling Abraham's son, Isaac, from their borders and by filling in his water supply. By the third generation, Jacob was able to say to Pharaoh: "Few and evil have been the days of the years of my life" (Gen. 47:9).

Driven by famine, Jacob's sons in the fourth generation accompanied their father into exile, and in the fifth, the Egyptian bondage began. Threat to survival came from two sources. Spiritually, many succumbed to idolatry, whereas physically, Pharaoh was bent on genocide. By ordering male infants to be drowned, national extinction was but a generation away, and the passage of decline would reach its ultimate conclusion.

Without a people dedicated to upholding monotheism, the ideal itself would also die, because people and religion are inextricably linked. The historical wheel, therefore, had made a full turn, for belief in a single God was equally endangered at the time of Moses, as it had been before Abraham.

# Time Span

## Chain of Tradition

## World History

**2000 B.C.E.**

### ABRAHAM
**THE PATRIARCHS**

**1**

Teachers of Monotheism

**HAMMURABI'S LAWS**

Hittite & Egyptian Empires

**DECLINE OF EGYPTIAN POWER**

**1500 B.C.E.**

### MOSES
**JUDGES**

**2**

Earlier Prophets

**BEGINNING OF PHILISTINE SETTLEMENTS**

Spread of Mediterranean Civilization

**1000 B.C.E.**

### DAVID
**KINGS**

**3**

Later Prophets

**RISE OF PHOENICIAN TRADE**

Mesopotamian Empires

**END OF BIBLICAL PERIOD**

**500 B.C.E.**

### EZRA
**ZUGOTH**

**4**

Joint leaders of the Sanhedrin and the rule of the Wise

**BEGINNING OF ROMAN REPUBLIC**

Spread of Hellenism

**END OF ROMAN REPUBLIC**

**0**

### HILLEL
**TALMUDIC PERIOD**

**5**

Compilation of the Oral Law

**BEGINNING OF ROMAN EMPIRE**

Spread of Christianity

**END OF ROMAN EMPIRE**

**500 C.E.**

### RAV ASHI
**THE GEONIM**

**6**

Heads of the Babylonian Academies

**BEGINNING OF MIDDLE AGES**

Spread of Islam

**DECLINE OF BAGHDAD CALIPHATE**

**1000 C.E.**

### RASHI
**THE RISHONIM**

**7**

Earlier Authorities: Commentators & Codifiers of Talmudic Law

**HOLY ROMAN EMPIRE**

Crusades

**END OF MIDDLE AGES**

**1500 C.E.**

### JOSEPH KARO
**THE AHARONIM**

**8**

Later Authorities: Commentators & Compilers of the Halacha

**RENAISSANCE & REFORMATION**

Spread of Western Civilization

**END OF OTTOMAN EMPIRE RETURN TO ZION**

**2000 C.E.**

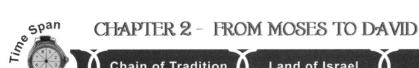

**1500 B.C.E.**
*Moses and the Exodus*

**40 years**

*Joshua*

**28 years**

*Judges*

*King David*

**1000 B.C.E.**

The covenant made with the Patriarchs was renewed with the entire people at Mt. Sinai, fifty days after the Exodus.

Moses, who led the people to Mt. Sinai, become know as The father of the Prophets, and observance of the commandments he received became an essential condition of the covenant.

After leading the people 40 years in the wilderness, Moses was succeeded by Joshua, his foremost disciple.

Joshua's successors were regional leaders only, called Judges. There were fifteen in all, and Samuel, who was the last, was also the greatest.

In answer to the people's request, Samuel established a monarchy, to check the Philistine threat.

If the first purpose of the Exodus was to bring the people into a covenant, the second was to bring them into the Land of Israel.

Only there could many of the commandments received at Mt. Sinai be observed, making it a spiritual center and not just a national homeland.

Peace within its borders would be the ultimate reward for keeping the Torah.

Joshua led the people across the Jordan, after which he spent 7 years in conquering Canaan and another 7 in dividing it among the tribes.

The many geographical areas into which the country is divided helped perpetuate tribal divisions after Joshua's death.

Ramses III prevented an invasion of his country by the Philistines, driven from their island home of Crete.

They then turned to the coastal plain of Canaan, where they established 5 city states.

The Philistines arrived about the same time as the Israelites under Joshua, and in the period of the Judges they advanced inland to threaten the entire country.

Saul, the first king of Israel, failed at the cost of his life to check their advance.

*Chapter Two*

# The Birth of a Nation

## From Moses to David (c. 1500-1000 B.C.E.)

"We believe that the most scientific view, the most up-to-date rationalistic conception, will find its fullest satisfaction in taking the Bible story literally and in identifying one of the greatest human beings with the most decisive leap forward ever discernible in the human story!"

The reference to "one of the greatest human beings" is Moses, and it was made by neither a biblical fundamentalist nor a Jew, but by Winston Churchill. His opinion is of importance because as a great man himself, he was aware of the extent to which great figures can alter history. And as Britain's most outstanding war-time Prime Minister, the famed defender of liberty, he could all the better evaluate a national leader who gave mankind one of its first lessons in freedom.

Churchill's essay on Moses, entitled "The Leader of a People," reiterates in general outline the biblical account. Moses, the greatest of the prophets who spoke with God, led the Israelites from bondage and through the perils of the wilderness, and brought them to the threshold of the Promised Land. He was also the supreme Law-giver who received from God the code on which the religious, moral and social life of the nation and of the civilized world were founded.

Moses' influence on history began when he stood before Pharaoh at 80 years of age but, unlike Abraham of whom little is known before he was 75, his life is recorded from birth.

When only three months old, his mother Jocheved saved him from infanticide by hiding him in an ark of reeds, and she continued to nurture him even after he was discovered and adopted by Pharaoh's daughter. In this way, Moses benefited from both maternal affection and royal upbringing, and ironically, the Israelite's future savior was raised by the daughter of their oppressor. Despite his privileged position, Moses maintained empathy with his people, which led him, when the occasion arose, to slay an overbearing Egyptian taskmaster. He fled to neighboring Midian and married Zipporah, a shepherdess and daughter of a priest named Jethro.

Like the patriarch Jacob, he too tended his father-in-law's flocks, until an incident occurred that transformed him into a shepherd of people. At the foot of a burning bush that remained unconsumed, he received a divine command to go to Pharaoh and seek permission to lead the Israelites from Egypt. Four times he tried to avoid the task, casting doubt either on his own ability or the people's faith, until finally Aaron, who was his elder by three years, was appointed to assist him. Once again, responsibility went to a younger brother, although on this occasion there was harmony between the two.

Apart from advanced years, there were other handicaps that might have disqualified Moses from leadership. He lacked both the gift of oratory and political experience and, without any personal ambition, he had never been appointed by the people. His sole claim to authority came from speaking in God's name and on that criterion alone his mission would either succeed or fail. Moses and Aaron's first meeting with Pharaoh was not a success, because it resulted in harsher conditions of slavery for the Israelites.

The purpose of the plagues that followed was to persuade the oppressor to release the oppressed, and to demonstrate to both the full extent of God's might. As the afflictions increased in number, so they increased in intensity. First the waters of the Nile were afflicted, and then all the land of Egypt. Discomfort to man and beast escalated into death. Following the slaying of the first-born, the tenth and most severe plague, the Israelites were expelled with a haste that left no time for adequate preparation.

### The Exodus

The Passover festival, which commemorates the Exodus, is the national Independence Day of the Jewish people. Most peoples gain independence by liberating their land from foreign domination, but only the Jews became independent while actually on foreign soil, celebrating the day they were able to leave. Nor were they ever obliged to fight for their freedom, because the Egyptians who pursued them were drowned in the Red Sea. Ever since, the Exodus has remained the cornerstone of Jewish faith, as the supreme example of God's intervention in history.

Yet despite its significance, if the Exodus had been an end in itself, the Israelites would have remained nothing more than a nation of freed slaves. Moses' request before Pharaoh "Let my people go," was invariably followed by the proviso "That they may serve me," thereby giving purpose to their freedom.

There were two reasons why the Israelites did not enter directly into the Promised Land by following the shortest route where Africa joins Asia. Firstly, they would have been no match for the warlike Philistines, who barred the way. Secondly, they were required to turn south towards Mt. Sinai. Even before the Exodus Moses had been told: "When you bring the people out of Egypt, you shall serve God on this mountain" (Ex. 3:12).

## *The Covenant at Mt. Sinai*

The original covenant with Abraham, later confirmed with Isaac and Jacob, was renewed with the entire people at Mt. Sinai. The commandments given at Sinai clarify the relationship between God, people and land that lies at the heart of the covenant for, if the people observed the commandments, they would be free to worship God in the Promised Land. Conversely, the ultimate punishment for neglect of the commandments would be exile.

Thus it was made clear that possession of the land was conditional, contrary to freehold without binding obligations. Such qualifications explicitly acknowledge that the land belongs to God, who exacts moral and ethical conduct from those who live in it. God moreover promised the land to future generations, placing an obligation on each one in turn to safeguard the inheritance of those yet unborn.

The covenant was given tangible expression in the form of two tablets of stone that Moses brought down from Mt. Sinai engraved with the Decalogue. Hence they are called "the tablets of the covenant" (Deut. 9:9) inscribed with "the words of the covenant" (Ex. 34:28) and placed in "the ark of the covenant" (Deut. 10:8). Two specific commandments, described as signs of the covenant, are circumcision and the Sabbath.

Because it represents the covenant, the Decalogue is seen as a summary of the other commandments.

The first tablet contains the duties of man towards God, whereas the second one deals with the duties of man towards his fellow man. But the two sets of duties are in many respects one, because the service of God also includes commandments such as to love the stranger and to allow the poor the gleanings of the fields. Thus Abraham's descendants became the only people bound by covenant, for example, to keep honest weights or to remember the needy.

Forty days (after receiving the Decalogue) proved too short a time to uproot the idolatrous influences of Egypt, because after that period the people asked Aaron to make a substitute for Moses, who had not yet descended from the mount. A golden calf was the result. Apparently all animals were held sacred in ancient Egypt, and Apis, the figure of a bull, was included when reverence was debased to actual worship. Certainly the influence of Egypt and the Egyptians, as well as the mixed multitude and converts who attached themselves to the Israelites at the time of the Exodus, is evident in the incident.

When Moses saw what had happened he broke the tablets of stone, representing the covenant that had been violated, and then ordered those who had remained loyal to punish the offenders. The Levites alone had not transgressed and, as a reward they and not the first-born, served in the Tabernacle when it was constructed. After the covenant was renewed, the ten "Declarations" were also inscribed anew (Ex. 34:28). (It should be noted that in Hebrew the term Ten Commandments is never found, simply because the commandments enumerated on the two tablets of stone number not ten but fourteen.)

## The Sanctuary

An exact plan of the Sanctuary or Tabernacle in which the tablets were kept can be made from the detailed description in the book of Exodus (ch. 25-31; 35-40). It was approximately 45 feet long by 15 feet wide, and divided by a curtain into two unequal parts. The "Holy Place" (in the proportion of a double cube) housed the candelabrum, the showbread and the altar of incense, while the "Holy of Holies" (a perfect cube) housed the Ark of the Covenant, containing the two tablets of stone. The entire construction was of timber supported by silver sockets and covered by curtains worked in a delicate tapestry.

There was a surrounding court (150 feet by 75 feet) and, whether dismantled when the people journeyed or set up when they encamped, the place of the Tabernacle was always symbolically in the center.

The tabernacle was dedicated during an impressive seven-day ceremony, immediately preceding the first anniversary of the Exodus. Shortly afterwards, the Israelites journeyed in a north-easterly direction towards Canaan.

## The Wilderness Years

The territory the Israelites entered on leaving Egypt, and which they were destined to inhabit for forty years, is known today as the Sinai Peninsula, partly bordered by the Gulf of Eilat (or Aqaba) in the east, and the Gulf of Suez in the west. It is widest in the north, where it borders on the Mediterranean Sea, and then tapers to a point 230 miles further south, resembling an inverted pyramid. In the north it is level and sandy, but towards the south, where Mt. Sinai is situated, there are high ridges.

There are two assessments of those who left Egypt. One is of "A people of erring heart" (Ps. 95:10), whereas the second praises the people for their faith in following Moses into a wilderness without visible means of support and vulnerable to attack by marauders. Thus Jeremiah declared in God's name: "I remember in your favor the devotion of your youth... when you went after Me in the wilderness, in a land not sown" (Jer.2:2).

On one level, the people's faith in leaving Egypt for an unknown destination is considered meritorious; on another, especially after the Sinaitic revelation, a higher level of conduct was expected of them.

It is a misconception to consider the wilderness years as a time of continuous wandering, for there were a total of forty-two encampments, accounting for most of the period. Most, if not all of the events that earned the people the epithet of an "erring heart," occurred in either the first or last years.

The first complaint by the Israelites took place immediately after leaving Egypt, at the Red Sea itself. They were surrounded on three sides either by the sea or border fortifications, while to the rear Pharaoh advanced at the head of 600 chariots. With a degree of irony, the people asked Moses whether he had led them into the wilderness because of a shortage of graves in Egypt. Another grievance centered on the lack of food and water, as the Israelites remembered the fleshpots of Egypt, but not the accompanying hard labor. Perhaps they longed not for fleshpots, but for the time when they were unencumbered by the commandments (Rashi to Numb. 11:5).

After leaving Mt. Sinai, which the Israelites reached in the third month after the Exodus and where they encamped for almost a year, they journeyed to Canaan's southern border. Twelve representatives, one from each tribe, were sent to spy out the land, and they returned with their report at the end of 40 days. The spies confirmed the picture of a land flowing with milk and honey, but concluded that the country was unconquerable. Only Joshua and Caleb dissented but were unable to check the general atmosphere of disillusionment and fear. The people wanted to appoint a new leader to take them back to Egypt, thereby rejecting Moses, the land into which he was to take them, and God Himself. As a consequence, they were condemned to remain in the wilderness for forty years, corresponding to the forty days taken to spy out the country. A new generation would enter Canaan.

The most serious challenge to Moses' leadership was made by Korah, although the year is not recorded. Korah was a Levite, a first born and a cousin of Moses, who resented the fact that Moses and his brother Aaron, the high priest, occupied the two most senior positions.

Many of Korah's supporters were descended from Reuben, Jacob's first born, and so may have resented the high rank assigned to the Levites after the incident of the golden calf.

A feature common to all the rebels was that although close to positions of authority by birth, in fact they possessed none. Some indeed retained positive spiritual aspirations – others had baser motives. Careful to conceal their frustrated ambitions behind ideological arguments, they claimed that Moses and Aaron had no right to arrogate the leadership to themselves, because the entire congregation was holy. The two brothers survived the insurrection, after which their personal authority was never again challenged. They still had to contend, however, with complaints about lack of food and water, even in the fortieth year.

### The Fortieth Year

A large part of the book of Numbers and all of Deuteronomy are devoted to describing the events of the last year in the wilderness. By that year a new generation encamped on the eastern side of the Jordan was ready to cross over into Canaan. During the journey, detours had been made, because local kings would not allow the Israelites to pass through their lands. Two Amorite kings actually attempted to check their progress by force, but they were defeated and forfeited territory from the Dead Sea to Mt. Hermon in the north. Because the area was good pasture-land, it was claimed by the tribes of Gad, Reuben and half the tribe of Manasseh, who were rich in flocks. These two and a half tribes were the first to be exiled in the period of the monarchy, when the kingdom of Israel came to an end.

Following the defeat of the Amorite kings, the king of Moab devised a new method of trying to halt the children of Israel, by hiring a Mesopotamian soothsayer called Balaam to curse them. The plan was a conspicuous failure, but Balaam was far more successful when, through his advice, the daughters of Moab and Midian enticed the Israelites into immorality and idolatry. The moral decline was checked by a zealous priest called Pinhas, who used a spear to kill a prominent offending Israelite and Midianite woman. Afterwards, on Moses' command, he accompanied an army of 12,000 (1,000 from each tribe) that exacted vengeance on the Midianites. Balaam, who was one of the victims, is best remembered for his prophecy regarding Israel: "Behold, a people that dwell alone, and shall not be reckoned among the nations" (Numb. 23:9).

The last year in the wilderness saw the deaths of Miriam, Aaron and Moses, in that order (although in order of birth Aaron was first). Of Aaron alone it is recorded that all the people mourned him, because of his reputation as a man of peace. He was succeeded as high priest by a son, but of Moses' two sons little is known. It was Joshua, his chief disciple, who was appointed successor.

Moses took leave of the new generation about to enter Canaan by delivering a farewell address. He reviewed major events following the Exodus and reiterated commandments applicable to a settled life in the Promised Land. The people's fate in that land or elsewhere, he stressed, depended on their own behavior. There, in the plains of Moab, Moses renewed the covenant made previously at Sinai.

After blessing each tribe, Moses ascended Mt. Nebo, a summit north of the Dead Sea, from where he saw the Promised Land. He was not allowed to enter, because of an incident shortly after the Exodus at a place called Meribah where he failed to sanctify God in satisfying the people's demand for water (Numb. 20:12). Moses' exact burial site on Mt. Nebo remains unknown. If it were otherwise, instead of being found in Rome, Michelangelo's famous sculpture of Moses (or something similar) might well be housed in a mausoleum built over the site, control of which would be a matter of contention for different faiths, if not a cause for war. It is best, therefore, that the site remains unknown, especially as Moses' legacy is more enduring than the hardest granite tombstone.

Through his legacy, as with that of Abraham's, monotheism advanced in giant strides instead of small steps, which is why both their lives serve as milestones in the intellectual, moral and spiritual development of mankind. The statement: "There arose not in Israel a prophet like Moses" (Deut. 34:10) testifies to his special place in history.

## Joshua

Following the incident at Meribah, where the people quarrelled with Moses over the lack of water, they were attacked by the Amalekites. From that time on, the Amalekites, who were descended from Esau, remained enemies of the Israelites until they were finally vanquished in the period of the monarchy. The commander who led the successful counter attack in the first ever battle forced on the Israelites was Joshua, who thereby fulfilled the role of soldier that would become more evident in the later conquest of Canaan.

After the victory over Amalek, Joshua as Moses' leading disciple, had accompanied his teacher for part of the way, during the ascent and descent of Mt. Sinai. The third time Joshua came into prominence was when he represented the tribe of Ephraim as one of the 12 spies who reconnoitred the land of Canaan. Together with Caleb, he opposed the negative report of the others, and they were the only two men of their generation who eventually crossed the Jordan.

It was not surprising therefore, that in a public ceremony not long before his death, Moses laid his hands on Joshua, appointing him successor. To this day, *Semichah* (Hebrew for laying of hands) is the name given to the granting of spiritual authority, although only with Joshua was the term applied literally.

Maimonides states in his Code (Laws of Kings 6:1) that before entering Canaan, Joshua offered its inhabitants three alternatives: To evacuate the land, to stay and make peace or to stay and make war. Peace was conditional on the renunciation of idolatry and the acceptance of Israelite sovereignty, but the offer was not accepted. "There was not a city that made peace with the Children of Israel" (Jos. 11: 19).

### *The Seven Years of Conquest*

It took Joshua seven years to conquer the country, which was entered by crossing the Jordan, just north of the Dead Sea. The first objective was Jericho, considered the gateway to the country and the oldest city in the world. It is also the world's lowest city with an ample water supply and an agreeable climate. The literal meaning of its name, City of the Moon, indicates its idolatrous origins.

Archaeological excavations confirm that Jericho's walls collapsed in a manner described in the sixth chapter of Joshua, after which it remained uninhabited for centuries. (Joshua placed a ban on its rebuilding, but apparently it was fully restored by the time of Cleopatra, who received its balsam gardens from Mark Anthony.) Jericho's capture and control of the Jordan's southern crossing point, guaranteed supply links with the tribes settled on the eastern bank, allowing the Israelites to advance inland.

In the capture of Ai, the second objective, Joshua compensated for the inability to lay a protracted siege by the use of strategy. After an initial setback, he used the cover of night and a feigned retreat to draw the defenders into an ambush, enabling the city to be taken. The two successive victories increased Canaanite demoralization, which had begun with reports of the Exodus and the military successes on the east bank. The Israelites now formed a wedge that separated the northern and southern parts of the country.

The different peoples inhabiting Canaan banded together to avoid falling piecemeal to the Israelites. The exception was the Gibeonites, who resorted to subterfuge to make a separate treaty, which saved them from war, but not from bondage. The king of Jerusalem led a five-part coalition in a punitive raid against the Gibeonites, who appealed to Joshua for help. Answering the call, he defeated the coalition in a single campaign before completing the subjugation of the south of the country.

Conquest of the north was more protracted, because of the rugged terrain and stronger resistance. Hazor, one of the larger settlements and a main fortress, led a wide based confederation containing cavalry and chariot units. Once again, Joshua achieved victory by surprise tactics. He took the battle to the enemy, burning their chariots and forcing them to flee.

Hazor was captured and archaeological excavations affirm that it was burnt to the ground. But the coastal strip, Jerusalem and the Jezreel Valley remained unconquered, leaving them as Canaanite enclaves. Even so, Joshua was in possession of sufficient territory to begin dividing the land, assisted by the elders.

## The Seven Years of Allocation

Moses had carried out the first stage of allotting territory when he allocated land on the eastern bank of the Jordan to the tribes of Gad, Reuben and half tribe of Manasseh. Joshua supervised the next two stages: first in Gilgal and then in Shiloh. Like the period of the conquest, the task lasted seven years.

Gilgal was the first Israelite encampment after the crossing of the Jordan, situated some 16 miles north of the Dead Sea. It served as a base for military campaigns, and was the first of several sites of the Sanctuary and the Ark, prior to the latter being permanently based in Jerusalem. There Joshua allocated the land by lots, according to the size of the tribes or families, as prescribed in the Book of Numbers (33:54). Judah, the largest and senior tribe, was allotted territory extending from the Mediterranean to the Dead Sea, with Jerusalem (then unconquered) in the north. The two tribes descended from Joseph, Ephraim (to which Joshua belonged) and Manasseh, occupied the center of the country.

After Gilgal the encampment moved to Shiloh, in the hill country of Ephraim, where the boundaries of the seven remaining tribes were determined. Benjamin had Jerusalem on its southern border, while Simeon, the smallest tribe, was absorbed into the territory of Judah. Issachar, Zebulun, Naphtali and Asher were given Galilee, with the latter two most northerly situated.

Last of all, Dan received land in the south, including Jaffa, one of the oldest ports in the world. (In the time of the Judges, Dan would migrate to the north, near one of the sources of the Jordan, and in 1909 C.E., Jaffa would give birth to the garden suburb of Tel Aviv.) Of the 48 cities given to the Levites dispersed throughout the country, six were designated as cities of refuge, three on either side of the Jordan.

## Joshua's Last Years

After allocating the land, Joshua served as leader for a further 14 years. His last recorded acts were to address two public assemblies, in the first to exhort the people to keep the covenant, and in the second to renew it. At both assemblies he reviewed past events, as Moses had done prior to his death.

Joshua's 28 years of leadership were unique in two ways - there were no incidents of idolatry, and his authority was never challenged. By the time he died aged 110, he had served his people as teacher, soldier, strategist and administrator.

Joshua was the first to use the expression "the Torah of Moses," just as he was the first to pass it on. The Mishnah states "Moses received the Torah at Sinai and passed it on to Joshua, and Joshua to the elders" (Ethics 1:1). The elders are generally identified with the Judges.

### The Judges

If, to quote a simile, Moses was like the sun and Joshua like the moon, then the Judges who followed were like meteors that only briefly illuminated the sky.

In general, the period of the Judges was a confused one, in which the worship of God and the practice of Canaanite customs existed side by side, leading to alternating periods of faith and regression. The confusion arose because after Joshua's death, the tribes were either unwilling or unable to complete the conquest, with the exception of Judah and Simeon. As a consequence, although the Canaanites were militarily subdued, culturally they were often the victors.

The Judges, who arose in time of need, were regional leaders only, varying in character and style. Samson's legendary strength enabled him to wage a one-man guerrilla war against the Philistines, while in the north Deborah possessed sufficient authority to forge a coalition of six tribes. Gideon was a farmer and Jephthah an adventurer. Samuel, the last and greatest Judge, was the only one whose authority was unanimously accepted. Despite the title of Judge, Deborah and Samuel are the only two of whom it is specifically stated that they administered justice.

Lacking the benefit of a strong, permanent leadership, the Israelites fell prey to different types of enemies. In addition to marauding tribes that crossed the Jordan to rob and plunder, there were others politically motivated, who denied the Israelite claim to the land.

A further threat was posed by the remaining Canaanites, who continuously sought to regain their supremacy. Yet the greatest danger of all was posed by the Philistines, who were not to be subdued until the period of the monarchy.

Undoubtedly the activities of the Judges overlapped. The only chronological certainty is that Othniel was the first, Samuel the last and that Jephthah lived 300 years after the entry into Canaan. Othniel is one of the Judges about whom little is recorded, in contrast to Deborah, Gideon, Jephthah and Samson, whose exploits are described in detail.

### Deborah

The valley of Jezreel is the largest in the country, stretching from the

## JUDGES

After Moses and Joshua, the people were led by Judges, who fought against a variety of enemies:

| JUDGE | TRIBE | ADVERSARY |
|---|---|---|
| Othniel<br>Ehud | Judah<br>Benjamin | Hostile peoples from the eastern side of the Jordan. |
| Shamgar | Not recorded | Philistines |
| Deborah | Ephraim | Internal Canaanite enemy. |
| Gideon | Menasseh | Midianites from the eastern side of the Jordan. |
| Avimelech | Menasseh | Gideon's son who committed fratricide to become "king." |
| Tola<br>Yair | Ephraim<br>Ephraim | "Minor Judges" not associated with any military exploit. |
| Jephthah | Ephraim | Defended Israelite claim to territory on eastern bank of Jordan. |
| Ibzan<br>Elon<br>Avdon | Judah<br>Zebulun<br>Ephraim | "Minor Judges" not associated with any military exploit. |
| Samson<br>Eli<br>Samuel | Dan<br>Levi<br>Levi | Fought against the Philistine threat to Israelite existence. |

Mediterranean in the west to the Jordan in the east, and thereby dividing the highlands of the Galilee from those of Samaria. Israelites, Persians and Egyptians would all fight here, as well as armies led by Tamerlane, Tancred, Saladin, Richard Coeur de Leon, Napoleon and Allenby, giving it the name of "the battlefield of the nations." But among this company, Deborah would remain the first and only woman commander.

By virtue of their large numbers and strong army, reinforced with iron chariots, the Canaanites in the area remained unconquered. For a period of twenty years they were powerful enough to harass the Israelites, until Deborah summoned Barak of the tribe of Naphtali to break their dominance. In accordance with Barak's request, she herself was joint leader of the army, which positioned itself on Mt. Tabor, while the Canaanites waited in the valley beneath.

Deborah's song of triumph after the victory speaks of heavenly intervention, suggesting a sudden storm that swept away the Canaanite chariots (Judges 5:21). (A similar situation in the Jezreel Valley occurred in 1799, when Arab troops fleeing Napoleon's forces, were caught in a flash flood and drowned.) Following their defeat, the Canaanites ceased to be a military threat, and Israelite farmers were free to descend from the high ground and cultivate the fertile Jezreel Valley. The respite lasted forty years, until a new threat arose.

### Gideon

> And the children of Israel did that which was evil in the eyes of the Lord....And He delivered them into the hands of spoilers who plundered them....Nevertheless the Lord raised up Judges who saved them (Judg.2:11-16).

These words typify the entire period, and so following Deborah there was a period of retrogression, when spoilers came in the form of the Midianites. For seven consecutive years they crossed the Jordan and entered the Jezreel Valley, the scene of Deborah's victory. From there they spread to the rest of the country, plundering the harvest of the Israelite farmers, and forcing them into hiding.

One of the farmers was Gideon who, as a sign of the confused times, destroyed his own father's idolatrous altar before setting about to rescue his people. The Midianites were compared to hordes of locusts in number and so expected any opposition to be counted at least in thousands. Gideon's first unexpected move was to attack with only 300 men, chosen for their integrity, and his second was to do so at night. The tactic worked because, caught by surprise, the Midianites were led to believe that they were surrounded by numbers comparable to their own. In the confusion of the night, they fought among themselves, and then fled into an ambush composed of several tribes at the Jordan's crossing. Gideon completed the victory by leading a coalition of tribes across the river, pursuing those who had escaped in their desert stronghold.

The men of Ephraim felt slighted, because they considered the part given them in the success insignificant. Only by tact and understanding did Gideon prevent an open conflict. Recognised as a military tactician and diplomat, as well as a man of God, Gideon was offered the crown. He refused it on the grounds that God alone was king.

## Jephthah

One of the earliest recorded territorial disputes involved the two and a half tribes on the eastern side of the Jordan, who had settled there in the time of Moses. The Israelites had taken the territory in a defensive war from a people that had in turn captured it from the Ammonites, who now wanted it back. Frontier change after a period of conflict is a perennial problem, and Jephthah at first attempted to resolve it by negotiation.

Jephthah's path to leadership was unconventional. He became an outcast and an adventurer after his half brothers had driven him away, euphemistically describing him as the son of another woman. When the Ammonites attacked the Israelites on the eastern bank of the Jordan, the latter invited Jephthah and his followers to come to their aid as mercenaries. From lack of choice, they accepted his condition that he remain their recognised leader if successful.

Jephthah's knowledge of history enabled him to engage in a series of diplomatic exchanges, in the course of which he explained to the Ammonites that at no time had they ever been wronged by the Israelites. This argument and others failed to convince the Ammonites and in the conflict that followed they were defeated. The men of Ephraim felt slighted because they had not been invited to participate in the battle, just as they had complained to Gideon in similar circumstances. Jephthah, however, lacked Gideon's patience and, instead of pacifying them, a short but fierce civil war ensued, in which Ephraim suffered heavy losses.

When those who escaped attempted to cross the Jordan, they were identified by their inability to say "*Shibbolet*" (pronounced *Sibbolet* by the Ephraimites) and were killed.

## Samson and the Philistines

The Philistines are mentioned in the time of the patriarchs, but their main wave of immigration reached the eastern Mediterranean about this period. Originally from Crete and the surrounding islands, they tried unsuccessfully to conquer the

Egyptians, who referred to them as the "Sea Peoples." From Egypt they turned to Canaan, where they occupied the southern coastal region and established a confederacy of five main cities centered on Gaza. The Philistine monopoly over the manufacture of iron gave them a distinct advantage, for their iron swords were far superior to the bronze implements of the Israelites, whose main occupation was farming. Even Judah, the largest and strongest of the tribes, was no match for the warlike Philistines.

Until the establishment of the monarchy, Israelite opposition was spasmodic and confined to individuals. Shamgar was one of the early champions, but his main achievement is that he resisted at all, especially as he was only armed with the goad of an ox. His exploit is described in a single verse, unlike the epic struggle of Samson, which takes up four chapters. Of all the Judges, only Samson and Samuel's lives are outlined from birth.

Samson came from Dan, the smallest of the tribes, that suffered an additional disadvantage of having the Philistines as neighbors. The Philistines, not being content with their coastal strip, moved inland and occupied Dan's city of Timnah.

There Samson married a Philistine wife and began his one-man resistance movement against her people. During the course of his 20-year activity, Samson came into contact with three Philistine women, each of whom provided him with an opportunity to take vengeance on Israel's most formidable enemy.

His advantage lay in his phenomenal strength, but he also suffered a major weakness, in that as the Mishnah puts it, "he went after his eyes" (Sotah 1:8). The encounter with Delilah, who worked in collaboration with the Philistine chiefs, proved to be fatal. She betrayed Samson to her masters, who blinded him and imprisoned him in Gaza. After a period of servile labor, the last scene of his life took place in a Philistine temple, where he was paraded before the crowd for amusement. With renewed strength, he supported himself on the two central pillars of the temple, and bringing them down, claimed more victims in death than in life.

Samson was the only Judge to be captured by his enemies and die in captivity, but had nevertheless shown that the Philistines were not invincible. Events were to prove that they would finally be defeated in the period of the monarchy, which was established by Samuel.

## Samuel

Like Samson, Samuel was a Nazirite from birth, but he was also a Levite, which enabled him to minister in the sanctuary of Shiloh to Eli, the aging high priest. In one of the recurring battles with the Philistines, the Israelites were defeated, the ark captured and Eli's two sons killed. Eli himself did not survive the shock, and the sanctuary of Shiloh came to an end.

The next sanctuary stood at Nob. After the Philistines returned the Ark it eventually rested in Kiryath Yearim, both places situated in the territory of Benjamin, not far from Jerusalem. Thus a precedent was established for separating the ark from the sanctuary. The latter remained at Nob throughout the period of Samuel's leadership, most of Nob's citizens being priests.

For the first time since Moses and Joshua, Samuel represented an authority accepted by all the tribes. This enabled him to convene national assemblies and, with his home in the center of the country as a base, he travelled extensively as a circuit judge. He also determined national foreign policy and so was king in all but name. His position however, was not hereditary and since his sons were unworthy to succeed him, the people requested a monarchy. A state ruled by a king would enjoy the stability of dynastic succession and someone to raise and lead a national army. For a people harassed by the Philistines these were prime considerations. They also wanted a type of government similar to that of other nations.

In a previous generation, Gideon had rejected the crown on the principle that God alone was king, and now Samuel presented the negative aspects of a monarchy. A king would impose conscription and expropriate property for his own benefit and for those who immediately surrounded him. Even so the people remained adamant and, to placate them Samuel anointed Saul as the first king of Israel. Henceforth, his own activities would be confined to the spiritual sphere.

In the history of the monarchy Samuel was king maker, but in the history of prophecy his role was supreme. He founded and taught schools of disciples, earning the title Father of the Prophets, comparable to Moses. The psalmist associated him with both Moses and Aaron in the verse: "Moses and Aaron among his priests and Samuel among those who call upon his name" (Ps. 99:6).

## Saul

Samuel's objection to the monarchy did not prevent him expressing personal admiration for Saul, whose physical stature suited him for high rank. He also possessed great humility and, even after his coronation did not neglect his original occupation of farming. But qualities suited for peaceful times were a disadvantage to Saul at the particular period in which he lived. Samuel's original approval of him turned first to disappointment and then to rejection, as the negative aspects of Saul's complex personality emerged. In addition to the contrast of physical stature and self effacement, he was courageous in battle but acted from fear of his own subjects. More critical, he fluctuated widely between the extremes of confidence and melancholia, symptoms in modern terminology of a manic-depressive. These and other factors would make him one of the most tragic figures in biblical history.

Three battles that Saul fought in Samuel's lifetime marked the deterioration in their relationship. The first, against the Ammonites, when Saul enjoyed Samuel's esteem, ended in victory. Prior to the second battle, inconclusively fought against the Philistines, Samuel had occasion to rebuke Saul, prophesying that his kingdom would not endure. The third battle was against Amalek, and because Saul failed to exploit the victory by following Samuel's instructions, the rift between the two was complete. At the beginning of his career, Samuel had told Eli that his dynasty would not last and, towards the end of his life he conveyed the same message to Saul.

After Samuel's death, Saul fought his final battle against the Philistines, which ended in defeat and his own death by suicide.

The scene was the Jezreel Valley, and although Saul was aware of the impending disaster, he prepared himself to die like a king by wearing the crown and royal armor. His remains, and those of three sons who died with him, were retrieved by the men of Jabesh Gilead on the eastern side of the Jordan, and given a fitting burial. The cycle was complete, for that was the first city Saul rescued after becoming king.

### The End of the Period

After Moses, Joshua and the Judges there followed a crisis of leadership. Or in the language of metaphor, after the sun, moon and meteorites, there was darkness. The darkness came with Samuel's death because no one since Joshua possessed his authority to unite the people. Not only was he the last judge, but also the greatest.

Without Samuel, the void in leadership was heightened by the failure of the monarchy. Much trust had been placed in Saul, Israel's first king, to eliminate the Philistine threat and inaugurate a new era of hope and security. But as high as these hopes had been raised, so was the depth of demoralisation when they failed to materialise. It is true that at first Saul created a standing army and enlarged the borders of the country but, in the end, the Philistines inflicted a crushing defeat. Saul and three of his sons were among the many Israelites who failed to survive the battle.

Without an army to protect them, fear spread to that part of the population closest to the Philistine threat. Those who fled abandoned their homes and in this way entire cities were taken over by the Philistines. There seemed in fact no impediment to the Philistines becoming virtual masters of the entire country. (Long after they had disappeared, the Romans still bore them in mind by calling the entire country Palestine, as mentioned elsewhere.)

Leaderless and dominated by a warlike people, national extinction was a distinct possibility, until a new king reversed the situation. While doing so, he ushered in a golden age.

| | | |
|---|---|---|

**2000 B.C.E.**

## ABRAHAM
**THE PATRIARCHS**

**1**

Teachers of Monotheism

**HAMMURABI'S LAWS**

Hittite & Egyptian Empires

**DECLINE OF EGYPTIAN POWER**

**1500 B.C.E.**

## MOSES
**JUDGES**

**2**

Earlier Prophets

**BEGINNING OF PHILISTINE SETTLEMENTS**

Spread of Mediterranean Civilization

**1000 B.C.E.**

## DAVID
**KINGS**

**3**

Later Prophets

**RISE OF PHOENICIAN TRADE**

Mesopotamian Empires

**END OF BIBLICAL PERIOD**

**500 B.C.E.**

## EZRA
**ZUGOTH**

**4**

Joint leaders of the Sanhedrin and the rule of the Wise

**BEGINNING OF ROMAN REPUBLIC**

Spread of Hellenism

**END OF ROMAN REPUBLIC**

**0**

## HILLEL
**TALMUDIC PERIOD**

**5**

Compilation of the Oral Law

**BEGINNING OF ROMAN EMPIRE**

Spread of Christianity

**END OF ROMAN EMPIRE**

**500 C.E.**

## RAV ASHI
**THE GEONIM**

**6**

Heads of the Babylonian Academies

**BEGINNING OF MIDDLE AGES**

Spread of Islam

**DECLINE OF BAGHDAD CALIPHATE**

**1000 C.E.**

## RASHI
**THE RISHONIM**

**7**

Earlier Authorities: Commentators & Codifiers of Talmudic Law

**HOLY ROMAN EMPIRE**

Crusades

**END OF MIDDLE AGES**

**1500 C.E.**

## JOSEPH KARO
**THE AHARONIM**

**8**

Later Authorities: Commentators & Compilers of the Halacha

**RENAISSANCE & REFORMATION**

Spread of Western Civilization

**END OF OTTOMAN EMPIRE RETURN TO ZION**

**2000 C.E.**

| Chain of Tradition | Land of Israel | Influence of World History |
|---|---|---|

**1000 B.C.E.**

*David*

*80 years*

*Solomon and the division of the Kingdom after his death*

*240 years*

*Northern Kingdom exiled*

*155 years*

*Southern Kingdom exiled*

*70 years*

*Return from exile Ezra*

**500 B.C.E.**

David captured Jerusalem and made it the capital of his kingdom. In the course of time it became a spiritual center for mankind and the eternal capital of the Jewish people.

David composed the Book of Psalms, and Solomon built the Temple in Jerusalem, which stood for 410 years before it was destroyed.

After David, the prophets were the nation's spiritual leaders. They warned that exile would be the ultimate punishment for neglecting the covenant.

The age of prophecy came to an end after the return from the Babylonian exile. About the same time, the high degree of intermarriage threatened the newly established community with extinction.

David eliminated the Philistine threat, and his reign combined with that of his son Solomon, is regarded as a golden age in Jewish history.

Their descendants ruled over the Southern kingdom of Judah after the country was divided into two.

The prophets taught in both sister kingdoms and biblical prophecy is associated solely with the Holy Land.

The Northern Kingdom of Israel was the first to be taken captive. The captives of the Southern Kingdom returned after a 70 year exile.

The sister kingdoms of Israel and Judah were often used as buffer states in the power rivalry between Egypt and Mesopotamia, where the empires of Assyria, Babylon and Persia followed each other in succession.

Assyria took the Northern Kingdom into exile, while Babylon later exiled the Kingdom in the South.

Cyrus king of Persia conquered Babylon, and allowed the Jews to return to their homeland and rebuild the Temple.

During Persian rule the Biblical period came to an end, some 1,500 years after Abraham.

*Chapter Three*

# From David to Ezra – The First Temple

The Period of Kings and Prophets (c. 1000-500 B.C.E.)

## *David and Saul*

After the final rift between Samuel and Saul, when it became obvious that a new king was needed, Samuel went to Bethlehem to anoint one of the sons of Jesse.

So imposing was the impression made by the eldest son, that Samuel automatically assumed he should be the new king, until told: "Look not at his countenance nor the height of his stature... for a man looks on the outward appearance, but the Lord looks on the heart" (I Sam. 16:7). While seven of Jesse's sons were being rejected, David, the youngest brother, was tending the flocks until almost as a last resort, he was brought before Samuel and immediately anointed.

Coinciding with the secret anointment, Saul began to suffer from bouts of depression that only music could assuage. Recommended to play before the king, David still found time to tend the flocks when not needed at court, while three of his brothers served in the army ranged against the Philistines. During a visit to his brothers, David heard a Philistine giant called Goliath taunt the Israelites, issuing a challenge for a decisive duel that no one had accepted in the course of 40 days. With Saul's permission, but armed only with a staff, a sling and five stones, David successfully took on Goliath. The victory was repeated in other encounters with the Philistines, earning David the popularity of the people, but the jealousy of Saul. Paradoxically, Saul needed David to assuage his bouts of depression through music, but as king he saw him as a rival to the throne and tried to kill him.

Fleeing from Saul, David became an outcast and leader of malcontents, finding refuge with the Philistines. They gave him a city in the Negev as base, where he posed as a rebel against his own people, but in practice protected Israelite settlements from marauding desert tribes. After Saul's death and the crushing defeat inflicted by the Philistines, David moved to Hebron, where his own tribe of Judah proclaimed him king. Other tribes remained loyal to Saul and rallied around Ish-Bosheth, his son and would-be successor. A civil war followed in which David gradually won the upper hand, and ended when Ish-Bosheth was murdered by two of his own men.

## Jerusalem

During the first seven and a half years of David's 40-year reign, he ruled from Hebron, where he was proclaimed king by all the tribes. Then he moved to Jerusalem, the former Jebusite city that he made his new capital from strategic, political and religious motives. Strategically, it was nearer the center of the country than Hebron, and commanded two major axes of communication. Politically, Jerusalem's central position made it a symbol of unity for the entire population, and situated partly in Saul's tribe of Benjamin, it offered the possibility of reconciliation.

David's religious motive was to provide a permanent home for the sanctuary. Previously, it had been set up in Gilgal (under Joshua), Shiloh (under Eli), Nob (under Samuel) and Gibeon (under Saul), and now David planned to build a temple on Mt. Moriah in Jerusalem, the site associated with Abraham's binding of Isaac. Although he made all the preparations for the temple's construction, it was actually built by his son Solomon, the man of peace. David succeeded, however, in bringing the Ark of the Covenant to Jerusalem, implying that the capital was to be the nation's religious *and* political center. In David's theocratic state, the king was also subject to a higher authority, and any abuse of power would also be a sin against God.

Only Jerusalem's northern side was unprotected by a valley, which David made good by building a defensive wall, among other improvements to the city. Through his influence, the new capital began to symbolise the new, united kingdom, instead of the insignificant and demoralised one he inherited. Today, the special connotation attached to the name of Jerusalem is unique among all the cities in the world.

In 1995, Jerusalem celebrated its 3000th anniversary as the City of David. Although some disagreed with the preciseness of the date, it was pointed out in official ceremonies that there could be no State of Israel without Jerusalem, just as there could be no peace without a united Jerusalem. Audiences were also told that the city has served as a capital only for the Jews, who turn towards Jerusalem whenever they pray. The names of Jerusalem and David occur in the Bible more then those of any other city or individual. (Moslems turn towards Mecca in prayer, and the name of Jerusalem is not found even once in the Koran.)

## *Victory over the Philistines and National Consolidation*

David's acts did not go unnoticed by the Philistines, who rightly came to regard him as a threat instead of a compliant ally. They moved inland to attack, advancing along the Soreq valley that would one day provide a railway route between the coastal plain and Jerusalem. The Philistines assumed the defenders would rely on Jerusalem's walls for protection, which is why they were unprepared when David's army left the city in two surprise assaults. The unusual tactic of taking the battle to the Philistines was successful, for thereafter they ceased to be a threat. According to some biblical commentators, the Kereti who served in David's army (II Sam 20:23) refers to the Philistines, but as a separate fighting force their dominance was broken.

With the main enemy vanquished, David gave his attention to securing and enlarging the country's borders. In the process he created an important kingdom on both sides of the Jordan, managed by competent administrators. Above all, he established a just legal system to protect the rights of all his subjects, and he himself took an active part, based on the principle: "The king by justice establishes the land" (Pr. 29:4). Unlike Saul, who continued to manage his estate even after his coronation, David gave all his time and attention to being a king. A unique feature of his court was the presence of prophets, who were free to remind him at all times that he was a man of God first and a king second.

## *David's Private Life*

If David had been with his troops campaigning against the Ammonites, instead of remaining in his palace from where he saw Batsheva, the well-known incident involving the two may never have occurred. The battle against the Ammonites, the external foe, ended in success, but not so the struggle with his own passions. Men of power in all ages have exploited their positions for personal benefit, but only David had Nathan the Prophet to offer rebuke, and only he is recorded as repenting and confessing, "I have sinned against the Lord."

Prophets not only reproved David, but also wrote his history (1 Chron. 29:29) and they saw in the incident with Batsheva a prime cause for subsequent tragedies. The child born to Batsheva died seven days afterwards, and three other sons from other wives would also meet a fatal end. The first was Amnon, who violated his half-sister Tamar, and was killed for the offence by her brother Absalom. Absalom himself was killed years later, after attempting to usurp the throne. By flattery and deceit he had built up a large following that he led into Jerusalem, forcing the aged king to flee to the eastern side of the Jordan. In a crucial battle there, Absalom was defeated and slain while attempting to escape, providing David with a bitter victory. He wanted his son vanquished, but not dead.

Adonijah was the third son to meet a violent death. Following Absalom's example, he tried to usurp the throne, frustrated because Solomon, although younger, was the designated heir. When Solomon became king, Adonijah was put to death for continuing to maintain seditious ambitions.

## Solomon

David was succeeded by Solomon, his son from Batsheva, and each ruled over a united kingdom for 40 years. During their successive reigns, the Israelites passed from a somewhat loose confederation of tribes into a settled nation, and Solomon especially, whose very name in Hebrew means peace, provided the peaceful conditions necessary for the transformation. Peace was achieved through foreign alliances, notably with Egypt and Phoenicia, and prosperity followed in the wake of trade on an international scale.

Solomon's kingdom controlled important trade routes by land and sea, with the port of Etzion Gever providing access to the Red Sea. It was the most southerly Israelite settlement, near Eilat on a modern map but within Jordanian territory, and provided a gateway to the African continent and the east. The ancient kingdom of Sheba in Southern Arabia also lay on an important trade route, between India and Africa, and so its queen's famed visit to Solomon may have been motivated by commerce. A large Red Sea fleet travelled for up to three years, returning with gold, silver and ivory.

Solomon fortified the strategically placed cities of Hatzor and Meggido in the north, and Gezer in the south. Archaeological excavations at the three sites have revealed common features in the gates and walls, and in the provision for horses and chariots. The horses and chariots came from Egypt, and for the first time, the Israelites possessed a cavalry force.

The Phoenicians were Solomon's second main trading partner, and their seamen dominated the Mediterranean. They reached as far as the Iberian Peninsula, and perhaps even the British Isles, to obtain tin. In the atmosphere of international co-operation, Phoenician craftsmen were employed by the Egyptians, and they were sent by Hiram, king of Tyre, to assist in the construction of the Temple.

## The Temple

Solomon's Temple was the highlight of the Israelite settlement of the land and the fulfilment of his father's ambitions and preparations, which included materials and building plans. At the beginning of the account of the construction, David is mentioned as having bought the site on Mt. Moriah from Aravnah the Jebusite. The end of the account describes how the Ark was brought from the city of David, or Zion, to the Holy of Holies (II Chron. 3-5.) But because David had been forced to fight and shed blood, the task of actual construction was left to Solomon.

Work on the Temple began in the fourth year of Solomon's reign, 480 years after the Exodus, and it took thousands of workmen and artisans seven years to complete. In plan it was twice the size of the Tabernacle but three times its height, and in addition had an entrance hall that faced east, towards the Mount of Olives. Two large columns flanked the entrance, perhaps symbolising the pillars of cloud and fire in the wilderness. The Temple's main hall housed the altar for incense, the table for the show bread and the seven branched candelabrum.

Pilgrims, who came from all over the country on the festivals, assembled in three adjoining Temple courtyards where they observed the priests and Levites performing the sacred service, and thus gained spiritual inspiration within their own lives. At the dedication ceremony Solomon spoke of the Temple also serving the spiritual needs of other nations, an idea taken up by Isaiah, who prophesied: "My house shall be called a house of prayer for all peoples" (Is. 56:7).

Other buildings that Solomon constructed were a royal palace with an ivory throne, and a hall of justice. A building called the House of the Forest of Lebanon, because of its numerous timber columns, probably housed the palace guard. Pharaoh's daughter had a special palace built in her honor, and her marriage with Solomon in itself indicated his importance, for in general, siblings of Egyptian royalty intermarried. Solomon married many foreign wives as a means of strengthening diplomatic or commercial ties, thereby ignoring the injunction: "Neither shall he (the king) multiply wives to himself, that his heart turn not away" (Deut. 17:7). As with his father, Solomon's deeds were recorded by prophets (II Chron. 9:29) who held him personally responsible for the worship of Astarte, Molech and other gods his foreign wives brought with them. In addition to appearing to condone idolatry, Solomon imposed heavy taxes, and both factors led to the division of the kingdom after his death.

## The Golden Age of David and Solomon

David and Solomon attained royalty despite being youngest sons who experienced opposition from older brothers and, taken together, their reigns form a golden age. Solomon consolidated the kingdom his father had established, and its southern and northern borders corresponded to those promised to Abraham "from the river of Egypt to the Euphrates" (Gen. 15:8). The Mediterranean formed the natural western border, while that in the east extended well beyond the Jordan. Never again would there be such extensive boundaries under a single rule. Within these borders, father and son engaged in a literary activity unique in the biographies of kings.

While still a shepherd, David was known for his musical ability, hence he was recommended to play before Saul. From musician he became composer, writing some poetry based on personal experiences recorded in the Books of Samuel and later included in the Book of Psalms. The psalms sung by the Levites in the Temple followed musical directions established by David (II Chron. 29:25-26).

Eventually, the psalms would transcend both time and place by speaking to, and on behalf of, all mankind. They do so by recording every human emotion from joy to grief and address God with expressions ranging from praise to contrition. *Tehillim* (as they are called in Hebrew) means songs of praise. Unlike prophetic literature that records God's words to man, the Psalms are a record of man speaking to God.

When the Jewish liturgy was later formulated, most of the psalms were incorporated, and the most important prayer (*Amidah)*, recited thrice daily, begins with a verse from Psalm 51:17 - "Lord, open my lips, and my mouth shall declare Your praise." A subsequent verse describes the efficacy of prayer: "The sacrifices of God are a broken spirit, a broken and contrite heart, O God, you will not despise." The 150 psalms are divided into five parts, corresponding to the Five Books of Moses.

According to the Talmud, the three biblical books associated with Solomon were edited in the reign of Hezekiah (Bava Batra 15a). Song of Songs was written in Solomon's youth, Proverbs in his more mature years and Ecclesiastes in his old age, and so between them, like David's psalms, they cover the full range of human experience. Other peoples in the ancient world, especially Egypt, also boasted of wise men, famous throughout the east for their understanding. Solomon, however, did not hesitate to ascribe his understanding to God, illustrated by the verse, "the fear of the Lord is the beginning of wisdom" (Pr. 9:10).

## *Rebellion*

Unfortunately, Rehoboam, Solomon's son and successor, did not inherit his father's legendary powers of judgment, and so in the very beginning made three fatal errors. Firstly, he declined to be crowned in Jerusalem and chose the northern city of Shechem instead, where the ceremony provided an excuse for a hostile assembly. Secondly, instead of listening to popular demand for a more lenient rule, as the elders counselled, he accepted the advice of young contemporaries with less experience. Following his reply "My father chastised you with whips, but I will chastise you with scorpions" (1 Kings 12:14) the northern tribes rebelled and "To your tents, O Israel" (v. 16) was their rallying cry.

The king's third error was to use his senior tax collector as an intermediary. The rebels responded by stoning the man who was the very symbol of their suffering

## The United Kingdom

| Kings | Prophets |
|---|---|
| Saul | Samuel |
| David | Nathan |
| Solomon | Gad |

## The Divided Kingdom

The 21 Kings of David's dynasty who ruled from Jerusalem

The 19 Kings from six dynasties who ruled in the north

### JUDAH

| Prophets | Kings |
|---|---|
| Shemaiah | Rehoboam |
| Iddo | Abijah |
| Azariah | Asa |
|  | Jehoshaphat |
|  | Jehoram |
|  | Ahaziah |
|  | Athaliah (Queen) |
|  | Joash |
|  | Amatziah |
| Isaiah | Uzziah |
|  | Jotham |
| Micah | Ahaz |
|  | Hezekiah |
| Nahum | Menasseh |
| Habakkuk | Amon |
|  | Josiah |
| Zephaniah | Jehoahaz |
| Huldah | Jehoakim |
| Jeremiah | Jehoakin |
|  | Zedekiah |

### ISRAEL

| Kings | Prophets |
|---|---|
| Jeroboam I | Ahijah |
| Nadab |  |
| Baasha | Jehu |
| Elah |  |
| Zimri |  |
| Tivni |  |
| Omri |  |
| Ahab | Elijah |
| Ahaziah | Micah |
| Jeroham |  |
| Jehu | Elisha |
| Jehoahaz |  |
| Jehoash |  |
| Jeroboam II | Hosea |
|  | Amos |
|  | Jonah |
| Zechariah |  |
| Shallum |  |
| Menahem |  |
| Pekahia |  |
| Pekah |  |
| Hosea |  |

End of northern kingdom: c. 720 B.C.E.

End of southern kingdom (c.586 B.C.E.)

| Ezekiel | 70 years of Babylonian exile |
|---|---|

## Return to Zion

| | Sheshbazzar |
|---|---|
| Haggai | Zerubbabel |
| Zechariah | Ezra |
| Malachi | Nehemiah |

End of biblical era: c. 500 B.C.E.

and, from fear of sharing the same fate, Rehoboam fled to Jerusalem. Only the tribes of Judah, Simeon and Benjamin remained loyal to the House of David, apart from the Levites whose main duties centered around the Temple in Jerusalem. Judah was the leading tribe and also the one from which David was descended, therefore the southern part of the country became known as the kingdom of Judah. The kingdom of the northern tribes was called Israel, after the name given to Jacob. Its first ruler was Jeroboam, who as a one time overseer of the northern tribes under Solomon, fled to Egypt after leading an unsuccessful rebellion. On Solomon's death, he returned to become spokesman for the north, and then king.

Shechem became Israel's capital, and Jeroboam's primary concern was to prevent his followers going on pilgrimage to Jerusalem, where they might renew ties with the House of David. Therefore, for political rather than religious motives, he set up golden calves in Dan and Beth-El, on his northern and southern borders, proclaiming: "Behold your gods O Israel, who brought you out of the land of Egypt" (I Kings 12:28). These were the same words used by the Israelites when they danced around the golden calf in the wilderness, and on both occasions the Levites refused to participate. In any case Jeroboam dispensed with the services of the Levites by appointing his own priests, and even acted as one himself. All these reforms were designed to encourage pilgrimage to Beth El instead of Jerusalem, and for the same reason he also amended the calendar.

The divided country was a weaker one, and encouraged invasion by Shishak, king of Egypt. By this time somewhat wiser, Jeroboam offered no resistance, but peace was bought at a high price. The royal and temple treasuries were plundered, and on a wall of the temple of Karnack, in central Egypt, there is a record of the tribute Shishak received following his excursion. Jeroboam, however, never relinquished his claim to the northern part of the country, and as long as he lived there were hostilities between the two kingdoms.

### The Kingdoms of Judah and Israel

There are detailed accounts of those who sat on the thrones of Judah and Israel, yet the imperishable legacy of the age is contained in the words of the contemporary prophets, who exhorted king and commoner alike to see beyond the transitory. It should suffice, therefore, to present only a brief summary of the two sister kingdoms. Rehoboam and Jeroboam were each followed by 19 successors but, whereas those in the south ruled from the same capital and belonged to the same dynasty, there were three successive northern capitals (Shechem, Tirzah and Samaria) and no less than six dynasties. Some dynasties consisted of no more than father and son, and frequently the founder was a military commander, who usurped the throne by murdering the deposed king and his family. To illustrate the instability of the northern kingdom, eight kings representing four dynasties were contemporaries of Asa, Rehoboam's grandson.

Stability and instability were also characteristics of the various empires that came into contact with the two sister kingdoms. Egypt to the south enjoyed secure government, and the 22nd dynasty founded by Shishak, the plunderer of Jerusalem, survived for two centuries. The empires to the east, along the banks of the Tigris and Euphrates were less constant, and in the period under discussion Assyrians, Babylonians and Persians occupied the same area. The endless rivalries between the empires situated on the Nile and the Euphrates influenced the kingdoms of Judah and Israel, because they were often drawn into coalitions and used as buffer states.

For their part, the kings of Judah and Israel were not averse to participating in alliances and international intrigue and often found themselves relying on false promises of help. Finally, after almost two and a half centuries of co-existence, the Assyrians exiled the northern tribes. The south survived alone for some 135 years longer until it too suffered the same fate at the hands of the Babylonians. The beginning and end of their dual existence was marked by war, but otherwise there were periods of friendship and co-operation, when the combined borders resembled those under David and Solomon.

As observers of the political manoeuvrings, the prophets declared that no treaty or coalition can shore up a state morally weak and unsound from within. Ultimately, signatories and guarantors of treaties are only motivated by self interest.

### The Prophets

After Samuel, there were four distinct stages in the history of prophecy. In the first, between Samuel and Hosea, schools of prophets were common, but prophetic statements were not recorded in separate books, and exile as a punishment was never threatened. Between Hosea and Jeremiah teachings were recorded in books that bear their authors' names, hence the term literary prophets. In this classical period of prophecy, as it came to be known, prophets were not associated with specific groups, but came from all classes of society. Isaiah was an aristocrat, Jeremiah and Ezekiel were priests, and Amos was a farmer and herdsman. The writings of the first three are the most extensive; therefore they are assigned separate books. Twelve others are known as Minor Prophets, because their books, ranging from one to fourteen chapters, are much shorter. During this second phase, exile is threatened as the ultimate punishment.

Jeremiah represents a watershed because, in addition to predicting exile, he actually experienced it. His eyewitness account of events, as described in the Book of Lamentations, is read in synagogues on each anniversary of the Temple's destruction.

The fourth prophetic phase began after the return from Babylon, when Haggai and Zechariah encouraged the work of national restoration. With Malachi, the age of prophecy came to an end.

The prophets were active in both kingdoms, but it was in the north that they fought hardest against idolatry. This was mainly due to the influence of Jeroboam and Ahab, who were respectively the first and eighth kings of Israel. Jeroboam set up golden calves on his northern and southern borders, more as a substitute for the Temple in Jerusalem than as an alternative for God. In Ahab's rule, instead of worshipping God in the manner of idolaters, idols were worshipped in their own right. When there were only 7,000 in the entire northern kingdom who did not bow to Baal, Elijah appeared on the scene.

## Prophets of the Northern Kingdom

### Elijah

As Elijah preceded the literary prophets there is no independent work that bears his name. The Book of Kings describes how the true source of idolatry in his time was Ahab's wife Jezebel, a princess of Phoenicia, who introduced her native gods of Baal and Asherah into the country. To serve these idols, she also brought hundreds of priests, and a special temple to Baal was built in the capital city of Samaria. Idolatry as the state religion meant that true prophets were persecuted, of whom one hundred were saved by a court official named Ovadiah, who hid them in a cave. Jezebel's native city of Sidon was one of the great Phoenician seaports, and the diplomatic ties cemented through her marriage to Ahab meant increased trade and prosperity. Many ascribed the favorable conditions to Jezebel's gods, which made the task of fighting idolatry in the Northern Kingdom all the more difficult.

Elijah is first mentioned when he appeared before Ahab to announce a drought. At a time when fellow prophets were forced into hiding, he actually confronted the king, although taking precaution to appear and disappear without notice, to avoid capture. The purpose of the drought was a punishment for idolatry, confirming Moses' warning: "Take heed lest...you turn aside and serve other gods... and He shut up the heavens that there be no rain, and the land yield not its fruit" (Deut. 11:16-17). Three years later, when the land was parched and water scarce, Elijah challenged the prophets of Baal to a contest of faith on Mt. Carmel in the north. Mt. Sinai and Mt. Carmel are both associated with the covenant. At the former, the

Decalogue began with the words "I am the Lord your God," which were reaffirmed by the people's declaration "The Lord He is God" at Mt. Carmel, after Elijah's triumph. The prophets of Baal were slain, the drought came to an end, but Elijah had to flee into the wilderness to escape Jezebel's wrath.

Mt. Horeb, which is another name for Mt. Sinai, was his eventual destination. The thunder and lightning that had accompanied the Decalogue, were reduced in the time of Elijah to a still, small voice. Twice he was asked: "What are you doing here, Elijah?" implying that a prophet's place is among the people, and not in the isolation of a wilderness.

Elijah's last meeting with Ahab was in Naboth's vineyard, adjoining one of the king's palaces in the Jezreel Valley. The king coveted the vineyard, but it was Queen Jezebel who acquired it for him, by judicial murder. Her plan of a fabricated charge and false witnesses has made her name synonymous in the English language with a shameless or scheming woman. It also led Elijah to ask the king rhetorically "Have you killed and also inherited?" and then predict the end of his dynasty. The house of Omri, of which Ahab was the most prominent member, was eliminated in the next generation.

Zeal is the word that most aptly summarises Elijah's activities. Virtually single-handed, he fought against idolatry in the Northern Kingdom, even though it meant suffering persecution by Jezebel. Yet for all his zeal, Elijah did not win the war against idolatry, only a battle, and when he departed it is not recorded that he died, but only that he ascended to heaven in a chariot of fire enveloped in a whirlwind.

## Elisha

Some of the tasks entrusted to Elijah were completed by his disciple, Elisha, and the two afford the only example of one prophet designating another as successor. (Moses had laid his hands on Joshua to appoint him leader, not prophet.) They are also the only two prophets for whom there is a physical description, for Elijah was "a hairy man, with a belt of leather about his loins" (II Kings 1:8) whereas Elisha was bald (II Kings 2:23).

Among their differences, Elijah was zealous and his appearances unpredictable, whereas Elisha used diplomacy and his home in Samaria served as a meeting place for the elders. It was also a base from where he visited different parts of the country, after the fashion of Samuel in the period of the Judges.

Elisha was active for almost 60 years, more than any other prophet, and his joint activity with Elijah spanned almost a century. He carried out the task originally given to Elijah of establishing two new dynasties. The first was in Damascus, the capital of Aram, which was roughly identifiable with present day Syria. Elisha travelled there to anoint Hazael, even though he foresaw that one day he would ravage Israel and Judah. Such was Elisha's reputation that even in Damascus he was known as "the man of God" (II Kings 8:8) and the incident provides the only example of a prophet anointing a foreign king.

The second dynasty established by Elisha was that of Jehu, and the anointing of a northern king by the command of a prophet was another unique event. Once appointed, Jehu set about eliminating the House of Omri, the very dynasty he had served as a senior army officer. His victims included Jehoram, King of Israel, Jezebel and her grandson, King Ahaziah of Judah who was visiting the north. The priests of Baal were also slain. Only one descendant of Ahab and Jezebel now survived, and that was Athaliah, mother of the murdered Ahaziah, and once queen consort to his father. She took the opportunity to seize the throne and rule in her own right but seven years later Jehoash, whom as an infant she had failed to kill in the coup, was crowned king in secret. Immediately afterwards, the only queen of the biblical period to rule alone lost her life.

During these various purges, Elisha represented stability and continuity. Universally recognised as the nation's spiritual leader, people came to him from all parts of the country for guidance and instruction. He even advised a king to treat some Aramean captives with consideration rather than severity, and a long period free of hostilities followed. Respectfully called "father," he established and led schools of prophets. In the following period, there is less biographical detail to describe the lives of the prophets, but in contrast, their actual words are recorded at greater length and in separate books.

### Hosea and Amos

The books of Hosea and Amos contain the teachings of two contemporary prophets and therefore reflect the same social and political background. The king most influential in their time was Jeroboam II, who reigned some 40 years, making him the longest reigning monarch of the longest reigning dynasty in the northern kingdom - the House of Jehu. During this period, weak kings on the throne of Assyria and an international power vacuum allowed the sister kingdoms of Israel and Judah to expand both in trade and industry. Prosperity was the result but, because it was unevenly distributed, the gap between rich and poor increased. To maintain their position, the affluent minority resorted to oppression and the perversion of justice, not realising that thereby they were preparing their own destruction.

Of the six kings of Israel who succeeded Jeroboam II, five died a violent death, including his own son whose assassination brought an end to Jehu's dynasty. Jeroboam's reign, therefore, proved to be the last period of security before Assyria overthrew the kingdom of Israel.

Hosea's activity bridged the last years of Jeroboam's reign and the subsequent period of anarchy. He saw in idolatry not merely aspects of social and national evils but the very source of injustice and a disastrous foreign policy. In Hosea's striking imagery, idolaters are compared to an adulteress seeking out lovers, with God portrayed as the devoted husband and Israel the faithless wife. The imagery was even depicted on a personal level, where his unrequited love for his own disloyal wife represented God's love towards Israel.

Despite his love, he divorced his wife and recovered the gifts he had given her; so would God appear to abandon Israel and revoke His benefits. Yet just as Hosea brought back his wife, God would restore Israel after a period of chastisement and contrition, and so his message is one of hope. The renewed relationship is described in the language of a wedding ceremony: "And I will betroth you to Me for ever... And I will betroth you to Me in faithfulness, and you shall know that I am the Lord" (Hos. 2:21-22).

Amos was Hosea's contemporary, probably older, but unlike him he was born in the south, coming from the town of Tekoa near Bethlehem. It is assumed that his family was not a distinguished one, because in contrast to other prophets, his genealogy is not mentioned. In Tekoa he was a herdsman and tended sycamore trees, until, as he himself describes, he became a prophet: "The lion has roared, who will not fear; the Lord God has spoken, who can but prophesy?" (Amos 3:8).

Although Samaria had been the capital of the north since the days of Omri, its seventh king, Beth El, site of the kingdom's main temple, predated it as a center for heathen worship. Consequently it was there that Amos mainly prophesied, denouncing the heathen altars and palatial homes of the rich, which were overlaid with ivory and built by exploiting the poor. When he threatened exile, and Jeroboam II himself with the sword, the high priest reported his words to the king as seditious. Jeroboam's response is not recorded, but to the high priest who told him to return and prophesy in Judah, Amos answered that he was neither a prophet nor the son of a prophet.

Although threats of punishment were justified against a background of oppression and immorality, they nevertheless created conflict for the prophets, who always sought the good of their own people. Therefore, twice Amos pleaded, "How shall Jacob stand, for he is small?" The change of heart that Amos sought on a national scale did not take place, unlike the exile that he predicted. But he also foresaw beyond the captivity to the period of return, when cities would be rebuilt, the soil made productive and the people never again taken from their land. In the tradition of the prophets, beginning with Moses, even the direst warnings were followed by a message of consolation.

# Prophets of the Southern Kingdom

## *Political Background*

For a number of years, while Jeroboam II sat on the throne of Israel, his counterpart in Judah was Uzziah, whose reign reflected the prosperity of the times. He built extensively throughout the country while creating a strong army, and such was his prestige that when he contracted leprosy, he was allowed to remain on the throne with his son Jotham acting as regent. Uzziah's 52-year reign was one of the longest in either kingdom, and when Jotham became king in his own right, he continued his father's domestic and foreign policies.

During the reign of Ahaz, Jotham's son, Assyria was fast becoming one of the mightiest empires of the ancient world. To create a counterbalance, the kings of Israel and Aram formed an alliance, inviting Ahaz to join. On his refusal, the coalition besieged Jerusalem, in an attempt to depose him, but the situation was saved by inviting Assyrian intervention. During his campaign, Tiglath Pileser III, the Assyrian king, captured Damascus, the capital of Aram, and the country became known as Syria, implying it to be a mere province of Assyria. He also led a large part of the northern population into captivity, and made Judah subservient.

Dependence on Assyria led Ahaz to adopt its style of worship, leading to innovations in the Temple and the setting up of heathen altars throughout the country. The spiritual decline was not checked until Hezekiah ascended the throne and introduced religious reforms. He also tried to regain national independence, which meant siding with Egypt, Assyria's main rival.

## *Isaiah*

As a witness to the rise and fall of empires and kingdoms, Isaiah became more involved than any other prophet in affairs of state. His freedom to address the court at any time confirms the tradition that he himself was an aristocrat.

He assured Ahaz that the coalition of Israel and Aram ranged against Judah would fail, and then advised him against inviting Assyria to come to his aid. When Assyria in turn threatened Judah in the reign of Hezekiah, and the king was inclined to turn to Egypt, Isaiah told him: "Woe to those who go down to Egypt for help, and turn not to the Holy One of Israel." The warning was heeded and Judah was saved, whereas the northern tribes that opposed Assyria were exiled.

The policy of deporting defeated nations was a common practice of the Assyrians, who established their empire by conquest. In the interchange of populations, a large foreign element was introduced into the territory of the former kingdom of Israel intermarrying with those who remained. Settling in the cities of Samaria, the land became a province of Assyria.

When Sargon, the founder of the last and greatest Assyrian dynasty died, a series of insurrections broke out throughout the empire and Sennacherib, his son and successor, spent most of his reign putting them down.

The members of Hezekiah's court advised him to join the rebellion and turn to Egypt for help, despite Isaiah's counsel to the contrary. The prophet saw in the Assyrians an instrument of God's wrath, before whom even Egypt would eventually fall. Sennacherib first put down the uprisings in the east, and then systematically those in the west until only Judah remained.

Lachish was the last stronghold to fall before Jerusalem was besieged, and archaeological evidence testifies to Hezekiah's preparations. In 1880 a 500 metre long tunnel was discovered, that connected the external Siloam spring to a large cistern within the city's walls, whereby Hezekiah provided Jerusalem with an adequate water supply. (An inscription by his workmen to commemorate the digging was transferred by the Turks from the tunnel after its discovery, and is now exhibited in the Istanbul Museum.) There is also evidence of a second defensive wall built to the north of Jerusalem where the even topography made Jerusalem most vulnerable.

A six-sided clay tablet found in Sennacherib's capital of Nineveh speaks of Hezekiah being "shut up in Jerusalem, like a caged bird." Isaiah also used the imagery of a bird when he said: "As birds hovering, so will the Lord of Hosts defend Jerusalem" (Is. 31:5).

Against every expectation, lsaiah's prophecy that the Assyrians would not enter Jerusalem was fulfilled, and the siege was abandoned overnight. The destruction of Sennacherib's army is ascribed by some to a plague, and Sennacherib himself was later murdered by his two sons. The deliverance of Jerusalem is regarded as a major event in Jewish history, not only because of the miraculous way it occurred, but also because of the implications. If the Assyrians had captured Jerusalem, as they took countless other fortified cities, there is little doubt its citizens would have disappeared in captivity, just like those of the Northern Kingdom. It is true that the population of Judah was exiled a hundred years later, but by then conditions were different, and in the intervening years a righteous king like Hezekiah reinforced national identity through a program of intensive Torah study. The additional hundred years of independence was due to Isaiah, for he instilled into the people, from the king down, the will to survive and outlive the invader.

Isaiah's activities came to an end with Jerusalem's deliverance, and even though many of his prophecies contain harsh judgements, true to prophetic tradition, they conclude with a message of consolation.

His description of the messianic age contains some of the most sublime passages ever written, as when, for example, he foresaw a time when peoples "shall beat their swords into ploughshares and their spears into pruning hooks. Nation shall not lift up

## PERSPECTIVE OF HISTORY - THE RISE AND FALL OF EMPIRES

The Book of Daniel views history as the rise and fall of successive empires. The boundaries of four such empires are illustrated below:

**The Babylonian Empire**
**c. sixth century B.C.E.**

**The Persian Empire**
**c. fifth and fourth centuries B.C.E.**

**The Ptolemaic Empire**
**c. third century B.C.E.**

**The Seleucid Empire**
**c. second century B.C.E.**

sword against nation, neither shall they learn war any more" (Is. 2:4). In that age: "The wolf shall lie down with the lamb and the leopard shall lie down with the kid.... for the earth shall be full of the knowledge of the Lord, as the waters cover the sea" (Is. 11:6-9).

## Micah

Isaiah influenced no one more than Micah, a fellow prophet and younger contemporary who did not hesitate to use some of his imagery. Unlike the aristocratic Isaiah, who spoke with princes and involved himself with matters of state, Micah was a man of the people. He came from a provincial town near the Philistine border, and devoted most of his attention to social affairs. Each prophet spoke in a distinctive style, even though a common purpose united them all. A striking feature of Micah's style is the way he refers to the needy and destitute not as the poor, but as "my people," in the sense that they are the people of God.

They were the victims, according to Micah, of greed and materialism, which he diagnosed as the main social malady. Because of greed, judges accepted bribes, priests taught for money and princes were corrupt. Because of greed, false prophets promised peace to whoever paid them. Micah spoke to the common people whose cause he championed, but his words also reached Hezekiah, (Jer. 26:19) thereby influencing his religious reforms.

In Micah's vision of the future, Zion would be the spiritual center and, like Isaiah, he saw that from there the word of the Lord would go forth. Adding a pastoral touch, he described the age of universal peace as a time when "every man shall sit under his vine and under his fig tree, and none shall make them afraid" (Mic. 4:4). Moses had asked: "What does the Lord your God require of you?" (Deut. 10:12) and, after repeating the question, Micah gave the definitive answer for all time: "to do justice, to love mercy, and to walk humbly with your God" (Mic. 6:8). This verse is regarded as the quintessence of Judaism, and for it alone Micah ranks as one of the great moral teachers of mankind.

## Political Developments after Micah

Manasseh followed his father Hezekiah on the throne of Judah and occupied it for 55 years, the longest reign of either kingdom. It was also one of the most disastrous, because he undid all his father's reforms and outdid the excesses of Ahaz, his grandfather. He set up altars to Baal and Asherah even in the Temple, and in accordance with heathen practice, burnt his own son. The kingdom of Judah reached a low spiritual ebb that was only equalled in the two year reign of his son Amon. Whether willingly or by coercion, the people participated in Manasseh's excesses, except for a faithful minority that resisted under the threat of death. Isaiah's own violent death is ascribed to this period.

Because of the many wrongs the prophets foresaw exile, but Judah would not suffer alone. Nahum, who was active about this time, spoke of the eventual downfall of Assyria and its capital Nineveh. Manasseh's reign corresponded to the height of Assyrian power, when dynamic kings extended the empire's borders to their limit. From its client states, the Assyrians expected both political and cultural subservience, for which reason they objected to Hezekiah's reforms, but encouraged Manasseh's idolatry. The decadence of Manasseh's reign, therefore, had its origins in his willingness to ingratiate himself with his Assyrian masters.

Nevertheless, at some stage he rebelled, possibly as part of a general uprising, and was led away in chains by the Assyrians. While in captivity, he had a change of heart, so that by the time he was restored to the throne, he tried belatedly to make good all the harm he himself had caused. Amon, Manasseh's son, was murdered in a palace coup and after the assassins in turn were killed, the eight year old Josiah was proclaimed king.

When he was twenty, Josiah began to cleanse the country of the idolatrous practices associated with his father and grandfather. Six years later, during extensive renovations to the Temple, the high priest "found a book of the Torah of the Lord, given by Moses" (II Chron. 34:14). These last three words in the Hebrew text can also mean "written by Moses," which is why some commentators state that the scroll was the actual one written by Moses and placed in the Ark (Deut. 31:26). During Manasseh's religions persecutions, when for the first time a graven image was set up in the Temple, the scroll had been hidden for safety, and was not found until Josiah's reign. The discovery made a great impact on the king, who read from it publicly, and used the occasion to renew the covenant.

He then instituted a program of religious reforms that rid the country of idolatry, and earned him a special place among the kings of Judah. He also guaranteed a proper judicial system, following the example of David and Solomon.

In a brief period of 40 years that began shortly before Josiah's reign and ended just prior to his death, Assyria passed from world domination to oblivion. The principle heir of the Assyrian empire was Babylon, but Egypt attempted to fill the vacuum by dominating Judah and Syria. When Pharaoh Necho led his army eastward in the confusion following the fall of Nineveh, Josiah was mortally wounded trying to check his advance at Megiddo. He was the last king of Judah to be buried near his ancestors in Jerusalem.

## Jeremiah

No one lamented Josiah's death more than Jeremiah, about whom more is known than any other prophet. Like Moses, he did not seek out his vocation, but God's word burnt within him like a fire that could not be contained and so in spite of himself, he began to prophesy at an early age.

He came from Anatot, a city of priests, and Zephaniah and Huldah, fellow prophets, were his contemporaries. Huldah was the prophetess consulted by Josiah when the scroll of the Law was discovered in the Temple and, in the period of reform following the discovery, Jeremiah began his activity. He naturally supported the reforms, but simultaneously criticised the superficial way in which they were often executed, especially by the leaders themselves. Contrary to what people wanted to hear, he predicted desolation and exile as a consequence of national guilt, and was forced to flee from Anatoth. Even in Jerusalem he became unpopular with every section of society, from the princes to common people, who at one stage were all united against him. The word "Jeremiad" derived from his name, meaning complaint or lament, is based on the fact that his summons to moral reform was backed by threats of doom.

The promised catastrophe would come from the north, by which Jeremiah meant the new power of Babylon, contrary to the message of the false prophets who cried: "Peace, peace, when there is no peace" (Jer. 6:14, 8:11). As long as Josiah lived, Jeremiah enjoyed his protection, but conditions changed when Pharaoh Necho fatally wounded the king in battle. The Pharaoh went on to fight a costly but inconclusive engagement with the Babylonians at Carchemish, in ancient Syria, and on returning deposed Jehoahaz and took him captive to Egypt. Jehoahaz, who had reigned for only three months, was replaced by Jehoakim, an older half-brother more sympathetic to Egypt.

In Jehoakim's fourth year, a Babylonian army led by Nebuchadnezzar defeated Pharoah Necho in a second battle at Carchemish, thereby definitely ending the Egyptian threat. Soon afterwards Nebuchadnezzar ascended the Babylonian throne, and found Jehoakim part of an anti-Babylonian coalition. The king of Judah was forced to accept his authority, following a punitive expedition, but this did not prevent him seeking the first opportunity to rebel.

Jeremiah realistically opposed resistance to Babylon, which placed him in opposition to the authorities, who forbade him to prophesy in the Temple. He evaded the ban by dictating his messages to Baruch, a disciple and scribe, who then read them before the priests, princes and people. Those who were pragmatic accepted Jeremiah's prophecies, but not so the king, who had the scrolls burnt and forced Jeremiah and Baruch into hiding.

When Jehoakim found the opportunity to rebel, Nebuchadnezzar sent a coalition of vassal states against Jerusalem. During the siege, the king died, and was followed by his son Jehoakin, who ruled only three months before surrendering Jerusalem to the Babylonians. Nebuchadnezzar himself had in the meantime joined the siege, and to forestall further rebellion, he took Jehoakin into exile.

Accompanying the king were other members of the royal family, Jerusalem's nobility and temple treasures, leaving only the poor and unskilled behind.

## *Jeremiah and the fall of Jerusalem*

The last king of Judah was Zedekiah, a third son of Josiah, and Jehoakin's uncle. Nebuchadnezzar, who put Zedekiah on the throne, intended him to be submissive, but instead he followed the example of his predecessors and turned to Egypt. Jeremiah continued to oppose the bankrupt policy and appeared in public with a wooden yoke on his shoulders, as a symbol of submission to Babylon. When the king's supporters broke it, he replaced it with another made of iron. He preached to neighboring kingdoms the same message of submission, because he was also a prophet to the nations. As for his compatriots in Babylon, he asked them to pray for its welfare, because on its peace, theirs also depended (Jer. 29:7).

The continued refusal to accept Jeremiah's appeals both for repentance on a national scale, and neutrality in foreign policy, hastened the end of the kingdom. Zedekiah allowed himself to be influenced by the pro-Egyptian party and rebelled against Babylon. Nebuchadnezzar responded by overrunning the country, and during the siege of Jerusalem, Zedekiah saw all Jeremiah's prophesies about to be fulfilled. This caused a change of heart in the king, and one particular commandment he persuaded the rich to keep was the release of bondsmen. But the rich quickly retracted during a short interlude, when the Babylonians lifted the siege to deal with an Egyptian army sent to Zedekiah's assistance. Jeremiah's reaction was to declare: "Behold, I proclaim a liberty to you, says the Lord, to the sword, to the pestilence, and to the famine" (Jer. 34:17).

By leaving Jerusalem during the temporary suspension of the siege, Jeremiah allowed his enemies to falsely accuse him of going over to the enemy. He was beaten, imprisoned and then lowered into a pit of mire, where he would have died if not rescued by a king's servant. When the siege was renewed, he suffered with the entire population of Jerusalem from the pangs of hunger, of which he later wrote: "those who died by the sword were more fortunate than those who died by famine" (Lam. 3:9). In the final overthrow, those who survived both sword and famine fled into the Judean desert under the cover of night.

Zedekiah was pursued, captured and then forced to watch his children's execution before he was blinded, the punishment reserved for traitors. Together with other captives and spoils from the Temple, he was led in chains to Babylon, to join the exiles of the previous deportation. Zedekiah was thus the last king descended from David to occupy the throne in Jerusalem, bringing to an end a dynasty of over 400 years, one of the longest in history.

With its last king deposed, the kingdom of Judah came to an end 850 years after the Children of Israel had entered the country under Joshua. Over the destruction of Jerusalem and the Temple, Jeremiah lamented: "Would that my head were water and my eyes a fountain of tears, that I might weep day and night for the slain of my people" (Lam. 8:23).

### The Final Tragedy

Even at this low ebb, other misfortunes were still to come. The Babylonians allowed a poor remnant to remain, to cultivate the land and provide food for their armies that might encamp in, or pass through, the country. Those who had fled to neighboring countries gradually returned and a semblance of normal life resumed. Gedaliah, whose father had been a courtier and one of Jeremiah's supporters, was appointed governor by the Babylonians.

The Ammonites, a marauding people living east of the Dead Sea and traditional enemies of the Israelites, looked with disapproval on a restored community. They wanted to incorporate Judah into their own territory, and so their king plotted Gedaliah's assassination. His accomplice was Ishmael, who traced his descent to David, and therefore resented someone without royal blood ruling over the country. Assisted by other accomplices he resorted to treachery to murder Gedaliah and a Babylonian garrison. Regarded as a tragedy, Gedaliah's death is commemorated in the Hebrew calendar as a fast day.

Fearing Babylonian reprisals, the remnant fled to Egypt, against Jeremiah's advice, putting an end to autonomous rule. Jeremiah and Baruch were forced to accompany the fugitives, and even in Egypt the prophet continued to condemn idolatry. But not even Egypt was beyond Nebuchadnezzar's reach, although there is no biblical record as to how he treated the Israelite refugees. According to Josephus, he took them to Babylon, where Jeremiah and Baruch spent the last years of their lives. (Antiquities, book 10, ch.9).

### The Babylonian Exile

A significant question is why the Jews, as the inhabitants of Judah came to be called, returned from Babylon after 70 years, whereas the numerically superior ten tribes disappeared after they were uprooted from their land. The question is strengthened when the comparison is made not with the northern sister kingdom alone, but with all the peoples of the ancient world who were taken into captivity and passed into oblivion. Individuals sometimes returned from exile but never, except for the Jews, a nation. If the explanation lies in a single word, then it is continuity, especially of leadership and worship, and both are associated with Jehoakin, the exiled king of Judah.

The books of Jeremiah and II Kings both conclude with the same words that describe how Jehoakin was released from prison after Nebuchadnezzar's death.

Evil-Merodach, the new king, reversed his father's policies on succeeding to the throne and, in addition to giving Jehoakin his freedom, showed him favors above any other exiled king at the Babylonian court. In effect Jehoakin became the leader of Babylonian Jewry and, whether or not he was given the title Exilarch associated with the position, it certainly became hereditary among his descendants. Thus the dynasty of kings that once ruled in Jerusalem became in Babylon a dynasty of Exilarchs, with David as the common ancestor. The presence of leaders descended from David reminded the exiles of a glorious past and hope in a messianic future as described by the prophets. In the more immediate future, one of the first groups of exiles to return to Jerusalem would be led by Zerubbabel, a prince from the House of David.

Continuity of worship was provided by the synagogue, and according to a famous letter written by Sherira Gaon in the late tenth century, Jehoiakin built the first synagogue in Babylon. He and some fellow compatriots laid its foundation with stones and earth that they had brought from Jerusalem, and they called the finished building by a composite name meaning "the Temple has been replanted in Babylon." Even before the exile, the synagogue existed contemporaneously with the Temple, but in Babylon it came into its own. Prayer took the place of sacrifice and in particular, prayers for the restoration of Zion preserved national aspirations. Whether in the synagogue or in isolation, the suppliant turned towards Jerusalem.

In the Yiddish language, the term for synagogue is "shul," which is clearly related to the English word school. Providing a place of learning was one of the prime objectives of the synagogue, where the exiles studied the sacred texts from Moses to their own day. The Torah thus became a portable "state" uniting the people through a comprehensive way of life, and in the synagogue it was read, explained and made accessible to all.

The prophetic teachings available to the exiles were not only contained in scrolls from the past, for there were also contemporary prophets to deliver or dictate the spoken word. They provided a continuity of spiritual leadership, bridging not only time but also space, because prior to the destruction of the Temple they addressed the two communities of Babylon and Jerusalem simultaneously. Ezekiel's words spoken in Babylon were conveyed to Jerusalem, and Jeremiah's words spoken in Jerusalem were conveyed in the opposite direction. Both were priests, and therefore specifically designated to teach the people.

## Ezekiel

Ezekiel's career began in Jerusalem, from where he was exiled to Babylon with Jehoakin and the city's elite, and from where he continued to address those left behind. He first prophesied in Babylon six years before the Temple's destruction, condemning the sins committed in Judah. Afterwards he spoke of national salvation and restoration, ending with a vision of the new Temple. His phraseology shows that he was familiar with all the sacred texts studied in Babylon, especially Leviticus and Jeremiah.

Ezekiel was listened to with greater respect than the pre-exilic prophets, some of whom had suffered verbal and even physical abuse. The changed attitude was due to changed circumstances that had been foretold by the prophets and therefore proved the truth of their teachings. Changed circumstances also led the exiles to believe that they were held accountable for the sins of the previous generation, as expressed by a proverb then widely quoted: "The fathers have eaten sour grapes, and the children's teeth are set on edge" (Ezek. 18:2). Ezekiel declared such belief mistaken, and spoke instead about personal responsibility and the concept that God sought the eradication of sin rather than the sinner: "Have I any pleasure that the wicked should die, says the Lord and not that he should turn from his ways and live" (Ezek. 18:33). True repentance, he taught, was strong enough to create a new heart and spirit in everyone.

More than any other prophet, Ezekiel used symbolism to convey his messages, just as more than any other he witnessed visions. Perhaps the most famous was that of the valley of dry bones, representing the House of Israel devoid of hope or future. Their resurrection and breath of new life was a promise of national revival. Exile profaned God's name, which would be sanctified, according to Ezekiel, with national restoration. He did not witness the day himself, for he died while Babylon was still a great power under Nebuchadnezzar, but the event was not long coming.

The Book of Daniel (Chap. 5) describes Babylon's final hours. Its last king, Belshazzar, made a feast, using vessels taken from the Temple by his father, Nebuchadnezzar. The ensuing idolatrous revelry came to an abrupt end with mysterious "writing on the wall" in the form of a cyptic message that only Daniel could decipher. Its meaning to the king was threefold: "G-d has numbered your kingdom and brought it to an end. You are weighed in the balance and found wanting. Your kingdom is divided and given to the Medes and Persians." (This dramatic scene would later be depicted in various art forms by Rembrandt, Byron, Heine and Handel.) That same night Balshazzar was slain and his kingdom brought to an end.

### Babylon falls to Persia.

Just as Assyria had fallen to Babylon, so Babylon fell to Persia, and in both cases the collapse was swift. The city of Babylon was situated on the Euphrates, and when Jeremiah once spoke of its waters drying up (Jer. 50:38) he may have been alluding to the way in which it was captured. The Euphrates formed a natural moat, and after the Persians diverted its waters, they were able to enter the city unopposed. Within a short space of time, one of the legendary cities of the world, known both for splendour and licentiousness, declined into insignificance.

The king who moulded the new empire was Cyrus, whose successors were prevented from advancing into Europe by the Greeks. Daniel, who lived under the Babylonians and Persians, saw beyond the biblical period to the time when Greece would succeed the kingdoms of the Fertile Crescent (Dan. 8:21). Whether in Greece, Persia, India or China, the East around the reign of Cyrus witnessed great intellectual ferment, for it was a time when new systems of ethical government were being established.

The Persian religion was very different from the polytheism of Babylon, far more idealistic and sympathetic to the monotheism of the Jews. Cyrus himself became a legend even during his lifetime, gaining fame as an able, merciful and practical ruler. He failed, however, to incorporate Egypt into his vast empire, and so it was in his interest to create a buffer state. To this end he encouraged the Jews to return to their homeland.

The proclamation by which Cyrus allowed the exiles to return was issued in 538 B.C.E., the year in which he conquered Babylon, and it is quoted in the last verse of the Bible: "Thus says Cyrus, king of Persia, the Lord God of heaven has given me all the kingdoms of the earth, and he has charged me to build Him a house in Jerusalem, which is in Judah. Whoever is among you of all his people, the Lord his God be with him, and let him go up" (II Chron. 36:23). Cyrus thus ended the 70-year exile prophesied by Jeremiah "until the land had made good her Sabbaths" (*ib.* v. 21). The "Sabbaths" refer to the 70 Sabbatical and Jubilee years desecrated by the Israelites from the time they entered the land until they were forced to leave.

In general history Cyrus is called the Great, but by the Jews he is called "God's shepherd" (Is. 44: 28) and "the Lord's anointed" (45:1) and they showed their gratitude to the Persians by never rebelling against their authority.

## *The Return to Zion*

With obvious editorial intention, the last words of the Bible "let him go up" are a clear invitation for the Jews to return to their homeland. Only a small minority, however, did so because the rest, especially the rich, were unwilling to uproot themselves and begin anew in a land still desolate. Those who returned did so in three main waves: two in the reign of Cyrus, and one in the reign of Artaxerxes I (the fifth king of Persia). The first wave of approximately 12,000 was led by Sheshbazzar, the second of 30,000 by Zerubbabel, and Ezra, who led the third wave, begins the next chapter.

Both Sheshbazzar and Zerubbabel were descended from David, a fact that aroused expectations for a full national restoration. It was the Samaritans, living in the north of the country, who did everything in their power to foil such hopes.

(After the exile of the ten tribes, the inhabitants of Samaria were first called Kutim, after a city of their origin in Mesopotamia. The Samaritans were members of a later sect who lived in the same area, but by talmudic times distinction between the two terms - Samaritans and Kutim - was blurred. In the following pages, the name Samaritan is applied retrospectively to biblical times.)

No sooner had the foundations of the new Temple been laid, than the Samaritans wanted to participate in its construction. True converts have always been welcomed (although not sought) by Judaism, both after the return from Babylon (Ezra 6:21) and ever since. The reason why Zerubbabel rejected the Samaritan offer, therefore, is because he did not consider them true proselytes. The Samaritans retaliated by accusing the Jews of sedition to the Persian authorities and as a consequence, the work of Jerusalem's restoration was halted. It was recommenced later through the exhortation of two prophets.

### Haggai and Zechariah

After Cyrus' death, general confusion surrounded the inheritance of the Persian throne until stability was restored by Darius I, a worthy successor of Cyrus who encouraged rehabilitation of the Jewish state. Haggai and Zechariah began to prophecy in the second year of his reign, by which time work on the rebuilding of the Temple had ceased for 18 years.

A task shared by both prophets was to encourage the work of restoration. Haggai rebuked the people for living in comfort while the House of God remained desolate, and he regarded the lack of rain and a poor harvest as punishment. Aided by Zechariah, he urged Zerubbabel, the governor of the province, and Joshua, the high priest, to restart building, and when they did so, the Samaritans renewed their opposition. The dispute reached Darius, who re-affirmed Cyrus' decree, and allowed the Temple to be completed (516 B.C.E.). It suffered in comparison to the first Temple, but even so Haggai promised that its glory would be greater.

A series of widespread insurrections at the beginning of Darius' reign threatened his empire, and so it was in Persia's interest to maintain Judah as a loyal autonomous state. From Zerubbabel's viewpoint, a disunited empire would have provided the opportunity to restore the monarchy, and both Haggai and Zechariah refer to the theme. But Darius proved to be an able administrator and the occasion never arose. Zerubbabel's post was not hereditary, and he was the last Persian governor or satrap from the House of David.

### The Story of Purim

Darius was succeeded by Xerxes I (485-465), who in the first five years on the throne brought Egypt once more under Persian rule, pillaged Athens and lost his fleet at Salamis. In Old Persian, his name resembles that of Ahasuerus in the Book of Esther, and if the identity is the same, then it was during his reign that Jews throughout the empire were threatened with genocide.

The threat originated with Haman, a senior courtier who made the king his accomplice with a gift of 10,000 talents of silver. He gained royal approval to destroy the Jews on the grounds that they were, paraphrasing his arguments, clannish, cosmopolitan, different, disloyal and dispensable. As an archetype for anti-Semites in every age, in the 20th century Haman would have argued that all Jews were communists, capitalists, revolutionaries and reactionaries, despite the glaring contradictions.

Haman's anti-Semitism began with animosity towards one individual Jew, who refused to bow down before him. This was Mordechai, cousin, mentor and guardian of Esther, Ahasuerus' new queen, and together they thwarted Haman's plans. Mordechai and Esther were also archetypes, especially of the 17th and 18th century court Jews, who used whatever influence they had over princes and rulers to avert anti-Semitic decrees. By royal command, Haman was hung on the gallows he himself had prepared for Mordechai, and the 14th day of Adar, when the Jews rested from their enemies, entered the Hebrew calendar as the Festival of Purim (Lots).

## Malachi and the end of the Prophetic Age

Although the precise date of Malachi's activity after the return from Babylon is not known, it is accepted that he was the last of the prophets. What is certain is that at the time he prophesied, Judah was both a material and spiritual backwater and for many of its social ills, he held the priests responsible. They neglected their duties in the Temple and towards the people, and as a consequence were held in contempt. They strayed themselves and misled others, especially with regard to mixed marriages that at best they failed to check.

Intermarriage posed the single greatest danger to the struggling community, and the problem was present from the very beginning, because the majority of returned exiles were males. Those who were single took foreign wives, and even those who were married did likewise, by either divorcing their Jewish partners or taking new ones. The choice fell mainly on Samaritan women, who were accepted without proselytization. No one denounced the practice more than Malachi, whose teachings, together with those of his fellow prophets, were ever after rejected by the Samaritans.

Often the foreign wives and their children were ignorant of Hebrew, leading to widespread ignorance and lack of religious observance. Whether in Jerusalem or the countryside, the Sabbath was neglected. When crops failed, poor farmers sometimes sold their children into bondage, because the wealthy imposed loans with impossible conditions. Instead of being censured, the unscrupulous were envied for their success.

Although the priests were partly responsible for the nation's plight by failing in their duties and setting a negative example, Malachi nevertheless still kept alive the image of the ideal priest as one whose lips "shall keep knowledge, and they should seek Torah from his mouth, for he is a messenger of the Lord of hosts" (Mal.

2:7). Fortunately for Jewish survival, someone who matched perfectly Malachi's description of the ideal priest journeyed from Babylon to Jerusalem to redeem the situation, for no one of lesser stature could have achieved the task.

### End of the Period

Malachi himself quotes some of the attitudes prevalent when the Second Jewish Commonwealth was in danger of dying at birth. "Everyone that does evil is good in the sight of the Lord and He delights in them... Where is the God of justice?" (2:17), "It is vain to serve God, and what profit is it that we have kept His charge?" (3:14). The widespread demoralisation was reminiscent of the time when the Israelites had been defeated decisively in battle by the Philistines, except that then the danger to national survival came from an external foe, whereas now the cause was internal weakness and intermarriage.

One reason why the joint reigns of David and Solomon may be regarded as a golden age is that for a brief period there was one united kingdom transcending the inter-tribal rivalry in the time of the Judges. But immediately following Solomon's death, the temporary union between the northern and southern tribes was broken, giving rise respectively to the Kingdom of Israel and the Kingdom of Judah.

Although idolatrous temples were at first built in the northern kingdom from political motives, idols were eventually worshipped in their own right, accompanied by social abuse and oppression. Frequent dynastic purges contributed to the northern kingdom's instability, until, weakened from within, it was exiled by Assyria. The turn of Judah to be exiled followed later at the hands of the Babylonians, Assyria's successor. Both kingdoms fell because they refused to heed the prophets, who insisted that national survival depends on moral laws, and not on political treaties or false promises of help.

When the Persians under Cyrus conquered Babylon, the Jews (as they were now called) were allowed to return, but the majority did not take up the offer. The Temple was eventually rebuilt, but in reduced splendor, reflecting the difficult conditions. Priests who served in the Temple failed to provide proper leadership, and at best did nothing to halt the widespread practice of intermarriage.

The struggling community centered around Jerusalem was in danger of disappearing, until the prophets found a worthy successor. The last exhortations of the prophetic era: "Remember the Torah of Moses my servant" (Mal. 3:22) was given meaning by a new type of leader.

Chain of Tradition — World History

**2000 B.C.E.**

### ABRAHAM
**THE PATRIARCHS**

**1**

Teachers of Monotheism

**HAMMURABI'S LAWS**

Hittite & Egyptian Empires

**DECLINE OF EGYPTIAN POWER**

**1500 B.C.E.**

### MOSES
**JUDGES**

**2**

Earlier Prophets

**BEGINNING OF PHILISTINE SETTLEMENTS**

Spread of Mediterranean Civilization

**1000 B.C.E.**

### DAVID
**KINGS**

**3**

Later Prophets

**RISE OF PHOENICIAN TRADE**

Mesopotamian Empires

**END OF BIBLICAL PERIOD**

**500 B.C.E.**

### EZRA
**ZUGOTH**

**4**

Joint leaders of the Sanhedrin and the rule of the Wise

**BEGINNING OF ROMAN REPUBLIC**

Spread of Hellenism

**END OF ROMAN REPUBLIC**

**0**

### HILLEL
**TALMUDIC PERIOD**

**5**

Compilation of the Oral Law

**BEGINNING OF ROMAN EMPIRE**

Spread of Christianity

**END OF ROMAN EMPIRE**

**500 C.E.**

### RAV ASHI
**THE GEONIM**

**6**

Heads of the Babylonian Academies

**BEGINNING OF MIDDLE AGES**

Spread of Islam

**DECLINE OF BAGHDAD CALIPHATE**

**1000 C.E.**

### RASHI
**THE RISHONIM**

**7**

Earlier Authorities: Commentators & Codifiers of Talmudic Law

**HOLY ROMAN EMPIRE**

Crusades

**END OF MIDDLE AGES**

**1500 C.E.**

### JOSEPH KARO
**THE AHARONIM**

**8**

Later Authorities: Commentators & Compilers of the Halacha

**RENAISSANCE & REFORMATION**

Spread of Western Civilization

**END OF OTTOMAN EMPIRE RETURN TO ZION**

**2000 C.E.**

**500 B.C.E.**

*Ezra*

*End of the Great Assembly*

*five generations of Zugoth*

*Hillel*

*Beginning of the Common Era*

*0*

---

Ezra, regarded as a second Moses, guaranteed national survival by restoring the authority of the Torah and renewing the covenant.

Together with Nehemiah and the last of the prophets, he founded the Great Assembly, which formulated prayers, edited books of the Bible and passed enactments.

The Sanhedrin succeeded the Great Assembly as the national legislative body, and at its head stood two leading scholars, known as the Zugoth or Pairs.

The Zugoth and upholders of the Oral Law became known as Pharisees, and their opponents Sadducees.

As the influence of the Sanhedrin declined in times of persecution, especially during the reign of Herod, national survival once again hung in the balance.

---

Ezra followed the same route as Abraham from Mesopotamia to the Land of Israel. His journey has also been compared to that of Moses, for both headed parties of returnees towards the Promised Land.

During the Greek period, the Maccabees fought for religious freedom, and in the process restored national independence for the first time since the kings of Judah.

Although Herod misruled the country, he consolidated the boundaries of the kingdom.

---

With the defeat of Persia by the Greeks, the Great Assembly was succeeded by the Sanhedrin. After the death of Alexander the Great in 333 B.C.E., his empire was divided among three generals.

The Seleucids in Syria and the Ptolemies in Egypt fought for domination of Eretz Yisrael, and during a period of Seleucid rule, the Maccabean revolt took place in 167 B.C.E.

Rome was the next world power, and in 63 B.C.E. Judea became one of its client states. Soon afterwards the Sanhedrin was temporarily abolished, and Herod (37-4 B.C.E.) ruled under Roman tutelage.

*Chapter Four*

# From Ezra to Hillel (c. 500 B.C.E. – c. 1 C.E.)

## The Men of the Great Assembly and Leaders of the Sanhedrin

### *A New Era*

Aclassical work on the Pharisees describes the influence of Ezra in the following words. "He marks in the long history of the Jewish people, the opening of a new period, a new stage of development, as important as the rise of prophecy, and only less important than the work of Moses...." Ezra stood forth at a most critical period to save the Jewish religion, and with it national life, from relapsing into decay through contact with gentile ideas and practices.

Moses had given the Children of Israel the Torah, generations of prophets had exhorted them to keep it, but Ezra devoted his life to teaching, explaining and interpreting it until it became the inheritance of every individual. Hence the full justification of comparing him to Moses. The Prophets had come and gone, leaving the world a collection of the most sublime thoughts ever uttered. Yet for all their grandeur, the people did not take the prophetic messages sufficiently to heart, otherwise there would have been no exile.

About this time, the people not only underwent a change of name (Jews instead of Israelites) but also a change of heart. Bitter experience taught them that if the Prophets had been right about foreseeing the exile, then they had also been correct in other matters. As Jeremiah put it (9:11-12): "Why was the land lost?... Because they forsook my Torah." Those who required further elucidation had merely to study one of the several scrolls containing prophetic teaching.

Prophecy came to an end, therefore, because anything a prophet might wish to say was already recorded. Neither was there any need for the denunciation of idolatry, simply because with the destruction of the Temple and subsequent exile, the temptations of idolatry ceased to exist. A new era required a different style of leadership, in which the emphasis would be placed on instruction instead of exhortation. And so symbolising the change of method, but not of principle, "thus the wise have taught" or "thus it is written" became the new introductory phrase, in place of "thus says the Lord" used by the Prophets.

## Ezra

When Ezra arrived in Jerusalem from Babylon, he addressed himself to the two major threats that jeopardised Jewish survival: intermarriage and ignorance. He was aware of the historic significance of his mission, because at the beginning of the journey he led some 10,000 returning exiles across the Euphrates, two days before Passover, reminiscent of Moses crossing the Red Sea. He arrived in Jerusalem to revive the community in Av, the month in which the city had been destroyed by the Babylonians.

Statistics lay behind the problem of intermarriage, in that among the 42,360 exiles who had returned at an earlier date under Zerubbavel, adult males predominated by more than two to one. When Ezra grasped the full scale of the problem, he openly mourned, but could have done little without the authority granted him by the Persian king, which exceeded that given to any predecessor. It is generally accepted that the Artaxerxes who invested him with power (Ezra 7:7) was the first king of that name (464-423 B.C.E.). The traditional policy of Persian rulers was to have a buffer state between their own kingdom and Egypt, which is why they encouraged an autonomous Jewish state. But beyond that, Artaxerxes showed Ezra special favor, demonstrated by empowering him to seek assistance from neighboring governors, and by sending gifts for the Temple.

## Public Assemblies

Acting within his authority Ezra convened a national assembly and, on the principle that drastic situations require drastic remedies, it was decided that foreign wives be divorced. Anything less would have proven ineffective, for what Ezra was attempting to create was a religious state, which is why, with the same authority, he also established a judicial system based on religious law. His ideal was that of all great Jewish leaders – to forge a nation devoted to divine service.

Sincere proselytes have always been accepted by Judaism, but the foreign wives who were divorced came under a different category. Ignorant of Hebrew and adhering to other customs, they would have passed on their ignorance and alien ways to a new generation, endangering its existence.

Ezra was a priest but the last thing he wanted to create was a priestly caste with a monopoly of the sacred, especially knowledge. After dealing with intermarriage, therefore, the most vital part of his reform programme was to spread Jewish teaching among every member of every household throughout the country. Toward this end, he made further use of public assemblies by reading from sacred scrolls. Not just reading however, because the texts required explanation, and for this purpose he was assisted by Priests and Levites, who were teachers by tradition. Parts of the books of Daniel and Ezra written in Aramaic reflect that it was then the official language of the Persian Empire and the one best understood by the people. Consequently, the first task of those who assisted Ezra at the public assemblies was to translate and then explain the more difficult passages.

With the same goal of making the Torah better understood, Ezra replaced the ancient Hebrew script with one he brought from Persia. The square shaped letters used today are based on his innovation, while the old script can still be seen in archaeological remains and Samaritan scrolls. By changing the alphabet, Ezra also made a further distinction between Samaritan and Jew. The Samaritans, for their part, demonstrated their opposition to the autonomous Jewish state, by attacking Jerusalem during a period of general unrest in the Persian Empire. They breached its walls, burnt its gates and destroyed some of the houses, leading to a reduction of the city's population. Outside Jerusalem in the rural areas, there was more opportunity for contact with gentiles, and gradually the foreign wives who had been divorced were taken back. By degrees Ezra's work was being undone and the harm continued until Nehemiah joined him.

### Ezra, Nehemiah and the Charter

When Ezra had first arrived in Jerusalem he prayed and fasted, and 13 years later in Persia, when Nehemiah heard of the city's plight, he did likewise. Nehemiah was Artaxerxes' cupbearer, and being close to the king enabled him to be appointed governor of the Jewish state, with restoring Jerusalem's walls the first priority. Nehemiah did not lead a party of returnees but on the king's instructions was provided with an armed escort and the authority to claim timber for building from the royal forests.

Three days after arriving in Jerusalem he made a night inspection of the walls and immediately ordered their repair. Sanballat, the governor of Samaria, led a coalition of neighboring peoples to halt the work and Nehemiah responded by distributing weapons among the builders. While half worked with spears and swords close at hand, the remainder kept guard. In 52 days, the work was completed, raising the morale of the Jews and disheartening their enemies, "For they perceived that this work was done by our God" (Neh. 6:16). A special dedication ceremony was held in the Temple, but the city remained under-populated and therefore vulnerable. To remedy the situation, Nehemiah determined by lots that one in ten of the rural population should move to the capital.

Nehemiah dedicated himself to reducing suffering no less than to repairing breached walls, by persuading the rich to restore the property of the poor and remit debts. The social gap had been exacerbated by a famine that forced farmers to sell fields and homes, and in extreme cases even their children into bondage. Nehemiah backed up his plea by personal example, and instead of placing the burden of his office on the people, which was the usual practice, he maintained it at his personal expense.

Ezra, the priest, scribe, legislator and supreme educator, was thus complemented in his work by Nehemiah, administrator and governor of the province, and their crowning success was the signing of a national covenant. The ceremony took place in the month of Tishri, 444 B.C.E., after Ezra had been in the country 14 years and Nehemiah one. Tishri contains more festivals than any other month in the Hebrew calendar, which explains why Jerusalem was full of pilgrims. From the New Year until after Tabernacles the people alternatively listened to Ezra's public readings and observed the holy days, after which they were prepared to renew the covenant first made at Mt. Sinai. The nation's leaders, beginning with Nehemiah, signed a charter "to observe and do all the commandments of the Lord our God" (Neh. 10:30). Following this general statement, certain commandments were stressed, such as the prohibition against intermarriage, obligations towards the Temple, observance of the Sabbath and the Sabbatical year, when debts were remitted.

Between Moses and Ezra, the covenant had been reaffirmed on several important occasions but never, as on this one, had it been ratified by signatories to a charter. The undertaking by rich and poor, priest and layman alike to accept the laws of the Torah could never have happened, if not for Ezra's preparatory work.

As for Nehemiah, after the signing of the charter he remained governor for just over a decade, before returning to Persia. A period of retrogression then followed, characterized by intermarriage, desecration of the Sabbath and neglect of the Temple, the very commandments previously singled out for special attention. The situation was such that Tobiah, an Ammonite opposed to Nehemiah, was installed in one of the Temple chambers, and a daughter of Sanballat, the Samaritan leader, married into the family of the high priest. Nehemiah therefore sought royal permission for a second journey to Jerusalem and corrected the abuses in a series of decisive actions.

It is not stated how long Ezra and Nehemiah lived, but it is known that their work was continued by a legislative body known as the Great Assembly, which they helped to establish.

## The Great Assembly

"Moses received the Torah from Sinai and passed it on to Joshua, and Joshua to the Elders and the Elders to the Prophets and the Prophets to the Men of the Great Assembly." This statement of the Mishnah (Avot 1:1) traces the line of transmission from Moses to the Great Assembly, which was the main legislative body in the Persian period. According to the Jerusalem Talmud, the Great Assembly comprised 85 members, a number corresponding to the 84 signatories to the national covenant described above, plus Ezra. It is more widely held, however, that its members numbered 120, similar to other autonomous legislative bodies in the Persian Empire.

Active at the end of the biblical period, the Great Assembly was able to bring the Bible close to its present form by assembling the writings of Moses, Joshua, Samuel, David, Jeremiah, the school of Hezekiah and Ezra, as well as its own contribution (Bava Batra 14a). The final editing, however, was not completed until the first century C. E. at Yavneh.

There is a connection between the arrangement of the Bible and that of the Prayer Book, with which the Great Assembly was also involved, because eventually entire biblical passages would become incorporated into the liturgy, giving it its unique style.

After the destruction of the Temple, prayers became a substitute for sacrifice and retained their importance even after it was rebuilt. The members of the Great Assembly appreciated that not all prayer can be spontaneous, and so they composed the Eighteen Benedictions, the most important part of the liturgy. It is also called the *Amidah* (Standing) after the upright position in which it is recited three times daily, and its composition in the plural form (Heal us... Bless us...etc.) reflects the fact that in Judaism, prayer is foremost a collective experience.

If Jews are known as the People of the Book, it would be justifiable to call those dedicated to faithfully passing it down as Men of the Book. That is even one way of translating the Hebrew word *Soferim*, which is the collective name given to scholars during the period of the Great Assembly. That word, however, is generally translated as scribes, as the name Ezra the Scribe testifies.

Doubtless, writing Torah Scrolls in the exact manner prescribed, free of error, was and remains an exacting and responsible task, but we see from the work of Ezra and his followers that their activity included much more. Going beyond the confines of merely copying, they explained, elaborated and expounded the text, conveying its full application. Whether known as Men of the Book or Scribes, the *Soferim* played a vital part in transmitting not only the Written, but also the Oral Law.

The Great Assembly came to an end with the Persian Empire, but it is difficult to determine a precise date, because the Persian period is one of the most obscure in Jewish history. What does emerge is that Ezra and the Great Assembly did their work extremely well, for by the time the Greeks became the new world masters, there were many Jews willing to fight and die for their faith.

### Simon the Just and Hellenism

When Alexander the Great defeated the Persian army in 333 B.C.E. and died ten years later, having established the largest empire the world had yet seen, Simon the Just was one of the last members of the Great Assembly. At the beginning of his conquests, when Alexander fought against Tyre, he requested and received assistance from neighboring peoples because the city, in modern Lebanon, was then situated as an island and difficult to conquer. Only the Jews did not send help, because they were still bound by an oath of loyalty to the Persian king. Fearing that Alexander would take vengeance during his advance on Egypt, they sent a delegation of priests to appease him.

The delegation, dressed in white, was led by Simon the Just, and as a consequence of his meeting with Alexander, Jerusalem was spared and the religious freedom of its citizens reconfirmed. The use of Alexander as a name among Jews dates from this time, as a token of their respect. Relations between Alexander and the Samaritans were less successful. They murdered his representative in Samaria, and as punishment the city was populated with Macedonians, while large tracts of territory were transferred to Judah.

It was Alexander's policy to use Greek culture as a uniting force throughout his vast empire and, as part of the same policy, he encouraged intermarriage between Greeks and Persians. Many officers and soldiers followed his example. Despite setbacks, efforts to unite the two sub-continents of Europe and Asia were generally successful. Alexander died of a sudden fever, at the early age of 33. A struggle for succession among his generals, known as the wars of the Diadochi, resulted in the murder of his wife and only son. Ultimately three generals emerged victorious: Seleucus, who inherited much of the former Persian Empire, Antigonus, who inherited Macedonia, and Ptolemy, who secured Egypt. Each general founded a dynasty that continued their rivalry into future generations, with the strategically placed province of Judah regarded as a special prize. In 301 B.C.E., in the midst of confusion and incessant warfare, it came under Egyptian sovereignty and would remain so for almost a century.

Simon the Just was high priest when Ptolemy breached Jerusalem's walls and took part of its population captive. We know how he reacted to the situation, because there is a special tribute to Simon in the Book of *Ecclesiasticus*, composed by a contemporary, Ben Sira. The offices of high priest and national leader were then combined and so in addition to praising Simon as the ideal priest, Ben Sira also relates that he repaired the damaged walls and provided Jerusalem with an adequate water supply. Then as now, without proper knowledge of how to channel water and exploit a limited rainfall, the country could hardly survive.

Simon was succeeded in turn by son and grandson as high priest, but his main disciple was Antigonus, whose Greek name is indicative of the new dominant culture. Simon and Antigonus are the first important figures in Jewish history after the biblical era.

## Conditions under the Ptolemys

Ptolemy Philadelphus (c. 283 - c. 246 B.C.E.) released the prisoners his father had brought from Judah, and the community they established in Alexandria soon became the largest and most influential of the Diaspora. Following the precedent of the biblical Joseph, also brought to Egypt against his will, many freed prisoners rose to high rank under the patronage of a king who was a noted administrator, economic reformer and builder. Alexander the Great gave his name to the port he built on the Mediterranean, but it was under the Ptolemies that Alexandria became a capital city, both politically and culturally, and the largest in the west. One factor that made it the cultural center of the ancient world was its famous library that contained about 490,000 scrolls, without counting duplicates.

To add to his literary collection, Ptolemy had the Torah translated into Greek by 70 scholars (or perhaps 72, six for each tribe) sent by the high priest specifically for the task. Through the *Septuagint* (Greek for seventy) belief in a single God and other teachings of the Torah were introduced into the non-Jewish world, and Diaspora Jews who spoke only Greek were served. In Egypt a festival marked the completion of the translation, but not so in Jerusalem. It was rightly feared that the *Septuagint* would discourage Diaspora Jews from learning Hebrew, alienating them from the original texts, and in general encourage assimilation. Furthermore, a translation can provide only a single superficial reading, while the original text can be understood at many levels.

Much of western civilisation is based on the aesthetic values of the Greeks, and the beauty of their language is acknowledged in the Talmud, which associates the name of Japheth, the ancestor of the Greeks, with the Hebrew word for beauty (Megillah 9b). There was, however a negative aspect of Greek culture rooted in paganism and licentiousness, which totally opposed Jewish values. The Olympic games, for example, were dedicated to Zeus and accompanied by pagan festivities. Training took place in the gymnasium, derived from a Greek word meaning naked, which describes how the competitors participated. Jewish participants tried to undo the mark of circumcision, because the pagans regarded it as a form of mutilation.

Because most Jews dissociated themselves from the negative elements of

Hellenism, their separatism led first to suspicion and subsequently to resentment and hatred, exacerbated whenever they enjoyed economic prosperity. Alexandria became the macrocosm of the meeting between the different cultures because of its large Egyptian, Greek and Jewish populations, and produced the first example of anti-Semitic literature, replete with fabricated accusations against the Jews and their beliefs.

In Jerusalem, the high priests themselves were the foremost advocates of Greek culture, and as they followed each other in quick succession, they ceased to be the nation's true spiritual leaders. There were 300 incumbents during the 420 year period of the Second Temple, and with two notable exceptions, one of whom was Simon the Just, they barely averaged a year each in office. The high priests also possessed the right to collect taxes, which explains why so many of them aspired to buy the position, and why worldly affairs interested them more than matters of the spirit. During the reign of Ptolemy III (c. 246-222 B.C.E.), a member of the aristocracy called Joseph outbid the incumbent high priest to become the new tax farmer. The Tobias family, of which Joseph was a member, benefited financially, as did Egypt, the recipient of the bribe, until Judah became the puppet state of a new master.

### Conditions under the Seleucids

In 203 B.C.E. Antiochus III of Syria (233-187 B.C.E.) took Judah from the boy king, Ptolemy V and, although he lost it soon afterwards, in 198 the country definitely passed to Seleucid rule. Any dreams he had of reviving Alexander's empire were dispelled when he disregarded the advice of Hannibal, then at his court, and fought against Rome. The fine imposed by the Romans after their victory was passed on to the peoples of his diminished empire, including the Jews. There was no relaxation when Seleucus IV came to the throne, and after he was murdered and was succeeded by Antiochus IV (175-163 B.C.E.), the situation severely deteriorated.

Jason became high priest by ousting his own brother, with promises to the Syrians of higher taxes and a pledge to turn Jerusalem into a Greek city, complete with gymnasium. As a member of the Hellenizing party, he adopted Greek customs and neglected Temple duties, until Menelaus bought the high priesthood by robbing the Temple treasury.

Two brothers contesting the throne of Egypt provided Antiochus IV with an opportunity to invade the country. He besieged Alexandria and would probably have taken it if a warning from Rome, answering an Egyptian appeal, had not forced him to withdraw. Frustrated, he marched on Jerusalem and slaughtered thousands of its citizens, as punishment for an uprising against Menelaus, following a false report of the king's death in Egypt. More beholden to Antiochus than ever, Menelaus led him into the Temple, which was plundered and desecrated by a pagan sacrifice.

Worse still, Antiochus attempted to Hellenize Judah and proscribe Judaism, which meant the death penalty for keeping the Sabbath, performing circumcision and declaring the New Moon, which determined the days the festivals were to be observed. A period of martyrdom followed, and among the many victims two are known by name. One was a 90-year old called Eleazar, who was killed for refusing to eat swine's flesh and the other was Hannah, who died with her seven sons because they refused to worship an idol. The Syrian king was known as Epiphanes, "god made manifest," but as a play on the title the Jews called him Epimanes "the mad."

## The Maccabee revolt and its aftermath

Widespread persecution led inevitably to rebellion. It began in a town situated in the Judean foothills called Modiin, where an elderly priest killed a renegade Jew about to offer a pagan sacrifice. The priest's name was Mattathias, of the Hasmonean family, and he died not long after he and his five sons attacked the Syrians, who had set up the altar.

The spark of revolt that he kindled became a flame under Judah, the first of the sons to inherit the leadership (165-160 B.C.E.). Judah is known to history as the Maccabee, which in Hebrew may either mean the Hammerer, or else forms an acrostic of the words: "Who is like unto you among the mighty ones, O Lord?" The Maccabees defeated four successive Syrian armies sent to crush the rebellion, after which they liberated Jerusalem. They compensated for inferior numbers and weapons by courage, mobility and superior knowledge of the terrain, but not least they fought for homes and ideals that they cherished more than life itself, thus meriting divine assistance.

After taking Jerusalem in 164 B.C.E., the Maccabees rededicated the Temple on the 25th of Kislev, a date incorporated into the Hebrew calendar as the Festival of Chanukah. Celebrated as a miracle, it commemorates the victory of the weak over the strong and of the few over the many. Almost 2000 years later, Judah's victories inspired the composer Handel to write an oratorio.

When Antiochus died, Judah exploited the confusion in Syria over the succession to liberate most of the country. Some Hellenizing Jews, favoring Syrian rule over the Maccabees, appealed to the regent Lysias for help. Elazar, one of the Hasmonean brothers, was killed in an ensuing battle, and Judah was forced to take refuge behind the walls of Jerusalem. Lysias was prevented from following up his advantage because domestic issues in Syria required his immediate return. Before doing so, he made an agreement with Judah granting the province full religious freedom.

The respite proved to be short lived. The Hellenized Jews were a fifth column that preferred the nation's enemies to their own leaders, and so when Demetrius I usurped the Syrian throne in 162 B.C.E. they invited him to overthrow the Maccabees. One army, led by Nicanor, was defeated, but a second led by Bacchides, sent to install a high priest called Alcimus, scored a military victory. Judah was killed and soon afterwards Johanan, his oldest brother, also died in battle. Of the five sons of Mattathias, only Jonathan and Simon remained.

Before his death, Judah had signed a treaty with Rome, and following his example, Jonathan entered into an agreement with both Rome and Sparta. Realising that they could not defeat Jonathan in battle, the Syrians invited him to a conference where he was treacherously murdered (143 B.C.E.).

Under Simon, the country enjoyed political independence for the first time since King Josiah in biblical times. He ruled over a grateful people as high priest and civil leader, but not as king, because he knew the title belonged to the descendants of David alone. Yet even in a period of peace, Simon died a violent death. He was invited to a feast by his son-in-law and then murdered, with two of his sons. Thus in the year 135 B.C.E., the first generation of Maccabean leaders came to an end.

The later generations of Hasmoneans were unworthy descendants. Instead of uniting the people, they increasingly became a source of dissension, until the country was divided by civil war. The true national leaders were the scholars and sages, who together with those who followed their teachings, were known as Pharisees. The ideological and often political opponents of the Pharisees were Sadducees and Essenes, and a knowledge of the three groups is essential for a full understanding of the period.

### The Pharisees

The Pharisees (*Perushim*) were the spiritual successors of Ezra and the Prophets. The word Pharisee itself means Separatist, recalling the references in the books of Ezra and Nehemiah to those who separated themselves from the surrounding peoples and remained faithful to the covenant. Previously they were known as *Hasidim* (pietists) and were foremost in the fight to regain religious freedom but, by the second generation of Hasmonean leaders, the term Pharisee was in use.

The Pharisees were of the people and for the people, and their main sphere of influence was the synagogue. There was only one Temple, situated in Jerusalem, but synagogues were found throughout the country, wherein the Pharisees could bring the message of the Torah to the people. Unlike the priests in the Temple who were qualified by birth, the eligibility of the Pharisee teachers depended solely on piety and learning. Through daily contact, the people became their followers and disciples.

The life of self-discipline that characterised the Pharisees went beyond the letter of the law, including observance of the laws of ritual purity and refraining from doubtfully tithed foods. In all matters they were guided by the Oral as well as Written Law and placed great emphasis on biblical exegesis. In a classic example, the Oral Law teaches that the statement "an eye for an eye" (Ex. 21:24) is not to be taken literally, but refers to monetary compensation. In another example, the Written Law speaks of the death penalty, which Pharisaic legislation virtually abolished - hence the saying "a Sanhedrin that condemned one individual to death in seventy years was called a bloody Sanhedrin" (Makkot 20a). Following biblical precedent, the Pharisees did not use imprisonment as a form of punishment, neither were trials presided over by a single judge, on the principle: "judge not alone, for none may judge alone except God" (Avoth 4:8).

The Pharisees' ethical teachings are found throughout Talmudic literature, but especially in one tractate of the Mishnah called Ethics of the Fathers (*Avot*). As an illustration, the following aphorisms are taken from the first chapter: "Judge all people in the scale of merit; Love work and hate lordship; Love peace and pursue peace, love one's fellow beings and draw them near to the Torah. On three things the world exists: on judgment, on peace and on truth." Undoubtedly there were some false Pharisees just as there had been some false prophets, and nowhere are they more denounced than in the Talmud itself. But this is a far cry from the historical distortion that as a class, the Pharisees were hypocrites and sanctimonious. In most dictionaries, this is how the word Pharisee is still defined, even though it is obvious that those originally responsible for the misrepresentation were polemical authors, most of whom were ignorant of Judaism and all set on prejudicing Greek and Roman audiences.

Above all, they could never forgive the Pharisees for influencing the people to remain steadfast in their faith. The fate of sectarians who opposed the Pharisees was either to abandon Judaism, or survive as an obscure sect.

### The Sadducees

A priest named Zadok in the Greek period, who rejected certain doctrines of the Pharisees, may have given his name to his followers, known as the Sadducees. They represented the priestly, wealthy stratum of urban society, sympathetic to Greek culture. They accepted only the Five Books of Moses as sacred and, as a substitute for the Oral Law, they produced their own code, called the Book of Decrees. Because they upheld the written word alone, the code abounds in severe forms of punishment, including the death penalty and the literal application of an eye for an eye. The net result was a sombre religious practice that had no appeal to the masses.

The Sadducees differed from the extreme Hellenizers only in their adherence to the Written Law, but otherwise both shared the Greek preference for sensual pleasures. Such behavior was anathema to the Pharisees, for whom worldly pleasures were not forbidden, but neither were they to be abused. It was the Essenes, the third contemporary group, that provided the extreme opposite of Greek hedonism.

## The Essenes

A reaction against worldliness encouraged the Essenes to withdraw into isolated communities, scattered throughout the country, with the main settlement near the Dead Sea. It was there that the famous scrolls associated with the sect were discovered in 1947, and subsequent excavations revealed a building for communal use, for a feature of their organisation was the doctrine of shared possessions. To avoid unnecessary speech the Essenes spoke little, and to avoid unethical pitfalls associated with trade and commerce, they engaged in handicrafts and agriculture, which also enabled their communities to be self-sustaining.

Instead of the "fence" that the Great Assembly built around the Torah as a form of protection, the Essenes constructed a large "wall" insurmountable for the majority. This expressed itself in the strictest observance of the Sabbath and in particular by stressing ritual cleanliness. They immersed before engaging in prayer and study, wore white garments as a symbol of purity, and abstained from conjugal relations. Marriage was tolerated solely for the purpose of procreation, not as a blessing in its own right, as the Pharisees viewed it. When numbers needed augmenting, orphans were adopted. The Essenes practised healing by incantation, which explains why their name in Aramaic means Healers.

Living in isolated communities, under strict rules that make the isolation absolute, runs counter to the spirit of Judaism, and it is probable that the Essenes were the subject of the contemporary statement: "Do not separate yourself from the community" (Avot 2:4). It is further probable that many of the sect eventually abandoned Judaism altogether, to join the new religion of Christianity with which they had much in common. After the end of the first century C.E., the Essenes ceased to exist.

## The Sanhedrin

Out of gratitude to the Hasmonean family for gaining religious freedom and political independence, Simon the last remaining brother of Judah the Maccabee, was appointed *Nasi* (President) and High Priest. The position was to be hereditary, and words to this effect were engraved in metal and fixed to a wall in the Temple compound. The council over which the Nasi presided consisted of priests and laymen, and is referred to on coins from the period as the Council of the Jews (*Hever Ha-Yehudim*), better known by the Greek name of *Sanhedrin*.

## THE RULE OF THE WISE

After the conquests of Alexander the Great (c. 330 B.C.E.), Hellenism spread throughout the former Persian Empire and in Judea, the Sanhedrin took the place of the Great Assembly. At its head stood the Zugoth (Joint Leaders), who were contemporaries of the Maccabees and their descendants.

| Contemporary Maccabean Rulers (Numbers refer to order of rule) | Zugoth — Leaders of the Sanhedrin | |
|---|---|---|
| | **Nasi** | **Av Beth Din** |

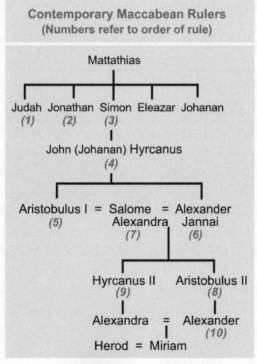

| | Nasi | Av Beth Din |
|---|---|---|
| | Yose b. Yoezer | Yose b. Yohanan |
| | Yoshua b. Perahia | Nittai |
| | Yudah b. Tabbai | Shimon b. Shetah |
| | Shemaiah | Avtalyon |
| | Hillel | Shammai |

The Common Era

Herod's kingdom

The Sanhedrin comprised 71 members, the traditional number of governing elders since the time of Moses (Numb. 11:16), and its three main functions were to expound the Torah, pass enactments and guarantee justice. It was situated near the Temple in the Chamber of Hewn Stones, although two lesser Sanhedrins of 23 members were also situated on the Temple Mount and others throughout the country. Matters too complicated for the provincial courts were brought before those on the Temple Mount, and if still unresolved, before the Great Sanhedrin, which thereby functioned as a supreme court.

In arrangement, the Sanhedrin was semi-circular, to enable its members to see each other, and to enable the Nasi to see them all, because he sat in the center facing the general body, flanked by two senior officials. Three rows of seats were also provided for students, who learnt by listening to the debates, thereby giving the Sanhedrin, which met on a daily basis except on Sabbaths and festivals, the additional role of a university.

In practice, autocratic kings ignored the Sanhedrin by placing themselves above the law, and a powerful empire like Rome, when inclined, suspended its activities altogether.

### The Zugot (Pairs)

For five generations, the Nasi or President of the Sanhedrin was assisted by a deputy (*Av Beth Din*), and together they are known as the *Zugot*, or Pairs. The more senior member is mentioned first, whenever their names are jointly recorded in the sources. The five generations of Zugot paralleled the five generations of Hasmonean leaders, and so the first pair, Jose ben Joezer and Jose ben Johanan, were older contemporaries of Judah the Maccabee. Jose ben Joezer, in the tradition of Ezra and Simon the Just, was an ideal priest, in contrast to the incumbent high priest, Alcimus, who happened to be his nephew. The Syrians, who were Alcimus' patrons, crucified Jose ben Joezer when they entered Jerusalem, about the same time that they killed Judah the Maccabee in battle.

Jose ben Johanan typified the Pharisee leader in his care for the people, as we learn from his statement: "let the poor be members of your household" (Avoth 1: 5).

### The Zugot in the reigns of Hyrcanus and Jannai

After Simon, the last of the Maccabean brothers, was murdered with two of his sons, he was succeeded by a third son called John Hyrcanus (135-104 B.C.E.) of the second generation of Hasmonean leaders. The Syrians, who had been invited into the country by the Hellenizers, besieged Hyrcanus in Jerusalem, and he bought them off by the payment of a tribute and by ceding former Philistine cities on the coastal plain. The setback proved to be temporary, for the Syrian empire was in the process of disintegration, racked by dissent from within and attacked by the Parthians from without. In the confusion, Hyrcanus retook the ceded cities and his act was recognised by Rome. The Romans renewed their ties with the Jewish state, because it was in their interest to support Syria's enemies.

Using foreign mercenaries in the style of Greek rulers, Hyrcanus subdued the Samaritans, destroying their temple on Mt. Gerizim in the process (c. 130 B.C.E.). Samaritan territory had divided the country and so the move was a strategic necessity, which cannot be said about his next conquest. This took place when Hyrcanus subdued the Idumeans (Edom), who lived in the mountainous area south of the Dead Sea. By forcibly converting them, he imitated the policy of Antiochus Epiphanes, against whom the Maccabees had initially begun their revolt. The result was to prove disastrous, because three generations later, King Herod of Idumean descent would cruelly persecute his Jewish subjects. Irrespective of the unhappy consequences, forced conversion is contrary to Jewish law, and this is the sole occasion it was ever applied.

Unlike his father's generation that had fought for religious freedom, Hyrcanus used his mercenaries for political purposes, and the distinction was not lost on his contemporaries. As the spiritual successors of the prophets, the Pharisees condemned Hyrcanus' military expeditions, and so he turned to the Sadducees for support. Eventually he identified with them completely, ruling as virtual king estranged from the people. His ideological turnabout became expressed in the saying: "do not believe in yourself until the day of death, for Johanan (Hyrcanus) served as high priest for 80 years, and in the end became a Sadducee" (Berachot 29a).

During Hyrcanus' reign, the name Pharisee made its first appearance, and while he still identified with them, he appointed Joshua ben Perahiah and Nittai of Arbeil, to lead the Sanhedrin. They formed the second generation of Zugot, when the Oral Law began to be handed down separately from the Written Law for the first time. The result was a series of statements terse in form but with wide implications, that depended for their authority on a reliable chain of tradition. Successive links were teachers and their disciples, all fully aware of their interdependent roles in maintaining the chain. Continuity was endangered, but not disrupted, when Joshua ben Perahiah and other Pharisee leaders temporarily fled to Egypt from persecution, after the Hasmoneans openly sided with the Sadducees.

Hyrcanus intended his wife to succeed him as head of state and his son Aristobulus as high priest, but after his death Aristobulus seized both positions. He set a precedent by being the first Hasmonean leader to call himself king, deliberately ignoring the tradition associating the monarchy with the tribe of Judah. In order to gain power, Aristobulus incarcerated his three brothers, but after a brief reign of one year (104-103 B.C.E.) they were released and the eldest married his widow, Alexandra Salome. The brother's name was Alexander Jannai (103-76 B.C.E.), who followed precedent by calling himself both king and high priest. Enlarging the kingdom on both sides of the Jordan, his military ambition destroyed any hope of reconciliation with the Pharisees.

The final rift with the Pharisees occurred in the Temple during Tabernacles, when Jannai desecrated one of the festival's ceremonies. He was pelted by an angry crowd and in retaliation, allowed his mercenaries to claim some 6,000 victims. With many of the Pharisee leaders either dead or in exile, the Sadducees gained control of the Sanhedrin, and implemented their harsh penal code laid down in the Book of Decrees. When the number of Jannai's victims reached about 50,000, his opponents appealed to Demetrius III for help. After the Syrian king entered the country, Jewish supporters joined his army, and an ensuing battle in which Jews fought each other on opposing sides shocked even those who had invited him. Gauging the extent of his unpopularity, Demetrius returned to Syria.

Jannai, however, was unmoved by loss of popular support, and on one occasion proved his cruelty by crucifying 800 opponents during a feast. A dissolute life hastened his end, and a parting advice to his wife was to fear neither Pharisee nor Sadducee, but hypocrites who expected reward for their misdeeds.

Jannai's preoccupation with conquest had left him little time for the high priesthood, and so Joshua ben Gamla, the deputy high priest, filled the role. It was for his contribution to education that Joshua is best remembered. He organised a network of schools throughout the country, and fixed the maximum number of pupils in a class at 25. Another leading figure in the field of education was Shimon ben Shetah, who was the first to make it compulsory. Jannai's persecutions resulted in a large number of orphans, and special care was taken to include them in the educational network.

Shimon ben Shetah (136-60 B.C.E.) the prominent Pharisee leader was allowed to remain in the Sanhedrin by virtue of being the queen's brother. He countered Sadducee influence as best he could, but in any case, during Jannai's reign the Sanhedrin had no influence in matters of the state.

### The Zugot in the reign of Salome Alexandra

When Alexander Jannai died, his widow Salome Alexandra became queen in her own right at over 60 years of age, and she reigned for nine years (76-67 B.C.E.). The exiled Pharisee leaders in Egypt were free to return, and one of them, Judah ben

Tabbai, was appointed head of the Sanhedrin, while Shimon Ben Shetah served as deputy. Together they formed the third generation of Zugot, and under their leadership the Pharisees once again controlled the Sanhedrin. One of its most important decisions was to abolish the Sadducean Book of Decrees, and replace it with an acceptable judicial system. By ensuring justice and guaranteeing widespread education in schools and synagogues, the Sanhedrin continued the work of the Great Assembly.

The Pharisees enjoyed the full support of the queen, resulting in a successful domestic policy. In external affairs, the only shadow was cast by Tigranes, the Armenian king, who dominated Asia Minor and threatened to invade the country. He was bought off by a large bribe, and then turned to defending his own country against the threat of Rome, but he was not strong enough to withstand Pompey and it was not long before the Roman general also intervened in internal Jewish affairs. The opportunity to do so was provided by rivalry between Queen Alexandra's two sons, Hyrcanus II and Aristobulus II. The confusing events of the period are made even more so by the fact that leading figures in succeeding generations often bore the same name.

Hyrcanus, the older of the two, who served as high priest, was well-meaning but weak. Aristobulus was an energetic and over-ambitious military commander, who sided with the Sadducees. When his mother fell ill, he plotted his own succession by secretly leaving Jerusalem to gain the support of over 20 garrison commanders, each one a fellow Sadducee. With their help, after his mother's death, he ruled precariously for four years (67-63 B.C.E.), but he was in every respect an unworthy successor. Salome Alexandra was the last monarch who deserved to be called a Hasmonean, and the peaceful conditions of her reign were not to return for 100 years.

Hyrcanus was defeated by Aristobulus near Jericho, and would probably have acknowledged his brother's supremacy, if a scheming adviser called Antipater had not manipulated him for his own ambitions. Antipater, of Idumean descent, persuaded Hyrcanus to receive help from an Arab king in exchange for the return of 12 cities taken in a previous reign. When people saw one brother supported by foreign troops and the other by Sadducees, they expressed contempt for both sides.

One particular incident during the civil war was regarded as ominous. When Aristobulus' supporters were besieged in Jerusalem, they lowered money from ramparts in a basket, into which Hyrcanus' men placed an animal for the daily sacrifice. On one occasion they placed a pig, which struck its claws into the walls as it was being drawn up. The animal was regarded as a symbol of Rome, poised to tear the country apart.

## The Beginning of Roman Domination

While the Hasmonean brothers were fighting among themselves, Pompey was engaged in bringing the entire area under some form of Roman domination. The two brothers sent delegations to Pompey's representative in Damascus and, because Aristobulus' bribe was the larger, Hyrcanus and his Arab ally were obliged to lift the siege of Jerusalem. Aristobulus pursued them, killing about 6,000. When Pompey himself arrived in Damascus, the brothers sent additional delegations with additional bribes, but on this occasion they were joined by representatives of the people, who wanted the office of king abolished and the ancient form of government under the high priest restored.

Hyrcanus and Aristobulus then travelled to Damascus for judgment, but before the verdict was passed the latter returned to Jerusalem. When Pompey came in pursuit, Aristobulus gave himself up, but his followers took refuge on the Temple Mount. After a siege of three months, they were massacred, and even the priests at the altar were among the victims.

Pompey entered the Holy of Holies (63 B.C.E.) but left the Temple undamaged. Hyrcanus, regarded as a friend of Rome, was reconfirmed as high priest and appointed civil ruler (63-40 B.C.E.). He was denied, however, the title of king, and cities on both sides of the Jordan were annexed to Syria. The effective ruler, under Roman patronage, was Antipater.

Aristobulus and two of his sons were taken to Rome but Alexander, the eldest, managed to escape on the way and raised an army to depose his uncle Hyrcanus. He was defeated by Gabinus the Syrian proconsul (57 B.C.E.) who then weakened the unity of the country by dividing it into five districts, each with its own Sanhedrin. For a short period, the Great Sanhedrin ceased to exist. After appearing in Pompey's victory parade, Aristobulus had two opportunities to return to power, both of which failed. The first was when he temporarily escaped from Rome and led an abortive rebellion in Judea. The second was when he was released from captivity by Julius Caesar to lead two Roman legions against Pompey, but was assassinated while still in Italy.

Before Caesar and Pompey led Rome into civil war (49 B.C.E.), they had formed, together with Crassus, the first Triumvirate. It was Crassus who succeeded Gabinus as the proconsul of Syria, and his love of money (by dubious means he had become the richest man in Rome) inspired him to plunder the Temple. He carried away gold coins and vessels, but soon afterwards his army was defeated by the Parthians, and following the disgrace he was murdered.

## Shemaiah and Avtalyon - the fourth of the Zugot

In such confused times, the Hasmoneans failed to provide meaningful leadership, and the same could be said of the high priests, who were at best functionaries. The people therefore looked to the Pharisees for guidance, and in particular to Shemaiah and Avtalyon, the leaders of the Sanhedrin.

Shemaiah and Avtalyon were both descended from proselytes, in contrast to their predecessors who were of noble birth. As a matter of policy they shunned political involvement, because after Alexandra, the Pharisees had no influential ally. The changed situation following the queen's death is reflected in Shemaiah's statement: "Love work, hate domination, and seek no intimacy with the ruling power" (Avoth 1:10).

The Pharisees' desire to remain aloof from affairs of state and their distrust of the reigning house were proved correct when the Sanhedrin tried Herod for murder.

## Herod's rise to power

Herod's rise to power was due to insatiable ambition, a complete lack of scruples and a genius for ingratiating himself with the leading figures in Rome, as it passed from republic to empire. His father, Antipater, had set the example by winning Julius Caesar's confidence, despite the fact that previously he had been patronised by Pompey, Caesar's arch enemy. The occasion arose when Caesar pursued Pompey to Egypt, where Pompey was assassinated and Caesar stayed to support Cleopatra's claim to the throne, against her rival who was both brother and husband. Antipater sent reinforcements to aid Caesar, while Hyrcanus encouraged the Jews of Alexandria to give him their support. Out of gratitude, Caesar reconfirmed the rights of Alexandria's Jewish community, the Jews of Asia Minor were guaranteed religious freedom, Hyrcanus' position as civil ruler was reconfirmed, and Antipater was appointed Rome's representative.

The authority invested in Antipater allowed him to make decisions in Caesar's name, and so he appointed Herod prefect in the Galilee and Phezael, another son, prefect of Jerusalem. Herod lost no time in exhibiting his cruelty by the way he put down a nationalist rebellion, inflicting the death penalty without trial. He was summoned before the Sanhedrin in Jerusalem to answer for his actions, and attended only on his father's insistence. Dressed in purple and accompanied by an armed guard, Herod intimidated all the members of the Sanhedrin except Shemaiah, who alone spoke out against the threat the accused posed to them all. Herod fled before the verdict was announced, but would return at a later date to justify Shemaiah's warning.

On the Ides (15th day) of March 44 B.C.E., Julius Caesar was assassinated, to the dismay of the Jews of Rome. Despite the benefits Antipater and his sons had received from him, they supported the conspirators on their arrival in Syria. When they, in turn, were defeated two years later at Philippi in Greece, Herod ingratiated himself with Mark Antony, Caesar's protégé and avenger. Antipater had in the meantime been poisoned, leaving Herod, his most ruthless and energetic son, with ambitions to rule as king. Any plans received a temporary setback when the Parthians placed Antigonus, Hyrcanus' nephew, on the throne of Judea (40-37 B.C.E.) The Parthian Empire, then at the height of its power, was strong enough to rival Rome, and even when Antony's legate drove them from the country, Antigonus remained king and high priest by virtue of a large bribe.

Herod travelled to Rome with lavish gifts to convince Octavius and Antony, both members of the Second Triumvirate, that he would serve Rome's interests best and the senate duly appointed him king of the Jews. No Senate vote, however, could make him popular with his intended subjects, who were content to be ruled by Antigonus, a direct descendant of the Maccabees. After inconclusive campaigning to obtain the throne, Herod asked Antony for reinforcements. Jerusalem was besieged for five months and, during that time, Herod married Miriam (Mariamne) Hyrcanus' granddaughter and therefore a Hasmonean princess. By this means he intended to strengthen his claim to the throne, but the people continued to stand by Antigonus. Many paid for their loyalty with their lives when Jerusalem eventually fell, and Antigonus was sent to Antony, who beheaded him at Herod's request.

The members of the Sanhedrin who had once tried Herod were also killed for their temerity. Shemaiah alone was spared, because during the trial he had forecast Herod's rise to power, and during the siege of Jerusalem he had advocated surrender to avoid bloodshed. Perhaps Shemaiah's popularity with the people also explains why he was saved, for it is related that on one occasion the high priest was attended by a large crowd as he left the Temple, but when the followers saw Shemaiah and Avtalyon, they left the high priest to accompany the two scholars.

### Herod's reign (37-4 B.C.E.)

Herod reigned for 33 years, and died just four years before the Common Era. For his Jewish subjects, he brought the period to a close on a note of despair, because he was responsible for many deaths and the introduction, or encouragement, of pagan customs throughout the country.

The first example of cruelty in Herod's domestic life occurred when his brother-in-law, Aristobulus III, was appointed high priest. His mother-in-law, Alexandra, was instrumental in the appointment (Alexandra was a granddaughter of the former queen of the same name.) She had exploited her friendship with Cleopatra of Egypt, who, in turn, influenced Mark Antony, whose word was decisive. Herod had reason to fear that the same sources of influence might one day bring the young and popular Aristobulus to the throne, and so he arranged his murder. When his brother-in-law was swimming in the Jordan, near Jericho, Herod had him drowned.

In 31 B.C.E. Antony and Cleopatra committed suicide after their combined forces were defeated by Octavius, the heir and grand-nephew of Julius Caesar. Herod travelled to Rome to justify his affiliation to the vanquished, but before setting out had his wife's grandfather, the 80-year old Hyrcanus murdered, lest he be crowned king in his absence. On his return, he executed his wife because she was accused, falsely, of treason, and when Alexandra attempted to avenge her murdered family, she too was killed. Thus through jealousy, suspicion and intrigue, the famous Hasmonean dynasty came to an ignominious end. Even afterwards, Herod's domestic life was never free of dissension, since he married ten times, and the different factions plotted continuously against each other.

In Rome, Herod proved once again his ability to flatter the winning side in a civil war, as Octavius accepted his homage. Octavius became the first Roman emperor, and among the honors bestowed on him by the Senate was the title Augustus (after which the eighth month of the year came to be named, just as the seventh commemorated Julius Caesar.) Herod honored his patron through the names he gave to two cities. One was Caesarea, with its imposing harbor on the shores of the Mediterranean, and the other was Sebaste (Greek for Augustus.) Sebaste was built on the site of Samaria, capital of the ancient northern kingdom, and its pagan temples were also dedicated to Augustus.

Herod was a prolific builder, especially when it came to building palaces for himself. He built one at Masada, overlooking the Dead Sea, a second near Bethlehem and a third in Jerusalem. In Hebron, he built a mausoleum over the burial site of the patriarchs, but his most famous structure was the Temple. The existing one, built after the return from the Babylonian exile, was not considered sufficiently prestigious, and so over a period of ten years Herod reconstructed it to twice its height and covered it with marble. Elsewhere in Jerusalem he built an amphitheatre and hippodrome, for in the style of Greek kings, he staged gladiatorial contests, and dedicated them to the Roman emperor.

Any good will towards the religious sensitivities of his subjects in rebuilding the Temple was more than offset when Herod placed a golden eagle above its entrance. In addition to being a graven image, it was a symbol of Imperial Rome, and an attempt was made to remove it on rumors of the king's death. The king proved the rumors false by executing anyone associated with the attempt and, to ensure that there would be true grief after his death, he planned a posthumous massacre. In his last years, Herod suffered some form of insanity that increased his cruelty. He executed two of his sons from Miriam, and then a third son from another wife, who had instigated the intrigues that led to their execution.

Herod was granted the Golan Heights by Augustus, which were part of the kingdom divided among his sons after his death. Augustus confirmed Herod's will, but it was fiercely contested by the brothers themselves. Their acrimony was only exceeded by the contempt in which the people held them, for as a general rule, Herod's dynasty produced neither good nor capable leaders. Archelaus received Judea and Samaria, but in 6 C.E. Augustus, following complaints from his Jewish subjects, removed him. Herod Antipas was appointed Governor of the Galilee and part of Trans- Jordan, but in the reign of Caligula he was banished (39 C.E.). Philip (d. 34 C.E.) whose kingdom was non-Jewish, ruled over territory east of the Galilee. His domestic policy was devoted to spreading Roman and Greek culture.

### End of the Period

If proof were needed that, for better or worse, individuals can shape history no less than movements and economic or social factors, then the figures who appear between Ezra and Herod (inclusive) provide sufficient evidence. It was said of Ezra that he would have been worthy of receiving the Torah if Moses had not preceded him (San. 21b), and there can be no greater testimony to his historical influence. Ezra was a priest and one of the founding members of the Great Assembly, whereas Simon the Just, a fellow priest, was one of its last members.

Simon guided his people during the turbulent times following the death of Alexander the Great, one of history's greatest generals who brought an end to the Persian Empire and spread Greek culture in its place. The period provides countless examples of peoples fighting for home and country, but only the Jews fought for their faith and conscience. Yet another priest, an aged one called Mattathias, gave the rallying cry for the struggle; "Though all the nations that are under the king's dominion obey him, and fall away every one from the religion of their fathers, yet will I and my sons and my brethren walk in the covenant of our fathers" (I Macc.2,19-20). Mattathias' five sons, led by Judah the Maccabee, showed how the few and under-armed can defeat entire armies, as long as they are morally strong.

The Pharisees, as the spiritual heirs of the Prophets, were the true national leaders during the Greek period. They were responsible for safeguarding Judaism, including prophetic teachings; hence their contribution to history is inestimable. Even though the majority remain anonymous, we still have the names of two Pharisee leaders in each of five generations who led the Sanhedrin.

Whereas the first generation of Maccabees fought for religious freedom, those who followed became increasingly involved in military exploits for personal ambition. When brothers became involved in power struggles, they thought nothing of leading the country into civil war. The later Maccabean leaders were Sadducees, the priestly aristocratic class too concerned with power and luxury to attend to spiritual duties. The main offenders were the high priests, who bought the position in order to act as tax farmers. At best they were mere puppets of foreign rulers, and at worst traitors to their own people.

But when it came to treachery, callousness and the ability to ingratiate himself to further personal ambition, none was the equal of Herod. It is true that his buildings were magnificent, especially the Temple, but he also constructed hippodromes for gladiatorial contests. In his private life, he murdered the last members of the Hasmonean family, into which he had married, while in the public sphere, he either killed the Pharisee leaders or forced them into exile. As a consequence, the Sanhedrin was rendered ineffectual, when it was not abolished entirely, reminiscent of the rule of the Roman proconsuls.

When Shemaiah and Avtalyon died, the chain of tradition comprising teachers and disciples in successive generations and essential for the transmission of the Oral Law was further endangered. The Oral Law was then in a formative stage, and its full development was essential if the Jews were to survive their next and longest exile.

Time Span

## Chain of Tradition

## World History

**2000**
B.C.E.

### ABRAHAM
**THE PATRIARCHS**

**1**

Teachers of Monotheism

HAMMURABI'S
LAWS

Hittite & Egyptian
Empires

**DECLINE OF
EGYPTIAN POWER**

**1500**
B.C.E.

### MOSES
**JUDGES**

**2**

Earlier Prophets

**BEGINNING OF PHILISTINE
SETTLEMENTS**

Spread of Mediterranean
Civilization

**1000**
B.C.E.

### DAVID
**KINGS**

**3**

Later Prophets

**RISE OF PHOENICIAN
TRADE**

Mesopotamian Empires

**END OF BIBLICAL
PERIOD**

**500**
B.C.E.

### EZRA
**ZUGOTH**

**4**

Joint leaders of
the Sanhedrin and
the rule of the Wise

**BEGINNING OF
ROMAN REPUBLIC**

Spread of Hellenism

**END OF ROMAN
REPUBLIC**

**0**

### HILLEL
**TALMUDIC PERIOD**

**5**

Compilation of the
Oral Law

**BEGINNING OF ROMAN EMPIRE**

Spread of Christianity

**END OF ROMAN
EMPIRE**

**500**
C.E.

### RAV ASHI
**THE GEONIM**

**6**

Heads of the
Babylonian
Academies

**BEGINNING OF
MIDDLE AGES**

Spread of Islam

**DECLINE OF BAGHDAD
CALIPHATE**

**1000**
C.E.

### RASHI
**THE RISHONIM**

**7**

Earlier Authorities:
Commentators & Codifiers
of Talmudic Law

**HOLY ROMAN EMPIRE**

Crusades

**END OF MIDDLE AGES**

**1500**
C.E.

### JOSEPH KARO
**THE AHARONIM**

**8**

Later Authorities:
Commentators & Compilers
of the Halacha

**RENAISSANCE &
REFORMATION**

Spread of Western Civilization

**END OF OTTOMAN EMPIRE
RETURN TO ZION**

**2000**
C.E.

Time Span

0
Hillel

200 years

Compilation of the Mishnah

300 years

Compilation of Babylonian Talmud begin by Rav Ashi

500 C.E.

Hillel, together, with his colleague Shammai, formed the last of the Zugoth but also the first of the Tanaim, as the scholars mentioned in the Mishnah are called.

His descendants served as leaders of the Sanhedrin for over 400 years, and represented the people to the Roman authorities as Nesi'im.

Rabbi Judah the Prince, in the seventh generation, compiled the Mishnah, which then served as the ultimate compendium of the Oral Law.

The Mishnah became the subject of debate in the academies of Eretz Yisrael and Babylon, and each center in turn produced its own version of the Talmud.

Scholars who lived between the compilations of the Mishnah and Talmud are called Amoraim, and by the end of their activity both centers had declined.

Hillel, like Ezra, came to Jerusalem from Mesopotamia, with the same mission of national rejuvination.

Roman governors misruled the country, and in the ensuing revolt the Second Temple was destroyed (68 C.E.).

Another rebellion took place in 132 C.E., and as a consequence of subsequent repression, the main center of Jewish life passed to Babylon after the compilation of the Mishnah.

By 425 "Palestina" was split into three provinces, and in the same year the last Nasi died.

Under Byzantine persecutions the Land was depopulated, as the Jews become a people of the dispersion.

Augustus Caesar, a contemporary of Hillel, was the first Roman emperor.

In Mesopotamia, the Parthians ruled between 247 B.C.E. and 224 C.E. and were generally favorable towards the Jews.

They were followed by the Persians (224 - 651 C.E.) whose kings, strongly influenced by Zoroastrian priests, persecuted the Jews and other minorities, in the style of their Byzantine counterparts.

In 313 Constantine adopted Christianity and transferred the capital of the empire to Byzantium, renaming it Constantinople.
With the empire divided between east and west, the first Byzantine emperor ascended the throne in 395. Under the Byzantines, the Jews in Eretz Yisrael suffered from progroms and anti-Semitic legislation.

*Chapter Five*

# From Hillel to Rav Ashi

## The Talmudic period (1-500 C.E.)

"When the Torah was forgotten in Israel, Ezra went up from Babylon to restore it; when it was again forgotten, Hillel the Babylonian went up and restored it" (Succah 20a).

To be precise, Hillel journeyed three times from Babylon to the Holy Land. The first occasion was as a child when he accompanied his father, on the second he studied under Shemaiah and Avtalyon and after the third he stayed permanently, as President of the Sanhedrin. There is a connection between the second and third visits because as a one time disciple of Shemaiah and Avtalyon, Hillel was able to quote rulings in their name. This was an essential requirement of the period when, as its name implies, the Oral Law was transmitted verbally and the validity of any teaching depended on the authority quoted and its transmission in an unbroken line. During the persecutions of Herod's reign, the chain of tradition became at best tenuous and Hillel formed an important link between past and future masters of the Oral Law.

The leaders of the Sanhedrin, known as the B'nei Betera, for all their virtues did not constitute a part of the unbroken tradition and, as soon as they recognised that Hillel did, they immediately resigned in his favor. This was in the year 29 B.C.E, the same year that Augustus was proclaimed the first Roman emperor, and eight years after Herod ascended the throne of Judea. Like his great-uncle, Julius Caesar, Augustus was held in high esteem by the Jews, and members of their family ruled as emperors until 68 C.E.

Hillel's dynasty lasted until 425 C.E., serving simultaneously as leaders of the Sanhedrin and official representatives of the people until the third century, when they relinquished the former position. The title they were given - *Nasi* - is the same word used for the princes of the tribes in the time of Moses. Like the kings of Judah in the biblical period, they traced their descent to King David.

### Hillel and the Oral Law

The Aramaic word for teacher is *tanna*, and those who taught the Oral Law until it was compiled seven generations (inclusive) after Hillel in the Mishnah, are known by the plural form as Tannaim. Although they date back to the Great Assembly, in a special sense Hillel is regarded as the first Tanna, because he was the first to arrange the Oral Law in a systematic order. He also established hermeneutic rules (such as analogy and inference) to show how, through exegesis, the Written and Oral Law are integrally combined.

Such type of reasoning is best understood by the initiated, but Hillel's appeal was universal when he paraphrased the commandment "You shall love your neighbor as yourself" (Lev. 19:18) to mean: "What is hateful to you, do not do to your neighbor." This, he explained to one would-be proselyte, is the quintessence of Judaism, while he persuaded another to accept the authority of the Oral Law.

Hillel's life marks a time of change, because in addition to being the first Tanna, he was also the last to share the leadership of the Sanhedrin. Hence he brought the period of the Zugot (pairs) to a close. At first his deputy was Menachem who for reasons not explained, vacated the position. One conjecture is that he led a group of disciples to join the Essenes but, whatever the reason, his place was taken by Shammai.

### Beth (the academy of) Shammai and Beth Hillel

In insecure times, when the Sanhedrin was either weak or abolished altogether, the vacuum was filled by the academy in Jerusalem led by Shammai. With Hillel's arrival a second major academy was established and the two were known respectively as Beth Shammai and Beth Hillel. Shammai's disciples were fewer, and tended to come from a more affluent stratum of society.

During their lifetimes Hillel and Shammai differed on only three points of Law but, in succeeding generations, the differences between their disciples multiplied to over 300. In all but 50 cases, Beth Hillel adopted the lenient view, yet the disagreements never endangered national unity, because they never reached a personal level.

Sometimes the debates touched on abstract subjects such as creation, reward and punishment. The ultimate question of this nature, that also occupied the philosophers of Greece and Rome, was whether it would have been better for man never to have been created. After two and a half years of deliberations, Shammai's negative opinion prevailed, with the added proviso that having been created, all should examine their deeds.

One of the few enactments recorded in Hillel's own name is the *Prosbul*, which was made against a background of financial burden exacerbated by heavy Roman taxation. As the Sabbatical year approached, when all debts were automatically remitted, the poor found it difficult to borrow.

To remedy the situation Hillel introduced the Prosbul which in effect transferred the collection of debts to the courts (hence the meaning of its Greek name: "in the presence of the court.") Because the law of remittance did not apply to the courts, the rich did not withhold their loans, thereby directly helping the poor and indirectly stabilising society.

## Political conditions during Hillel's last years.

Hillel served as *Nasi* for 40 years, and saw Herod succeeded by Archelaus (4 B.C.E.). Unfortunately for his subjects Archelaus inherited his father's faults, including cruelty and a gift for intrigue. To prove to the emperor Augustus that he was strong enough to rule, he provoked a disturbance in order to have it forcibly put down. The incident occurred on Passover eve, while his father's massacre of those who had attempted to remove the eagle from the Temple was still mourned. Archelaus sent foreign mercenaries into the Temple court, with the full knowledge that they would be expelled, for the act was forbidden even by Roman law. The second time they were sent in, on the pretext of keeping order, a massacre took place, resulting in thousands of deaths. Another massacre occurred when Archelaus travelled to Rome for a meeting with Augustus.

During the meeting Archelaus was cautioned to govern with understanding and received the title Ruler of the People instead of king. But since he was either unwilling or unable to act on the advice, Augustus banished him to Gaul in 6 C.E., and placed the province under direct Roman rule. For the next 60 years, 14 procurators, subordinate to the Syrian legate, governed in Caesar's name. Their main residence was in Caesarea, but when in Jerusalem they ruled from Herod's palace, and foremost among their responsibilities was the collection of taxes. Payment of the tribute to Caesar became one of the most emotive issues of the time.

Coponius was the first procurator, but whether he, Archelaus or Herod governed the country, Hillel was looked upon as the true national leader. Whereas they were at best unpopular, he was universally revered, and when he died, all the people mourned. The most fitting tribute was to call him "the disciple of Ezra."

## *Rabban Gamliel the Elder*

### The first Generation of Tannaim (20-40 C.E.)

Little is known of Simon, Hillel's son, and so it is assumed he did not live long. In effect, Hillel was succeeded by his grandson Gamliel, who was called Rabban (our master) as a sign of respect, and also the Elder, to distinguish him from other descendants of the same name. As a general rule, the patriarchs were called Simon and Gamliel in alternate generations. During the first decade of his presidency, the Sanhedrin met in the Chamber of Hewn Stones, which was part of the Temple complex and where alone capital cases were tried. But 40 years before the destruction of the Temple the Sanhedrin changed its place of meeting, as a sign that it was no longer able to judge murder trials, due to the prevalent lawlessness. Henceforth the Romans alone inflicted the death penalty and crucifixion was one of their standard methods.

Rabban Gamliel developed Hillel's concern for society's weaker elements through enactments that aided widows, divorcees and gentile poor. He also corresponded with scattered Diaspora communities, and travelled when necessary to Antioch, to represent the people before the Roman authorities.

## *Rome's Influence*

About the time Rabban Gamliel assumed office, Augustus was succeeded by his stepson, Tiberius Caesar (14-37 C.E.). This second emperor reformed the tax situation in the provinces and reduced public shows and other expenses, thereby making himself unpopular in Rome. He retired to the island of Capri from where he ruled the empire by correspondence during the second half of his reign. The arrangement left Sejanus, the captain of the guard, with a great deal of power which he used to plan a campaign against the Jews throughout the empire. Shortly after Tiberius became emperor, Sejanus had persuaded him to expel Rome's Jews but this new threat was potentially much more serious. It was foiled after Tiberius suspected treason and had his captain of the guard executed.

Perhaps Sejanus' greatest disservice to the Jews was to appoint Pontius Pilate governor of Judea in 26 C.E., the same year that Tiberius left Rome for Capri. All the procurators were at best insensitive and at worst rapacious and bloodthirsty, with Pilate in the second category. In the Galilee he executed patriots without trial and deliberately angered Jerusalem's population by setting up images of the emperor. They were transferred to Caesarea after the Jews protested to Rome but following complaints by the Samaritans he was removed from office. His dispersal of a Samaritan assembly on Mt. Gerizim had resulted in many deaths, yet for all his cruelty, Pilate is best remembered for a trial over which he presided.

### The Origins of Christianity

Misrule, first by the House of Herod and then by the Roman procurators, encouraged nationalistic aspirations. There were some, like John the Baptist, who proclaimed the immediate coming of a savior, whereas his cousin Jesus (born between 8 and 4 B.C.E.) actually had messianic pretensions. Jesus spent most of his life in the Galilee, but around the year 30 he went to Jerusalem with a group of followers to celebrate Passover. The festival of liberation and his own second name, which means savior *(christos)*, provided much symbolism and some zealots saw in him a future king able to deliver them from Roman oppression.

To control Jerusalem's population, always enlarged on the festivals, Pilate brought in extra troops and their mere presence increased the existing friction. In the midst of this tense atmosphere, Jesus was brought before the high priest and later Pontius Pilate for trial, and before both he maintained his messianic claims. Only Pilate could condemn anyone to death, and the punishment for all those who rebelled against Rome was crucifixion.

The high priest, Caiaphas, at the head of a special 23-man Sanhedrin, approved Pilate's verdict, which was hardly surprising. All its members were Sadducees, who as a class were out of touch with their own people and therefore dependent on Roman good will for all the privileges they enjoyed. As a consequence, they were puppets of Rome, with whom they fully collaborated despite the treachery involved.

Above Jesus' cross was a sign that read "King of the Jews." His followers dispersed, but the idea spread among them that he was not dead, a belief that eventually identified them as a separate sect. At first its members were all Jews and known as Nazarenes, alluding to the town of Nazareth in lower Galilee. The later name of Christian is derived from the Greek word for savior as mentioned above.

When belief in Jesus was taught to the gentiles, the question arose whether they too were obliged to observe the commandments of Judaism. Paul of Tarsus declared them free, thereby enabling the new religion to spread rapidly and making him in the eyes of many its true founder. In his youth, Paul had been a disciple of Rabban Gamliel and in that period of his life was called Saul. Christianity spread the name of God throughout the Roman world, but it offered nothing to the Jews that they could accept or did not already possess. The original sect of Jewish Christians, nowhere welcomed, was doomed to disappear. Its members either returned to Judaism or assimilated among the gentiles.

### King Agrippa I (d. 44 C.E.)

The province of Judea received a respite from oppressive Roman procurators when Agrippa ascended the throne in Jerusalem. He was a grandson of Herod and

Miriam, the Hasmonean princess, and had been educated at the court of Rome during the reign of Tiberius. While there, he befriended Caligula and Claudius, two future emperors, and when the former ascended the throne he made Agrippa king over territories east of the Galilee.

After only eight months as emperor, Caligula suffered an illness that may have impaired his sanity because afterwards he began to build temples wherein he was to be worshipped as a god. When Agrippa passed through Alexandria on the way to take up his appointment, an anti-Semitic uprising took place. The Roman governor ordered statues of the emperor to be set up in synagogues, and refusal led to further rioting. On Agrippa's intervention, the governor was removed, but anti-Semitic activity did not let up under his successor. Apion, the foremost Jew baiter of the time, led a delegation to Rome, while Philo, the philosopher who tried to synthesise Jewish and Greek teachings, led a counter delegation to protect the rights of Alexandria's Jews.

While the various representatives were in Rome, Caligula ordered his image to be set up in the Temple. Following protests by the Jews, the Syrian governor ordered to implement the command appealed to Rome to have it rescinded. The command was repealed but only through the intervention of Agrippa, who had travelled to Italy specifically to intercede. Caligula was assassinated shortly afterwards and, fortunately for the Syrian governor, news of his death arrived before an order from the now deceased emperor for him to commit suicide.

The guards who killed Caligula found his uncle Claudius hiding behind a curtain and, without consulting the Senate, proclaimed him emperor. The Senators felt slighted but a crisis was avoided by Agrippa's intervention. A grateful Claudius confirmed Agrippa in his possessions and added to them Judea and Samaria. The unity of the kingdom on both sides of the Jordan, last achieved in Herod's reign, was thus restored.

Whatever his lifestyle had once been in Rome, when Agrippa ascended the throne he became a model king. He allowed himself to be influenced by Rabban Gamliel, and followed the sages in all matters of observance. On Shavuot (the festival of Weeks), he himself carried the first fruits into the Temple like any ordinary farmer, and at the end of the Sabbatical year, he publicly read from the Torah. This was a commandment for the king alone, and remembering his Idumean descent, he wept when he came to the verse: "You shall not set a stranger over you" (Deut. 17:15). But the people consoled him by calling him their brother. During the decade that Pilate governed the province, there were no less than five high priests, and the office was similarly exploited by other procurators. Agrippa remedied the abuse, but unfortunately his reforms came to a premature end when he died aged 54 in 44 C.E.

About this time the first generation of Tannaim came to an end. The teachings of most scholars were recorded under the collective names of Beth Hillel and Beth Shammai, but one specific name that stands out is that of Jonathan ben Uzziel. He was a disciple of Hillel, and is remembered for translating the writings of the prophets into Aramaic, a spoken language since the days of Ezra.

Agrippa II, who was 17 years old at his father's death, was not appointed successor although, in 52 C.E., Claudius gave him the northern part of the country where, as a true descendant of Herod, he succeeded in alienating his subjects. The death of Agrippa II brought to an end the last period of stability before the destruction of the Temple, for once again the province came under direct rule from Rome.

## *Return of the Procurators*

This meant the return of the procurators, who came from the Greek speaking section of Roman society, noted for its anti-Semitism. During Caminus' rule (48-52) which was marked by murder and bloodshed, the idea of rebelling against Rome first took root. Agrippa II followed his father's example in appealing directly to Rome to recall its representative, but none of the successors were better. The spirit of rebellion increased with every new cause for discontent until it could not be suppressed.

In Jerusalem and other centers, there were bands of Sicarii, so called after the Latin name for the short sword they concealed in their garments. They were assassins who did not differentiate between Roman and Jew and not a few victims were killed solely for their money. Even the procurators sometimes hired the Sicarii to circumvent the formalities of a trial.

As long as Claudius lived, there was hope of avoiding open conflict because through the intercession of Agrippa II he was able to restrain the procurators. Claudius, however, was succeeded by Nero (54-68) who was brutal enough to murder his own mother. At first he listened to able advisers and the government was fairly tolerable but, when unworthy counsellors took their place, the situation deteriorated. Nero was suspected of burning half of Rome (64) in order to provide a background for his recitation of the fall of Troy. According to another rumor, he used fire as the surest and speediest method of slum clearance, enabling Rome to be rebuilt on a magnificent scale. Four years later, after a revolt, he committed suicide.

The year Rome burnt, Gessius Florus was appointed governor of Judea, and not long afterwards he himself started a conflagration that would consume Jerusalem and the Temple. He personally did not apply the torch but his actions produced the same result.

### Prelude to War

Florus (64-66) proved to be the last procurator before the war with Rome. Caesarea, from where he governed, was a center of friction between Greeks and Jews but particularly so after Nero declared it to be a Greek city. Instead of mediating, Florus openly opposed the Jews who were, in his eyes, nothing but a source of revenue and plunder. On one occasion, he demanded 17 talents of silver from the Temple, and when the request was met with public derision, he marched on Jerusalem to take vengeance. Unable to identify those who had mocked him, he exacted indiscriminate punishment, leaving some 3,000 dead.

Florus' common tactic was to goad local populations into open opposition and then order his troops to intervene. Benefiting personally from the spoils, he always justified the use of force on the pretext of keeping order. The Jews complained about Florus to the Syrian Legate, and Agrippa travelled to Jerusalem in an attempt to calm the situation. He advocated continued payment of the tribute to Caesar but after he left the city the zealots gained control. The sacrifice in Caesar's name was abolished in the full knowledge that the act was tantamount to rebellion.

Roman troops garrisoned in Herod's palace felt threatened and, despite assurances of safe passage if they laid down their arms, they were massacred as they left. On the same day, other Roman troops in Caesarea stood by as Greeks killed Jews, and the scene was repeated elsewhere. In Alexandria the Roman commander was an apostate Jew whose troops actively participated in the disturbances. When Gallus, the Syrian Legate, arrived in Jerusalem to restore order, his troops were forced to retreat. They were attacked again on the hills outside the city but the legate himself and a large part of his force escaped under the cover of night. Euphoria following the victory encouraged many former moderates to join the war party, even though no one doubted that the Romans would return to avenge their defeat. Those who feared the most left Jerusalem.

### Rabban Shimon ben Gamliel (died c. 68 C.E.)

Once war became inevitable the responsibilities of government were assumed by the Sanhedrin, which was led at this stage by Shimon, Rabban Gamliel's son. Regional commanders were appointed, and Joseph ben Mattathias, better known as the historian Josephus, was placed in charge of Galilee. Despite Rabban Shimon ben Gamliel's personal opposition to the choice, Josephus nevertheless respected the patriarch and refers to him in his writings as a prudent and honest leader.

R. Shimon was a moderate who would have preferred a compromise with Rome, but like many others, he was swept along by events that led inexorably to war. At some stage in the conflict, he was captured and executed by the Romans, and his death is recorded in the liturgy for the Day of Atonement and the Ninth of Av. The Romans realised that a leaderless people is easier to subjugate, and so for about a decade they did everything in their power to bar a successor, especially from the house of David.

## War

When Jeremiah declared: "Out of the north the evil shall break forth upon all the inhabitants of the land" (1:14), he was referring to Babylon, but many subsequent invaders, including Vespasian, also entered the country from the same direction. Vespasian, one of Nero's most successful generals, brought an army of 60,000 troops to crush the Jewish revolt (67 C.E.), and in Galilee he was joined by Agrippa II. Agrippa, who was the last important member of Herod's dynasty, was rewarded with additional territory after the war and eventually achieved the rank of praetor.

Even before fighting broke out, the northern part of the country was in effect lost to the Romans, for two main reasons. Firstly, as soon as Josephus had formed his army, he should have eliminated the threat posed by Agrippa. His failure to do so gained him many critics, none more vociferous than John of Gush Halav (Gischala), a fellow officer. Thus, from the very beginning, the northern command was divided. Secondly, the strategically placed stronghold of Sepphoris went over to Vespasian, who used it as a springboard to capture the rest of Galilee once fighting commenced.

When conflict did begin, Josephus' inexperienced force was no match for the Roman legions, who restricted the opposition to isolated strongholds. The most difficult one to conquer was Jodpata, whose defenders at first managed to burn the siege towers, but eventually succumbed to hunger and disease. 40,000 were slain and 12,000 taken captive by the Romans but a small group, including Josephus, managed to escape and take refuge in a cave. They killed each other by drawing lots, until there were only two survivors who then passed over to the Roman camp. Whether by luck or design, one survivor was Josephus, who convinced Vespasian that his actions had always been in Rome's interest, which in practice was true. On becoming Vespasian's adviser, Josephus adopted his patron's name of Flavius, and although he attempted to mediate between Rome and the Jews, the latter always regarded him as a traitor.

## Jerusalem Under Siege

With the north under his control, Vespasian marched south. He allowed his troops a short rest and then captured the towns and cities of Judea, prior to besieging Jerusalem. In the capital, feelings of despair over the loss of Galilee were matched by contempt towards Josephus, and those responsible for his appointment were no longer heeded. The Zealots took control, which meant anyone advocating peace with Rome was summarily executed. There is much credibility in the statement that fraternal hatred was the true cause of Jerusalem's destruction, and certainly the internecine fighting saved the Romans much work. Opposing factions burnt each other's food stores, which otherwise could have been sufficient to withstand a protracted siege and, instead of using their combined strength to fight the Romans, they wasted lives and energy in fighting each other. By bringing about starvation, disease and self-inflicted wounds, Jerusalem's defenders were their own worst enemies.

To add to the tragedy, events in Rome required Vespasian's return, whereas a compromise peace, if one had been offered, would have served his interests. Turmoil followed Nero's death as three emperors seized power in quick succession. By choosing Vespasian as emperor, the legions in Syria and Egypt established the new Flavian Dynasty and, before returning to Rome to consolidate his position, he gave command of the siege to his son Titus.

## The Fall of Jerusalem

Titus attacked after Jerusalem's defenders had accomplished much of the task for him. Having burnt their own stores, the terrible scenes of famine described in the Book of Lamentations, at the time of the First Temple's destruction, were repeated. The streets were filled with corpses, and those killed by the sword were more fortunate than those who died of starvation.

Towards the end of the siege, resistance became confined to two main groups. One was led by John of Gischala, the former commander in Galilee and critic of Josephus, whose men occupied the Temple complex. The second faction was led by Simon bar Giora, who held the upper city. Whereas Titus had the advantage of being able to rest his troops and replace losses, the defenders fought continuously and each fighter was irreplaceable. In addition, the Romans possessed siege equipment and exemplary discipline, all of which combined to make the fall of the Temple inevitable.

Battering rams were ineffectual against the Temple's massive stonework, but there was sufficient combustible material for Titus to order the use of fire. On the ninth day of Av a Roman soldier threw a flaming torch into the Temple's wood store, and nothing could stop the flames from spreading. Rather than fall into enemy hands, many defenders threw themselves into flames that burnt into the following day. The Romans greeted the Temple's destruction (68 C.E.) with shouts of triumph, but the Jews have commemorated it as a national day of mourning ever since.

The upper city fell a month later, when the Romans breached its walls and burnt the houses. Anticipating the Warsaw Ghetto by almost 2,000 years, many defenders sought refuge in underground hideouts, but when hunger forced them into the open, they were slain without mercy. After five months, the siege of Jerusalem came to its tragic end.

## Aftermath of the War

Estimates of those who died in the conflict vary from 600,000 (Tacitus) to one million (Josephus) for, when the siege began, Jerusalem was crowded with Passover pilgrims. Yet even the lower reckoning equates the number of victims with the combined casualties of Hiroshima, Nagasaki, Rotterdam, London and Coventry in World War II. In addition to those who died in the siege, thousands of captives were sold into slavery or died of starvation, while others were killed in arenas by wild beasts and in gladiatorial combat.

Titus designated three towers, once part of Herod's palace, for the use of the tenth legion, stationed to garrison what remained of Jerusalem. (The base of one tower still stands, mistakenly called the Tower of David.) With the bulk of his army Titus proceeded to Caesarea and Syria, where he celebrated his victory, but the main festivities were reserved for Rome. There, on the Arch of Titus, can be seen sculptured in stone the seven-branched candelabrum and other Temple vessels carried in the triumphal parade. (Details are not necessarily correct, because the arch was built in the later reign of Domitian, Titus' brother.) Vespasian, who shared the glory, gave instructions for the vessels to be placed in a Roman temple, where they probably remained until 455, when the Vandals sacked Rome. Africa, the home of the Vandals, may also be where the Temple vessels are still hidden. The main exhibit in Titus' triumphal procession was Simon bar Giora, whose execution provided the highlight of the festivities.

The last stronghold to fall in the war against Rome was Massada, once Herod's winter palace, situated on a plateau overlooking the Dead Sea. Constructed to be impregnable, any conqueror would first have to overcome the height of the plateau and then a stone perimeter wall protected by 38 towers. At the northern end were three strong buildings, each situated on a steep rocky terrace where the 960 defenders held out with ample arms and provisions. The commander of the tenth legion, who besieged Massada, built a wall almost five kilometres (three miles) long around the base of the plateau, to cut off the besieged, and nearby the remains of eight military camps can still be seen. Using unlimited captive labor, he then constructed a giant ramp to reach the peak, but the fortifications were never tested to the full.

After three years, when the besieged realised defeat was inevitable, they committed mass suicide. According to Josephus, ten were chosen by lot to slay the rest, and by the same rule killed themselves. When the site was excavated in 1963-65, a synagogue, ritual immersion pools and sacred scrolls were among the finds, testifying to the piety of the defenders. The Romans themselves admired their courage. Jewish soldiers of the modern state proclaim at the site in formal ceremonies: "Massada shall not fall again."

## Rabban Johanan ben Zakkai
### (The Second Generation of Tannaim, 40-80 C.E.)

To Rabban Johanan ben Zakkai and the second generation of Tannaim fell the task of national rehabilitation. Realists foresaw the outcome of the conflict from the very beginning, and understood the need for a new spiritual center. Only Johanan ben Zakkai knew how to bring this into being, by persuading the Romans to recognise a town called Javneh on the coastal plain as the new seat of the Sanhedrin. The zealots had allowed no one to leave besieged Jerusalem and so, to gain an audience with Vespasian, he had his disciples spread false reports of his death, and then carry him out of the city in a coffin.

Outside Jerusalem, ben Zakkai was brought into the Roman camp, where he greeted Vespasian as emperor. When news arrived immediately afterwards that the legions had indeed elected Vespasian to rule Rome, he agreed to spare Javneh and its sages.

With the Temple and Jerusalem in ruins, most of the country desolate under Roman occupation and a large part of the population dead or in captivity, the scholars of Javneh set about their task. Following the example of the sages after the destruction of the first Temple, prayers were substituted for sacrifice and emphasis was placed on study. The main school of learning was called Kerem be-Javneh, the Vineyard of Javneh, because the rows of scholars resembled the layout of vines in a vineyard.

Johanan ben Zakkai received the title Rabban because he was president of the Sanhedrin, but he was always aware that both the title and the position rightfully belonged to Hillel's descendants. He had asked for that dynasty to be reinstated when he stood before Vespasian and so, at the appropriate time, he resigned in favor of Gamliel. By the time he stood down, Javneh's authority was complete, for at first it had been neither automatically nor universally accepted. His disciples were the leading scholars of the next generation, and one of them (Elazar ben Azariah) earned his praise for declaring a good heart to be the most favorable attribute (Avoth 2:9).

Many of Rabban Johanan Ben Zakkai's enactments were designed to preserve the memory of the Temple, but took the new situation created by its destruction into account. His achievements are best understood by his statement: "If you are planting trees, and someone tells you that the Messiah has arrived, first put in the saplings, and then go welcome the Messiah" (Avoth of Rabbi Nathan Chap. 31).

## *Rabban Gamliel of Javneh*
### (The Third Generation of Tannaim (80-110)

Rabban Gamliel had personally witnessed the nation's sufferings during the war with Rome and so was fully aware that internal strife had contributed to the disaster. One of his main goals, therefore, was to achieve unity, especially in the Sanhedrin, where individual opinion was to be subordinate to that of the majority. He sought respect not for his own sake, but for the office he represented. At one stage his colleagues even temporarily deposed him because they thought him too authoritarian and, after being reinstated, he was obliged to share the presidency.

At Javneh members of Beth Hillel and Beth Shammai debated together for the first time in a Sanhedrin free of Sadducean influence. The 316 differences that had developed between the two schools in the course of a century were examined, and the *halachah* (Law) decided by majority vote in favor of Beth Hillel, with 18 exceptions. The Mishnah, which later recorded the differences, also mentions Rabban Gamliel's name 68 times, as evidence of his contribution towards its development.

In addition to the expansion of the Oral Law, the scholars of Javneh also dealt with the written text when they gave the Bible its final form. They determined its 24 component books which are divided into three parts: *Torah, Neviim* (Prophets) and *Ketubim* (Writings). *Tanach*, the resulting acronym, is the Hebrew name for the Bible. The English word Bible comes from the Greek *biblia*, which means little books, for in effect the Bible is an entire library spanning over one and a half millennia, from the time of Moses to the final editing at Javneh. More than 60 different kinds of writing have been detected, ranging from narrative to poetry and wisdom literature. The theme common throughout is the existence of one God, before Whom there can be no other. This is the Bible's most sublime teaching, and it gives purpose both to the account of the creation and the subsequent historical narrative. The relationship between God, man and the creation is an historical one, expressed in successive covenants with Noah (as the representative of mankind) and the ancestors of the Jewish people.

Works not considered sufficiently authoritative for the Bible, were placed in a separate compilation, called the Apocrypha. In Alexandria the Jews included some of these books in their Greek version of the Bible, one example being the Wisdom of Ben Sira, which is quoted extensively in the liturgy for the Day of Atonement.

Just as the compilation of the Bible completed the work begun centuries earlier by the Great Assembly, so the scholars of Javneh gave final form to the most important part of the prayer book, known as the *Amidah* or Eighteen Benedictions. Of the last two benedictions to be added, one is a prayer for the restoration of the

House of David, a common theme in Jewish liturgy, and the other is directed against slanderers. The danger posed by slanderers who maligned Jews to the ruling authorities, began with the Samaritans and was taken up at a later date by the Sadducees. By the period of Javneh a major threat was posed by the Jewish-Christians, who denounced the Jews to the Romans. Under Rabban Gamliel's direction, the benediction against yet another hostile dissident sect was reformulated.

Rabban Gamliel was also responsible for the compilation of the *Haggadah* which is recited at the Passover *seder*. Other festivals also received distinctive customs that reflected the changed situation after the Temple's destruction.

Following Hillel's precedent, the scholars at Javneh continued to study and formulate the Oral Law and, in its enactments, the Sanhedrin inclined towards leniency. To alleviate the harsh conditions of Roman rule, farmers were allowed to work their fields right up to the Sabbatical Year. But among the prohibitions, they were not allowed to sell their land to Roman veterans who wished to remain in the country, in order to keep it in Jewish possession.

From many aspects the achievements of Javneh were the most productive in the entire period of the Tannaim and, by the time of Rabban Gamliel's death, it was firmly established as the new national center.

## Judaism in the Roman World

When Rabban Gamliel and others travelled abroad, it was mainly to the court in Rome but, in the city itself, discussions were often held with philosophers and others about belief. The Roman practice of adopting foreign gods, such as Mithras from Persia and Iris from Egypt, encouraged superstition and low moral values, which in turn led to increased dissatisfaction with paganism. Women in particular were attracted to Judaism by such practices as kindling the Sabbath lights, and the husband of one such proselyte was Flavius Clements.

He is of importance because he happened to be the cousin of the emperor, and as a reaction, Domitian (81-96) banned conversion to Judaism. In order to have the edict revoked Rabban Gamliel led a delegation to Rome.

Outside the Roman Empire, another famous proselyte was Helena, the Queen of Adiabene (in modern Iraq). She moved to Jerusalem (c.45 C.E.) where she built a palace to live with her children and, in the war against Rome, her husband fought on the Jewish side. After her death, Helena was buried outside the walls of the city with other members of her family, in a site known today as the Tomb of the Kings.

Domitian was succeeded by Nerva (96-98), whose reign proved to be a landmark. Previously, some of the emperors had been worshipped as gods, but subsequently, the custom became commonplace. Emperors who believed themselves divine also laid claim to absolute truth, and the Jews had no choice but to reject both assumptions. Consequently, they were often accused of disloyalty and suffered from punitive decrees, and when this occurred, further delegations travelled from Jerusalem to Rome to seek reprieve.

## Rabbi Akiva

### (The Fourth Generation of Tannaim 110-135)

Simon ben Gamliel was not ready to assume leadership on his father's death, and so the responsibility passed to Akiva ben Yosef, the foremost scholar of the age and one of Jewish history's outstanding figures. The period was not an easy one, because Roman suspicions of a new revolt were quickly aroused. While the Sanhedrin changed its venue between Javneh in the south and Galilee in the north, leading scholars taught in their own academies, and none was more famous than Rabbi Akiva's.

Akiva's rise to prominence was not an easy one. Of proselyte descent, he moved from upper Galilee, where he was born and where ignorance was widespread, to work as a shepherd in the south. He married Rachel, whose rich father opposed the match and for many years cut off the pair from his immense wealth. Rachel nonetheless encouraged her illiterate husband to study and eventually he surpassed his teachers at Javneh. Having mastered every aspect of Jewish learning from exegesis to mysticism, he formed another major link in the chain of tradition, and several disciples were required in order to pass on his comprehensive knowledge.

R. Akiva's learning was matched only by the variety of his accomplishments and activities, which ranged from supervising charity for the poor to education for the young, and from accompanying delegations to the court of Rome to refuting sectarians. In addition, R.Akiva was an ardent nationalist, who gave all his support to the struggle for independence in the next war against Rome.

## The Bar Kochba Revolt (132-135)

In the period between the destruction of the Temple and Hadrian's ascension (117), conditions in Judea were always difficult, but afterwards they became impossible. Hadrian was a proponent of Greek culture, and as such believed that circumcision was a mutilation of the body. He held it to be even more objectionable when performed by the Jews because it increased their separateness. For this reason, he proscribed the practice on the pain of death when he introduced a policy of Hellenization throughout the empire. He also proposed to set up a shrine to Jupiter on the Temple site, and created a general situation similar to the one that had provoked the Maccabean revolt three centuries earlier.

When rebellion became inevitable Rabbi Akiva travelled extensively to major centers of the Diaspora in Asia Minor, the Arabian Peninsula, Egypt and Mesopotamia. The army formed afterwards comprised soldiers from these same places, and so it may be assumed that the purpose of his visits was to appeal for funds and volunteers. Hadrian also travelled extensively, and while he was in the eastern part of his empire the revolt was postponed. In 132 C.E. he returned permanently to Italy, and in that year the war began.

The commander of the Jewish forces was Simon Bar Kosiba, known better as Bar Kochba (Son of a Star), after the verse "A star shall arise out of Jacob" (Numb. 24:17). His virtues included physical strength and courage but they were outweighed by his arrogance for, in a prayer ascribed to him, he asked God not for help but only not to hinder his efforts. Even so, Rabbi Akiva remained a fervent supporter, placing in him messianic hopes.

At first Bar Kochba gained victories in the south and then in the north of the country, and when Jerusalem was liberated, a special coin was minted, depicting the Temple. (A star shown overhead is thought by some to portray Haley's comet, which entered orbit about that time.) Any euphoria however was short-lived, because peace in other parts of the empire allowed Rome to concentrate all its forces on Judea.

Overall command of the Roman army was given to Julius Severus, then serving in Britain, and one of Hadrian's most successful generals. True to his name, he quashed the rebellion with a severity that turned Judea into a desert. The Romans conquered the country piecemeal, because Bar Kochba's inferior forces made it impracticable to engage in decisive pitched battles. Towards the end, only a natural fortress called Betar situated in the Judean hills remained unconquered.

Betar withstood three and a half years of siege, and eventually fell not by direct assault, but because a Samaritan showed the Romans a hidden way into the city. Both sides suffered heavy casualties, with 600,000 defenders slain, and survivors sold into captivity. When Severus reported his victory to the Senate, he omitted the customary phrase "I and the army are well." Significantly, Betar fell on the ninth of Av, the date associated with other tragic events in Jewish history.

In an attempt to erase Jewish identity, the Romans proscribed observance of the festivals, public prayer, the teaching of Judaism and the ordination of disciples. Many secretly and some openly defied the prohibitions, even at the cost of their lives. Rabbi Akiva was the first to appreciate that Judaism and national survival were intertwined, and so he continued teaching until captured and imprisoned in the Roman administrative center of Caesarea. On the eve of the Day of Atonement in 135 C.E., the year that Betar fell, he was tortured to death while proclaiming the unity of God.

## Main Centers where the Mishnah was developed

**Usha**  In Galilee, became the new center after the Bar Kochba Revolt (c. 140 c.e.).

**Shefaram**  Witnessed continuous Jewish settlement until the 19th Cent.

**Bet Shearim**  Where Rabbi Judah the Prince, in the 6th and last generation of the Amoraim, edited much of the Mishnah.

**Tzipori (Sepphoris)**  The largest city in the Galilee, and last home of Judah the Prince.

**Tiberias**  Spiritual capital of the Galilee where the Mishnah was completed c. 200 c.e.

**A Samaritan zone, in the center of the country, separated Judea from the Galilee.**

**Jerusalem**  Where the Sanhedrin met in The Chamber of Hewn Stones.

**Yavneh**  Seat of Sanhedrin after destruction of Temple.

**Lod (Lydda)**  Famous seat of Jewish learning.

**Bnei Berak**  Where Rabbi Akiva taught and arranged the Oral Law.

**The Holy Land**

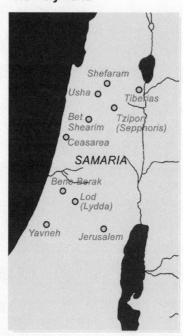

## Main Centers where the Talmud was developed

**Caesarea**  Where parts of the Jerusalem Talmud were edited.

**Tiberias**  Where the debates between Rabbi Johanan and Resh Lakish formed the basis of the Jerusalem Talmud, where it was edited c. 400 c.e.

**Nehardea**  Where Samuel taught in the first generation of Amoraim. The city was destroyed in 259, and students went to Pumbeditha and Mehoza.

**Sura**  Academy established by Rav, Samuel's colleague, and where later Rav Ashi and Ravina II compiled the Babylonian Talmud.

**Pumbeditha**  Together with Sura formed the two main diaspora centers.

**Mehoza**  Where Jews constituted most of the city's inhabitants.

**Babylonia (Modern Iraq)**

Rabbi Akiva's students joined him in supporting the revolt and so, after his death there was not one left who had been ordained. Continuity was preserved however by Judah ben Bava, who ordained five of R.Akiva's leading disciples at the cost of his own life, because the act was proscribed.

## The Disciples of Rabbi Akiva
### (Fifth Generation of Tannaim – 135-170)

The five ordained disciples of Rabbi Akiva became the leaders in the fifth generation of Tannaim, when the center of Jewish life passed to Galilee. Cities and towns in the south, including Javneh, remained desolate. Greek style theatres were built in an attempt to spread pagan culture. A shrine to Jupiter was even set up on the Temple Mount and Jerusalem, where Jews were forbidden to set foot, was renamed Aelia Capitolina (Aelius was one of Hadrian's first names). The name of the province itself was changed to Syria-Palestina. Syria indicated that the country had no independent identity, and the name Palestina was meant to humiliate the Jews by calling the country after their traditional enemy in biblical times.

The situation changed three years after the defeat when Hadrian died and was succeeded by Antoninus Pius (138-61). The empire enjoyed peace and much was done to ease the burden in the provinces. This meant the end of persecutions in Judea, and the prohibition to bury the slain of Betar was lifted. To commemorate the event, a special blessing was added to the Grace after Meals prayer. The Sanhedrin reassembled at Usha in the lower Galilee, with R.Shimon ben Gamliel as president. After spending much time in hiding from the Romans, he was ordained by the disciples of Rabbi Akiva, thereby restoring the presidency to a descendant of Hillel.

Unlike his predecessors, Simon did not use the title of Rabban but, even so, his name is mentioned 20 times in the Mishnah. Rabbi Akiva's disciples are quoted collectively hundreds of times; the most prominent was Rabbi Meir who, like his teacher, was of proselyte ancestry. His wife Beruriah was a personality in her own right; from her he learnt to pray for the eradication of sins, not of sinners. Rabbi Meir was primarily responsible for developing and passing on Akiva's arrangement of the Oral Law to Judah, Simon ben Gamliel's son, who used the material in the compilation of the Mishnah. Judah, however, did not study under Rabbi Meir, because of a disagreement between the latter and the patriarch's family. Instead he attended the academy of Rabbi Shimon ben Yochai, another of Rabbi Akiva's disciples.

Rabbi Shimon ben Yochai (or bar Yochai) is closely associated with the *Zohar*, a mystical commentary on the Torah in Aramaic, known in English as the "Book of Splendour." Study of the work is mostly confined to students of mysticism -

*Kabbalists* - but sometimes statements are found that are comprehensible to all, such as: "A man should so live, that at the end of every day he can repeat: 'I have not wasted my day.'" The Zohar was publicised by a thirteenth century Spanish mystic called Moses de Leon, whose claim that the original parchment copy of the Zohar was found in a cave in the Holy Land, recalls the famous 1947 discovery of the Dead Sea Scrolls.

The revolt made Rome more intolerant of criticism than ever, but this did not prevent bar Yochai from voicing disapproval of the ruling power. He was denounced and forced into hiding for 13 years. His son Elazar, who hid with him, later became a colleague of Judah the Prince, the most famous scion of Hillel's dynasty.

## Rabbi Judah the Prince
### The sixth generation of Tannaim (170-200)

Judah, the seventh patriarch, was called Rabbi like his father, and not Rabban. In the hierarchy of titles applied to the scholars during this period we are also able to detect a gradual descent in authority as we move further away from the Sinaitic source. The title of Prince alluded to Judah's wealth and knowledge, which he combined to a degree seldom equalled. Notwithstanding Rome's might, he spoke with emperors as an equal. This was the golden age of the Roman Empire, following the tyrannical reign of Hadrian and preceding the long period of decline.

Judah's contemporary was Marcus Aurelius, one of Rome's Antonine emperors, and an unusually noble one. Amongst examples of his humanity were concern for the poor, clemency towards political criminals and disapproval of gladiatorial combats. His saintly personality led him to reject paganism and, in his travels to the east, he combined affairs of state with quest for wisdom. Marcus Aurelius first met Judah the Prince on a journey to Egypt, and a strong friendship developed between the two. Latin or Greek provided a common tongue for their exchanges of correspondence or private meetings that took place in Galilee, where both had residences. Matters of faith formed an important part of their discussions and, as a result, the emperor learnt much about Judaism. According to one source, he even became a secret proselyte (Jer.Tal. Megillah 3:2).

It was clear even at the time that the peaceful conditions might never return, and so the opportunity was taken to compile the vast body of material surrounding the Oral Law. Earlier generations had been able to absorb and retain the vast mass of material, commentary and explanations of the Written Law, but by now its retention by memory had become well-nigh impossible.

Judah the Prince was born in the year Rabbi Akiva died, and the latter's disciples formed a bridge between the two by passing on the oral traditions of previous generations. There were in addition customs and enactments since the time of the prophets which also needed to be formalised and recorded.

Judah the Prince therefore produced a compilation, called the *Mishnah*, derived from a verb meaning to repeat, to teach or to learn. It comprises 63 tractates, arranged in six main categories or Orders. The tractates themselves are subdivided into chapters, and the chapters into separate Mishnayot (plural of Mishnah). The six main categories are: *Zeraim* (Seeds: Laws relating to Agriculture); *Moed* (Seasons: Laws of Sabbaths, Festivals and Fast days); *Nashim* (Women: Laws of marriage, divorce and vows); *Nezikin* (Damages: civil and criminal legislation), *Kodoshim* (Holy matters: Laws concerning the Temple and ritual slaughter; *Taharot* (Purities: Laws of ceremonial purity and impurity). Laws of the Nazirite are included in the Order of Nashim (Women), to teach that even those who practise self-denial should not refrain from marriage. Ethics of the Fathers is included in the Order of Damages, because ethical behavior is the most effective method of preventing injury.

The Mishnah's style is clear, concise Hebrew although, as a concession to contemporary languages, it also contains some Aramaic, Latin and Greek words. After the Bible, it is the most important stage in the development of Hebrew; just as in the history of the Oral Law it marks the most important stage since Ezra.

Rabbi Judah the Prince completed his monumental work about 200 C.E. at Beth Shearim in Galilee, which was also the seat of the Sanhedrin. The last 17 years of his life were spent in Sepphoris, because its climate better suited his health. The Sanhedrin joined him there; it was also close to Tiberias, where the emperor sometimes stayed. The friendship between the two was a major reason why the province enjoyed more autonomy than at any period since the destruction of the Temple. The poor received assistance from the patriarch's own wealth, and scholars were granted tax relief. It is little wonder then that in addition to the respect he inspired, his death was mourned by all sections of the population.

Judah the Prince was buried in Beth Shearim, where the most fruitful period of his life had been spent. Excavations there have revealed the remains of a large synagogue and a catacomb with the names Shimon, Gamliel and Anina (Hanina) found in a side chamber. These are the three names mentioned by Judah in his dying instructions:

> My son Shimon shall be *Haham* (head of the Academy); my son Gamliel shall be *Nasi* (Patriarch) and Hanina ben Hana shall preside over the Sanhedrin (Ketubot 103b).

### Rabbi Hiya and the Generation of Transition  (200-220)

In accordance with Judah the Prince's wish, the positions of head of Academy and

Nasi were separated for the first time among Hillel's descendants. The generation they represented was one of transition that fulfilled two tasks: the first to complete the editing of the Mishnah and the second to make separate compilations from the vast amount of material not included. These compilations were given the general name of *Beraitot* (extraneous Mishnah) and were made by some of Judah the Prince's leading disciples, each in his own academy. The foremost scholar was Rabbi Hiya, whose compilation is called the *Tosephta* (Addition).

By definition, the extraneous and additional works are not as important as the Mishnah itself, and have been compared to the books omitted from the Bible, which were relegated to the Apocrypha. The analogy, however, is not exact, because the Apocrypha is not an aid to understanding the Bible, whereas the *Beraitot* and *Tosephta* are often quoted in order to fully understand the Mishnah. They amplify where the Mishnah is brief, or may quote a biblical source omitted from the Mishnah, which is intentionally terse.

Apart from his compilation, Rabbi Hiya is remembered as an educator. He established a nationwide network of schools, caring especially for orphans. As a result, compulsory education began at the age of six for all children, producing an unparalleled degree of literacy. Following the precedent of Ezra and Hillel, he came from Babylon to revitalize Jewish life, and his sons who accompanied him continued his work. Rabban Gamliel, Judah the Prince's successor, did not live long, and a son also called Judah inherited the role of Nasi. Judah II, followed by the Sanhedrin, moved to Tiberias on the shores of Lake Galilee, where he continued Rabbi Hiya's work in the field of education. His philosophy was: "Children should not be interrupted in their lessons, even for the rebuilding of the Temple"(Shabbat 119b).

Judah II was the last patriarch who was also a recognized scholar, and his death brought the work of the Tannaim to a close. Those who followed are called *Amoraim*, or interpreters of the Mishnah. There were six generations of Amoraim in the Holy Land, and eight in Babylon.

## *Rav and Samuel*

### (The First Generation of Amoraim in Babylon - 220-250)

After the compilation of the Mishnah, the community that had existed in Babylon since biblical times came into its own, and the figure associated with the change was Abba ben Ido. Better known as Rav, he was born in Babylon and accompanied his uncle, Rabbi Hiya, to the Holy Land where he was ordained and served as a member of the Sanhedrin. Following the death of his teacher, Judah the Prince, he returned to Babylon and henceforth Babylon remained the main center of Jewish life for centuries.

Like so many great figures of Jewish history, Rav's fame lay in his scholarship, which he passed on to his students in the academy he established in Sura, an otherwise obscure town in southern Babylonia. The subject of study was the Mishnah, which Rav brought to Sura from Galilee and, by comparing it to other compilations of the Oral Law, its meaning was clarified and apparent contradictions reconciled.

Before establishing his academy, Rav held an official position as inspector of markets, which enabled him to travel widely and observe the general lax standard of religious observance. At this stage he declined to head an academy in Nehardea, in favor of a younger colleague called Samuel, with whom he was destined to lay the foundations of the Babylonian Talmud.

The Jewish community of Nehardea was the oldest in Babylon, and Samuel, its leading figure, was both physician and astronomer. He claimed that the paths of heaven were as familiar to him as the streets of his native city. Babylon led the ancient world in astronomical knowledge, and Samuel was careful to distinguish between astronomy and astrology, by declaring that good deeds, and not the stars, governed human affairs (Shabbat 156b). He never received ordination and, whenever he disagreed with Rav, a later generation would decide, apart from monetary matters, in the latter's favor. Samuel's dictum, "the law of the land is law," binds Jews to observe the civil code of the country in which they live.

There was no central legislative body in Babylon corresponding to a Sanhedrin, and so discussions in the different academies often took a theoretical rather than practical course, similar to analytical and applied methods in mathematics. Students ordained in the Babylonian academies were called Rav (great), and not Rabbi (my teacher), the title used in the Holy Land, that bestowed greater authority.

### Persian Rule in Babylon

The Parthian Empire was founded in 250 B.C.E. and, at the height of its power, when it was able to challenge Rome, included Babylon. When Trajan reorganised the eastern part of his empire (c. 115 C.E.), the Jews sided with the Parthians, and for their support experienced Roman cruelty. In 226 C.E., about the time Rav returned to Babylon, the Persians became the new masters, and a strong central government superseded the Parthian feudal system under local leaders.

A single dynasty of kings, called the Sassanides, ruled the new Persian Empire, and they used the ancient religion of Zoroastrianism as means of unification. At times, attempts were made to revive the glories of Cyrus and Darius in a previous age, and the combination of religion and nationalism resulted in the persecution of Jews and other minorities.

The adherents of Zoroastrianism believed in a god of good (truth, light and sun) and a god of evil (darkness and night), and were guided by priests who were subordinate to the king alone. The priests forbade the Jews to use light during Persian festivals; thus the Chanukah candles were kindled in secret. Likewise, they forbade burial, in the belief that corpses contaminate the ground, and so Jewish cemeteries were destroyed. (The Parsees of India, the last surviving Zoroastrians, continue the practice of placing their dead in towers, to be devoured by vultures.) Shapur I, the second Persian king, was a strong ruler who fought both Rome and the influence of the priests, and his friendly relations with Samuel ensured religious freedom for the Jews.

When Rav died in 247, many of his disciples went to Samuel's academy in Nehardea, making it the main seat of learning in the Jewish world. But after Samuel's death a decade later, Nehardea was destroyed by Palmyra, a state wedged between the mighty empires of Persia and Rome. It was later resettled, but the academy never regained its glory. Its place was taken by the academy in Pumbeditha, a prosperous commercial city with a long established Jewish community.

Until approximately the year 1,000 C.E., the two Babylonian academies of Sura and Pumbeditha provided spiritual guidance for the entire Diaspora.

### The Earlier Amoraim in Eretz Yisrael

The stability enjoyed by Babylonian Jewry under Persian kings was lacking in Eretz Yisrael, due to the decline of the Roman Empire. Between 235-268 there were 12 emperors, most of whom met a violent death, and the army instead of the Senate usually chose the successor. Internal confusion was compounded by border warfare, especially against Persia.

Whenever Roman armies marched, the responsibility of food supply fell on the local populations and, if quotas were not met, entire towns and villages were punished. At best the punishment resulted in economic hardship and, at worst, physical destruction. The Jews were affected more than most because their country frequently served as a bridge between warring armies. Under such circumstances, when life was at stake, the sages would allow bread to be baked on the Sabbath and work in the fields was permitted during the Sabbatical year.

The conditions of the time are reflected in the life of Resh Lakish (Rabbi Simeon ben Lakish) who had studied under Judah the Prince in his youth but afterwards had to rely on his strength and wits for survival. According to different accounts, he was either captured by outlaws and forced to join them, or else fought gladiatorial contests. Afterwards he met Rabbi Johanan, a one time fellow student, who persuaded him to return to study and gave him his sister in marriage. Rabbi Johanan was head of the academy in Tiberias where the two debated and taught, and among their disciples were Gamliel IV and Judah II, son and grandson of Judah the Prince. Rabbi Johanan and Resh Lakish even attracted students from Babylon, temporarily reversing the trend in the opposite direction, and their discussions are quoted extensively in both the Jerusalem and Babylonian Talmuds.

Both brothers-in-law lived to old age and, although Resh Lakish was the younger, he died first. Rabbi Johanan had outlived ten sons, but on his brother-in-law's death he was inconsolable and died soon afterwards (247).

### Political Developments in the Roman Empire

A decade after Rabbi Johanan's death, Diocletian became emperor (284-305) and checked Rome's decline through a series of reforms and military victories. As a test of loyalty, he introduced a form of emperor worship, but exempted the Jews out of respect for their religious principles. In contrast he persecuted the Christians, whom he suspected of trying to dominate the empire. They in turn blamed the Jews for the discrimination.

Diocletian formally divided the empire to make it more manageable and, after he retired, a power struggle ensued bringing Constantine to power in the eastern part. The Christians were by now a dominant force, and in 313 Constantine, together with his counterpart in the west, issued the Edict of Milan. The edict officially recognised Christianity throughout the empire and its followers were permitted to hold public office. When Constantine became sole emperor he used the church as an instrument of unification and, in 326, transferred the capital of the empire from Rome to Byzantium (in modern Turkey.) Four years later he dedicated the city as Constantinople in his own honor.

After Constantine's death in 337 the empire was again divided, with Judea part of the eastern half, ruled from Constantinople. The Christian emperors of the Byzantine Empire, as it was called, were all hostile towards the Jews, in contrast to only some of the pagan emperors, who had formerly ruled from Rome. The emperors were influenced by an anti-Semitic clergy who taught that Christianity had superseded Judaism, and only stubbornness prevented the Jews from accepting the new situation. The Jews were then ascribed inferior status, which was cited as proof, in a confusion of cause and effect, that God had rejected them.

The Edict of Milan, by which Christianity was tolerated, also recognized Judaism, yet the Jews were made to feel anything but equal as they suffered increasingly from discriminatory legislation and mob violence. In their own country they were denied access to Jerusalem, and monasteries or churches were built on sites identified by Helena, Constantine's mother, whose enthusiasm never failed to convince her that whatever sites and relics she found were exactly what she was looking for.

At the Council of Nicaea, convened by Constantine in 325, the Sabbath was changed from the seventh to the first day of the week. Sunday (the Sun's day) was chosen because Constantine once worshipped the sun (which also appeared on his coins) and the change was designed to further separate Christianity from its Jewish roots.

### The Later Amoraim in Eretz Yisrael

Rabbi Abbahu represented the third generation of Amoraim (290-320). He taught in Caesarea, the Roman administrative capital and an important center for early Christianity. The Christians, who enjoyed official protection, often initiated theological debates, anticipating the great disputations of medieval Europe. On such occasions Rabbi Abbahu's wide knowledge, which included Greek, cast him in the role of defender of Judaism against its detractors. The polemical nature of the times is reflected in his explanations of certain biblical verses, as when he interpreted the words "apart from Me there is no God" (Is.44: 6) to mean: "I have no son." On the verse "God is not a man" (Numb. 23: 18) he comments that anyone who claims to be God is lying.

In his youth Rabbi Abbahu had studied under Rabbi Johanan in Tiberias and, as Galilee entered into decline, so Caesarea increased in importance. In the year 351, all centers of Jewish life in the country suffered from a new and harsh wave of persecution. The Byzantines destroyed Sepphoris, Tiberias and Lod, forcing many to flee to Babylon and increasing the general desolation. Soon afterwards the Sanhedrin was abolished and with it the ceremony of proclaiming the new moon by eye-witness.

In order to make the new moon, and hence the festivals, independent of observation by witnesses, the patriarch Hillel II produced a fixed calendar. In the Hebrew year, the orbit of the moon around the earth determines the months, whereas the orbits of the earth around the sun determine the festivals. (Passover for example, is always a spring festival, and Tabernacles an autumnal one.) To produce a fixed calendar therefore requires resolving the eleven-day discrepancy between the lunar and solar years, and Hillel solved the problem by adding an extra month (Adar II), seven times in a nineteen-year cycle.

The Julian solar calendar, which was used in his time, accumulated an error of ten days by 1582, when it was replaced by the Gregorian reckoning. Hillel's calendar, by contrast, has never needed adjustment. In the Moslem Lunar calendar, the fast of Ramadan progressively falls in different seasons, whereas Hillel II determined over 1,500 years ago that the Hebrew festivals always fall at the same time of the year.

Hillel II was a contemporary of the Byzantine emperor Flavius Julianus (361-363), better known as Julian the Apostate. He was a successful general, a just administrator and a scholar whose studies led him to abandon Christianity. He even attempted to restore paganism, before his short reign came to an end when he died in a skirmish with the Persians. The Jews mourned his death because they saw in him a friend. In a letter to Jewish communities, he had announced the abolition of an unjust tax and went so far as to propose the rebuilding of the Temple. He referred to Hillel II as his brother but, within a few years both were dead, and conditions once more deteriorated.

Even if an emperor wanted to protect the Jews, the hostile attitude of the clergy prevailed. While some priests preached inflammatory sermons, others led mobs that destroyed synagogues and entire villages. Massacres had also taken place in pagan times but now they were rationalized by accusations of deicide. Laws were passed excluding Jews from state office or the army, while accepting proselytes or intermarriage with Christians became a capital offence.

When the Byzantines applied anti-Jewish legislation to the Samaritans, a revolt broke out that led to the destruction of Christian communities. In return, a Byzantine army massacred the Samaritans, and the cycle of violence came to an end only when the Samaritans ceased to exist as a separate group. (Today, remnant communities can be found in the town of Nablus - ancient Shechem – and the Israeli city of Holon.)

## The Jerusalem Talmud

Such times were hardly conducive to study, and certainly not in the intense manner of the Babylonian academies. What people wanted to hear were messages of hope and consolation, or ethical and moral rules, which formed the content of contemporary literature. The academies either reduced their numbers or closed altogether, as the population diminished with each generation. After six generations of Amoraim, the Talmud of Eretz Yisrael was compiled (c. 400 C.E.), while conditions still allowed. The work was completed in Tiberias and Caesarea, and not in Jerusalem, which was then forbidden to Jews. Nevertheless, it is called the Jerusalem Talmud, in order to identify the rest of the country with the capital city. It was compiled in haste and with insufficient resources, and although agricultural laws are covered more extensively, it is only about one seventh of the size of the more authoritative Babylonian Talmud.

## The Last Nasi

Soon after the completion of the Jerusalem Talmud, the office of Nasi came to an end. Its last incumbent was Gamliel VI, who offended the Byzantine authorities by building a synagogue without special permission. As punishment he was removed from office and, when he died without an heir ten years later (425 C.E.), the emperor Theodosius II allowed no successor to be appointed.

In 356 C.E. the Byzantines had partitioned the province of Palestina into two and, in the year Rabban Gamliel died, they divided it further, into three districts.

The purpose of smaller, independently administered areas was to blur national identity.

## *The Babylonian Amoraim and the Completion of the Talmud*

After the death of Rabbi Johanan and Resh Lakish towards the end of the third century, the center of Jewish learning returned to Babylon. There Rabbah headed Pumbeditha for 22 years, and his debates with Rav Yosef, who eventually succeeded him, became in themselves the subject of study in other academies. The number of students at Pumbedita at this time, including those who studied part time, reached about 12,000. Rabbah and Rav Yosef both taught the former's nephew nicknamed Abbaye who, like his uncle, was poor, but the knowledge he accumulated, even while combining farming with study, enabled him to succeed as head of Pumbeditha.

Abbaye's friend, colleague and academic rival was Rava, a rich merchant from the commercial city of Mehoza, where he established his own academy. Their period of activity, corresponding to the fourth generation Amoraim (320-350), is regarded as a watershed in the development of the Talmud. Early Talmudic debate had analyzed the Mishnah, but now emphasis was given to reaching practical conclusions. Deference was at first given to earlier authorities but, after Rava and Abbaye, later scholars being better informed were considered more authoritative. Discussions between the two are recorded extensively throughout the Talmud, with Abbaye the more lenient. The law, however, with six exceptions, was later determined according to Rava's opinions.

Rav Nachman followed Rava at Nehardea, while Rav Papa, another disciple, who established his own yeshivah near Sura, began to compile the Babylonian Talmud. This was a time when other academies were also set up, but none took the lead until Rav Ashi (d. 427) re-established that of Sura in a nearby location. He remained its principal for 56 years, sufficient time to make two complete revisions of all the material that had accumulated around the Mishnah, based on the debates of the academies in Babylon and Eretz Yisrael. Because the subject matter was by now too vast to be memorised, Rav Ashi committed it to writing in précis rather than verbatim form, resulting in the Babylonian Talmud.

Rav Ashi utilized a period of peace to carry out his work, just as Judah the Prince had done to compile the Mishnah, and no one in the period between the two combined scholarship and wealth to the same degree. Rav Ashi's son continued the work of editing, as did Ravina II in the eighth and last generation of Amoraim in Babylon, bringing the talmudic age to a close in the year 500.

The *Talmud* (meaning Study or Learning) comprises the Mishnah, written in Hebrew, and the *Gemara* (meaning Completion) written in Aramaic, the spoken language of the time. The Gemara summarizes the centuries of debates around the Mishnah, and therefore serves as a giant commentary but, in addition to its legal discussions (Halachah), it also contains parables and allegories (Aggadah). Additional subject matter such as astronomy, history and geography make a precise definition of the Talmud difficult. It is not even literature in the conventional sense, because its estimated 2,500,000 words are written in a terse style without punctuation or paragraphs. To complete the statistics, its 2,693 pages contain the names of more than 2,200 Amoraim.

Evidence of editing in the Talmud is subtle. As one example, the final words of its first and last sections both quote the same verse: "The Lord will bless His people with peace" (Ps. 29:11) to stress that peace is the most important of all blessings.

### The End of the Period

About the time of Rav Ashi's death, Byzantium took upon itself the role of universal protector of the Church, while Persia was the guardian of Zoroastrianism. The Jews suffered under both. The Persian king Jezdegerd II (d. 457) prohibited observance of the Sabbath and Festivals, and forbade the recitation of the Shema (the unity of God). His son Peroz was even more intolerant, because during his reign synagogues were destroyed and children forcibly abducted to be converted to Zoroastrianism. In 468 the Exilarch and many scholars were executed, and after Peroz' death the academies were closed, as revolution hastened internal dissolution.

About this time the Jews had become a minority in their own land. The process began when Titus destroyed Jerusalem and continued two generations later with the revolt against Hadrian, when Jerusalem was rebuilt as a Greek city. Each conflict left the population decimated because of the large numbers slain or exiled, while the country itself was gradually denuded.

Intermittent hardship under the pagan emperors became everyday experience under the Byzantines. The church was divided over matters of doctrine and, as different factions plotted and fought against each other, the Jews were the last to be granted peace.

Following physical violence and legal discrimination, Jewish national existence in a recognised homeland ceased to exist. Individuals have always remained, allowing Jews to claim a continuous presence in the Holy Land ever since the time of Joshua in biblical times. But as a people, by the Middle Ages they were to be found in settlements throughout Europe, North Africa and Asia Minor, which constituted in effect the then known world.

In an age when travel was slow and means of communication limited, the danger existed that different centers would remain isolated, perhaps ignorant of each other's existence. Under such circumstances, not only individuals but entire communities could lose their identity, or else survive merely as obscure religious sects destined for oblivion.

## 2000 B.C.E.

### ABRAHAM
**THE PATRIARCHS**

Teachers of Monotheism

**HAMMURABI'S LAWS**

Hittite & Egyptian Empires

**DECLINE OF EGYPTIAN POWER**

**1**

## 1500 B.C.E.

### MOSES
**JUDGES**

Earlier Prophets

**BEGINNING OF PHILISTINE SETTLEMENTS**

Spread of Mediterranean Civilization

**2**

## 1000 B.C.E.

### DAVID
**KINGS**

Later Prophets

**RISE OF PHOENICIAN TRADE**

Mesopotamian Empires

**END OF BIBLICAL PERIOD**

**3**

## 500 B.C.E.

### EZRA
**ZUGOTH**

Joint leaders of the Sanhedrin and the rule of the Wise

**BEGINNING OF ROMAN REPUBLIC**

Spread of Hellenism

**END OF ROMAN REPUBLIC**

**4**

## 0

### HILLEL
**TALMUDIC PERIOD**

Compilation of the Oral Law

**BEGINNING OF ROMAN EMPIRE**

Spread of Christianity

**END OF ROMAN EMPIRE**

**5**

## 500 C.E.

### RAV ASHI
**THE GEONIM**

Heads of the Babylonian Academies

**BEGINNING OF MIDDLE AGES**

Spread of Islam

**DECLINE OF BAGHDAD CALIPHATE**

**6**

## 1000 C.E.

### RASHI
**THE RISHONIM**

Earlier Authorities: Commentators & Codifiers of Talmudic Law

**HOLY ROMAN EMPIRE**

Crusades

**END OF MIDDLE AGES**

**7**

## 1500 C.E.

### JOSEPH KARO
**THE AHARONIM**

Later Authorities: Commentators & Compilers of the Halacha

**RENAISSANCE & REFORMATION**

Spread of Western Civilization

**END OF OTTOMAN EMPIRE RETURN TO ZION**

**8**

## 2000 C.E.

# CHAPTER 6 - FROM RAV ASHI TO RASHI

**500 C.E.**

*Rav Ashi*

*The Geonim*

*Rashi*

**1000 C.E.**

Rav Ashi and his disciple Ravina II were responsible for the redaction of the Talmud, and its final editing was carried out by a group of scholars known as Saboraim. Talmudic Law bound the scattered communities of the Diaspora together with a common code, enabling them to preserve their identity.

After the great Moslem conquests of the 7th and 8th centuries the Babylonian academies became the center for all Jews in the Arabic speaking world, including North Africa and Spain.

The heads of Sura and Pumbeditha were called Geonim, whose answers to queries sent from different communities formed a new genre of literature called the Responsa.
They disseminated knowledge by regulating a curriculum of learning for thousands of full and part time students. Hai and Sherira Gaon were the last effective heads of Pumbeditha and with their deaths the Babylonian center entered its final decline.

Around the year 500, Mar Zutra brought a copy of the Talmud from Babylon to the land of Israel, from where it reached Italy and other parts of Europe.

Although the Talmud's redaction took place in Babylon, it was based on the Mishnah of Eretz Yisrael and quotes many of its scholars.

In 636 the Arabs conquered the country from the Byzantines, to the relief of all its inhabitants. It became a military district called Falastin, ruled from Ramle, the only town founded by the Arabs. The Temple Mount was converted into a Muslim place of worship.

From the end of the 9th century, and for the next 200 years, the heads of the academies in Eretz Yisrael were also called Geonim, but they did not reach the stature of their Babylonian counterparts.

In Galilee, the Masorites determined the authoritative text and system of vocalization for the Bible.

Byzantium continued the tradition of Rome even after the collapse of the Western Empire. Its influence spread throughout Europe through the Code of Justinian, which was compiled about the same time as the Talmud. This code, based on Roman Law, included all the prevalent anti-Semitic enactments, influencing legal systems throughout the Middle Ages.

The new religion of Islam spread quickly after the death of its founder Mohammed in 632. At its height, Arab culture outshone that of Europe, and the Jews contributed to, and benefited from, the revival of learning. For over 200 years, Baghdad was the center of the Arab empire, and the Jewish community including the academies, benefited from the prestige.

In the tenth century, the Arab empire began to disintegrate, and the accompanying decline of the Baghdad caliphate contributed to the eclipse of Mesopotamia as the center of the Jewish world.

*Chapter Six*

# From the compilation of the Talmud to Rashi (c. 500-1000)

## *The period of the Geonim*

The Middle Ages began with two codes, the Talmud and the Code of Justinian. The first preserved the Jews, whereas the second contained laws giving them permanently inferior status.

Soon after Christianity was adopted throughout the Roman Empire (313), its emperors, encouraged by churchmen, issued a series of humiliating enactments against Jews, based on the false assumption that they were guilty of deicide and ought therefore to be segregated from Christians. Theodosius II, the emperor who abolished the office of patriarch and excluded Jews from public office, embodied all anti-Semitic legislation in a code that bears his name (438), upon which the more famous Code of Justinian was based (535).

Justinian's code influenced subsequent legal history throughout Europe, but of more significance for the Jews, it sanctioned discrimination against them from the Middle Ages to modern times. They were to be kept apart and afforded inferior status, although protected against total extinction, in order to be converted to Christianity at a later date. Countries like France, Germany and Poland, from which the Jews were never completely expelled, maintained an unbroken tradition of anti-Semitism from the time of Justinian, one of the greatest anti-Semites in any age, up to the Holocaust.

Discriminated against and dispersed in communities from the Atlantic Ocean in the west to the Persian Gulf in the east, the Jews found an antidote against national extinction in the Talmud. No matter where they lived, they were united by the same code of conduct and discipline of thinking, which provided a substitute for geographical borders.

Yet mere survival, it may be observed, can be an affliction unless accompanied by a positive attitude towards life, and this the Talmud also provided. In an age when illiteracy and ignorance were widespread (the Emperor Justin, Justinian's uncle, could neither read nor write) Jews needed to be decidedly more than literate to relive the debates of Sura and Pumbeditha when studying the Talmud, and all who observed its laws, customs and ceremonies thereby infused their lives with spiritual content.

A corollary of monotheism is its uncompromising abhorrence of idolatry and, as a consequence, the sages forbade participation in pagan festivals and the use of wine associated with idol worship. Detailed dietary laws in any case restricted social contact with gentiles, causing no little resentment in the Greco-Roman world and ever since. Yet the fact that successive Roman emperors found it necessary to forbid conversion is evidence in itself that many admired Judaism's refusal to countenance gods that were no gods and, attracted by its universal message of a kingdom of one God to be established on earth, became proselytes.

Contemporary Byzantine and Persian empires represented anything but an ideal, forcing many Jews to find refuge in the nearby Turkish Kingdom of the Khazars, situated between the Caspian and Black Sea. Under their influence, about the year 740, many leading Khazars adopted Judaism and, during the 300 years of its existence, the very idea of an independent Jewish state had a stimulating effect throughout the Diaspora. Shortly after their conversion the Khazars upheld the Talmud when a fierce debate over its authority took place in Babylon.

Justinian's code and the Talmud both entered Europe via Italy, and when the Byzantine armies conquered that country in 555, the Laws of Justinian were automatically introduced and soon adopted by other states. The introduction of the Talmud from Babylon into Europe was more complicated. In 513, an Exilarch called Mar Zutra rebelled against the Persians and established the Jewish Kingdom of Mahoza, preceding the Kingdom of the Khazars by more than two centuries. Mar Zutra's independent state, however, was of much shorter duration; after only seven years he was captured and crucified.

Mar Zutra's son of the same name escaped to Tiberias, bringing with him the Talmud, from where it reached Rome, Northern Italy and other European centers. It could never have reached Europe directly from Babylon, because national boundaries and barriers of language severely limited communication between the two parts of the world. By contrast, there was constant contact between the Jews of Rome and the Holy Land, ensuring that the communities of Babylon and Europe, as well as Asia and North Africa, were all united by the same code.

As a descendant of David, Mar Zutra was looked up to as a national leader and established a dynasty that survived for seven generations, but it was only a pale reflection of the glorious age of the *Nesi'im* (leaders of Sanhedrin) who had followed Hillel.

## The Saboraim

The scholars who lived in the period following the compilation of the Talmud are known as *Saboraim* (Explainers). Our information about them is vague, corresponding to the confused and troubled times in which they lived. After the decline of Sura and Pumbedita, a place called Firruz Shapur became a temporary center where the Saboraim completed the editing of the Talmud. They made some minor additions to the text and gave it its final form, but they were not innovators and produced no new rulings.

The next creative period is associated with the Geonim, which began when conditions in Persia became more settled, and lasted until the decline of the Babylonian center.

## The Geonim

The academy of Pumbeditha was reopened in 589 and that of Sura two years later. The heads of the two academies were called *Geonim* (plural of Gaon, meaning Excellency, after whom the period is named.) Their primary task was to spread knowledge of the Talmud, which they did in three ways. Firstly, by virtue of their position, they taught thousands of students who attended their academies. Student numbers were particularly high for two months every year (*Yarchei Kallah*) in the spring and the fall, when work in the fields was slackest. But, in addition to farmers, artisans and merchants also participated in the study of different tractates chosen for study each time. In modern Israel, some yeshivot continue the practice in modified form.

The Yarchei Kallah were convenient times for the Geonim to answer questions sent from the Diaspora on all aspects of Jewish knowledge. In the course of time, the accumulated answers numbered thousands, and when collected together created a genre of literature known as the Responsa. Many Responsa were devoted to explaining difficult passages of the Talmud, thus becoming the second method by which the Geonim disseminated its knowledge. Towards the end of the 19th century, a large number of Responsa dealing with legal and communal matters were found among thousands of other manuscripts in the storeroom (*genizah*) of a synagogue in ancient Cairo. Many of these documents can be seen today in the libraries of Cambridge, St. Petersburg and New York.

The third way Talmudic lore reached the Diaspora was by codification. Educated laymen can master Talmudic debate, but only the expert knows how to derive specific rulings. The Geonim were the recognised experts throughout the Jewish world and some of them made the first attempts at codifying Talmudic Law.

Two major difficulties often faced by Diaspora communities when corresponding with the Babylonian academies, or even with each other, were language and political boundaries. Spanish speaking centers, for example, found it difficult to communicate where only Persian was spoken, and even populations that shared the same tongue might be divided by political borders. These and other handicaps disappeared in a comparatively short space of time with the Arab conquest of the seventh century.

## Islam and the Arab conquests

Mohammed, the founder of Islam, was born in Mecca about the year 570. Orphaned as a small child, he was uneducated, growing up in relative poverty. When aged 24 he married a wealthy widow much his senior and, until the age of 40, led an uneventful life tending her camels. Then he began to teach the futility of idolatry after claiming to have seen the angel Gabriel, and declared himself the first Arab prophet. The citizens of Mecca rejected his belief in a single God, because much of their revenue depended on pilgrimage to the Ka'ba, a small windowless shrine, regarded as sacred by pagans. Because of opposition in Mecca, Mohammed fled to Medina (then called Yathrib). Islam reckons its years from 622 C.E., the date of his flight. In Medina Mohammed received help from Jews, who formed a large part of the population, and from them he borrowed many customs and teachings that were incorporated into the new religion of Islam. Islam means "Submission to God" and, as the name implies, the Jewish teaching of a single God forms its fundamental precept. Being illiterate, Mohammed took from Judaism only what he saw or heard, the same applying to Christian teachings. Whenever there are differences between Jewish, Christian and Islamic texts, his followers regard the first two as corrupt, even when in the Koran, Pharaoh asks his vizier Hamon to erect a "Tower of Babel."

Mohammed made Medina a theocratic state and his influence quickly spread, but he was disappointed when the Jews rejected his claim to be a prophet. To show his displeasure, he substituted Mecca for Jerusalem as the direction for prayer, and the day of rest was changed from the seventh to the sixth day. He further appropriated much Jewish property, because his first victories were over the Jewish tribes of Arabia that he either expelled or decimated, sometimes taking women and children captive. Like Christianity, Islam is a daughter religion of Judaism that attempted matricide.

Mecca became Islam's holiest city, and within it the Ka'ba the holiest spot,

## The Babylonian Academies in relation to the Moslem Empire (c. 750)

The Moslem Empire, which reached its peak about 750 with Baghdad as its capital, greatly facilitated communication between different Jewish communities and the academies of Sura and Pumbeditha. Six examples illustrate how far and in what matters their authority extended.

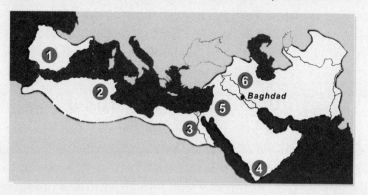

**1 Spain**   Paltoi, the Gaon of Pumbeditha (842-858) sent out a copy of the Talmud with explanations. Natronai (853-856) and Amram (855-874) heads of the Sura academy, sent out respectively an arrangement of the daily blessings and the first complete Order of Prayers.

**2 North Africa**   Sherirah the Gaon of Pumbeditha, (968-998) sent out a responsum tracing the development of the Talmud, since acknowledged as a classical source for a history of the Oral Law.

**3 Egypt**   During the period of the Geonim, the Karaite schism spread westward from Babylonia to Egypt. One of the greatest threats ever to traditional Judaism was checked by the Geonim.

**4 Yemen**   Saadia head of Sura, (928-942) whose scholarship covered every branch of Jewish knowledge, translated the Bible into Arabic. The translation was particularly appreciated by the Jews of Yemen, and is read by their descendants to this day.

**5 Land of Israel**   The scholars of Eretz Yisrael tried to assert their authority over the Geonim by initiating their own calendar calculations. Saadia maintained national unity by refuting their claims.

**6 Babylonia**   In Babylonia itself, the Geonim spread the knowlege of the Talmud by encouraging thousands of part time students to study in the academies for two set months each year. In those months they also formulated responsa to thousands of queries sent from throughout the diaspora.

making it the greatest object of pilgrimage in the world. While still banned from Mecca, Mohammed gained access to the Ka'ba for his followers by making a ten year treaty with the Korayish, the city's ruling tribe. After only two years, however, when strong enough to march in, the treaty was ignored, but the act set a precedent in Islamic Law. An agreement with infidels is valid for only ten years, but may be broken any time before, if and when considered necessary. (In recent history, the late P.L.O. leader Yasser Arafat quoted the precedent to justify his signing the Oslo Accord with Israel.)

After Mohammed's death (632), his teachings were collected into the Koran, the sacred book of Islam. Its attitude towards the Jews is ambivalent, reflecting Mohammed's own opinions at different stages in his life. What is clear is that the Koran offered a code far superior to the corrupted Christianity of Byzantium or the decaying traditions of the Persian priests. Most important, it united the Arabs to a degree never before achieved, and inspired them to conquer the world. As an additional incentive, Mohammed also promised those who died facing the enemy a direct passage to Paradise.

The Arabs broke out of the desert into the fertile valleys and, although inferior in numbers, their mobile forces easily defeated the armies of Persia and Byzantine. Omar, Mohammed's brother-in-law and successor who personally accepted Jerusalem's surrender, achieved the main victories. By the time he died in 643, the Muslims had conquered the Holy Land, Syria, Armenia, Egypt and Persia, creating in the process a new empire.

Conquests in Africa opened up that continent to trade and commerce, including traffic in slaves. Although the Arabs did not introduce slavery, which is as old as history itself, they did develop networks that supplied the Islamic world and beyond with human chattels.

### The Jews under Islam

By the time of the Arab conquest, the Jews of the Holy Land had suffered so much that any change was for the better. In 611 the Persians had invaded the country and three years later captured Jerusalem. The Jews, who had supported them, were massacred when the city was retaken by the Byzantine emperor Heraclius (629). When the Arabs entered Jerusalem in 638 they were welcomed as liberators who brought stability and a greater degree of tolerance.

The Arabs forced conquered peoples to adopt Islam, except Jews and Christians, who were allowed to retain their own beliefs, because once they were custodians of the truth and are still known as the People of the Book. They were accorded second class status, however, because they rejected Mohammed whose followers alone are considered true believers. Omar, who laid out the administrative base of the empire, issued laws that forbade Jews to hold public office, employ Muslim servants or repair synagogues. They were also required to wear a yellow patch on their sleeves to set them apart, but in effect, none of these restrictions were applied with the same rigor as in Europe at a later date.

Following the Arab conquests, the academies of Sura and Pumbedita became more accessible to the Diaspora. Different countries that had once been ruled by Vandals, Visigoths, Persians and Byzantium were now part of one great empire united by a common border and language. Consequently, distant communities in Africa or Spain corresponded more easily with the Geonim in Babylon. Another result of Moslem rule was the reinstatement of the Exilarch as the representative of Babylonian Jewry.

## The Exilarchs

"The Babylonian Exilarchs were like kings who possessed the authority to rule Israel in every place and to administer justice even without consent. Every judge worthy of the title who had received permission from the Exilarch was automatically authorised to adjudicate throughout the Jewish world, even without the agreement of the litigants."

So Maimonides, in his famous code, describes the powers of the Exilarch. The Exilarchs were like kings both in their authority and life-style, for they dressed in clothes of silk and gold, and travelled to and from their palaces in a coach of gold accompanied by guards. The day of their inauguration was an occasion for special ceremony, and afterwards they were given a place in the Caliph's court among the highest dignitaries. These men, treated like royalty, were actually descended from one of the last kings of Judah who was exiled to Babylon, and so they traced their lineage to David himself.

The House of David often served as a barometer indicating the attitude of the authorities towards the Jews. During the Hadrianic prosecutions, for example, the office of Patriarch was suspended, but when Judah the Prince enjoyed the friendship of the Roman emperor, the entire province lived in peace. In Persia, where the last kings persecuted the Jews, one of them attempted to eliminate David's descendants by killing the Exilarch and his family. When the Arabs conquered the country and inaugurated a period of tolerance, they began by installing a new Exilarch. Their choice was Bustenai, a surviving member of the murdered Exilarch's family.

Bustenai (d. 660) was both an historical figure and the subject of much legend. According to one account, the Caliph Omar gave him a Persian princess in marriage but, as she was not his only wife, there were different branches of succession. When one particular branch came to an end a century later, a dispute over succession split the Jewish community.

### The Karaite Schism

Anan ben David was due to become Exilarch, but because he rejected the authority of the Talmud, his candidacy was rejected in turn by the Geonim, who appointed a younger brother instead. Anan's like-minded supporters nevertheless continued to recognise him, leading to his arrest. By opposing his brother, who was a senior official at the Caliph's court, he faced the charge of treason. In defence, Anan claimed to be the founder of a new religion, thereby absolved from any allegiance to the Exilarch. The Caliph sat in judgment and accepted the argument, because as a Shiite Moslem, he himself rejected the Suna, the Islamic Oral Law.

Originally known as Ananites, the members of the breakaway sect were called *Karaites* (Scripturalists) by a later generation, because they only accepted the written word of the Bible. Their first appearance may have been in medieval Persia, but their spiritual roots reached back to Second Temple times, when the Sadducees denied the validity of the Oral Law. Just like the Sadducees, they observed Shavuot (the Festival of Weeks or Pentecost) on a different date from the majority of Jews, and did not observe the festival of Chanukah at all because of its post-biblical origin. But both Sadducee and Karaite traditions show clearly that acting on the written word alone leads to restriction and religious anarchy, instead of emancipation.

Thus the Karaites allowed no light in their home on the Sabbath, even when kindled beforehand; neither on that day did they step outside their homes. Anan tried to instil some conformity of observance among his followers by producing the Book of Precepts, equivalent to the Sadducean Book of Decrees, but both works ended in oblivion.

Whatever unity Anan did accomplish, was cancelled out when he said, "Do not rely on my opinion," which opened a floodgate of different biblical interpretations among his followers. Not until the ninth century and culminating in the twelfth, when the sect began to decline, was conformity of observance achieved. This was due to a series of codes, based partly on exegetical methods the Karaites themselves originally condemned. The codes of the Geonim, by contrast, were part of a tradition that spanned millennia based on the *Halachah*. This is a word usually translated as Law, but a more literal and faithful rendering would be "the [proper] way."

### Jehudai Gaon (d. 764) and Paltoi Gaon (d.858)

The first Gaon to make a compilation of the Halachah was Jehudai, head of the Sura academy. His work was necessary because in the new Arabic-Persian culture, Aramaic, the language of the Talmud, ceased to be spoken. The Talmud therefore was not always understood, and even when it was, few knew which particular opinion, found in any one of thousands of folio pages, was law. This marked a further stage in the diminution of the generations since Sinai. The Geonim were equipped to overcome the difficulty, because as principals of the famous academies they were required to know the Talmud by heart. Jehudai's achievement was even more remarkable because he was blind. His Compendium, written in Aramaic, and which he dictated to his disciples, only contains laws applicable after the destruction of the Temple.

Some hundred years later, Paltoi, the Gaon of Pumbeditha, sent a copy of the Talmud with explanatory notes to the Jews of Spain. This was needed in an age when manuscripts were laboriously written by hand, making books scarce. Even an isolated tractate of the Talmud free of copyist's errors was a rarity. Paltoi's Responsa illustrate how even in the furthermost parts of the Muslim empire, contact was maintained with the Babylonian academies.

The period of the Geonim cannot easily be divided into generations because they were advanced in age when appointed, and only held office for an average of ten years. There were some 50 heads of Pumbeditha and 38 in Sura and, although we know their names, their contemporaries remain anonymous. The situation in the Talmudic period was reversed, for among the names of thousands of scholars, few are identified as heads of academies.

### *Amram Gaon (d. 874)*

Amram Gaon is best known for producing the first *siddur* (prayer book). In an early stage of the synagogue service, many prayers were improvised, which explains why some of the early Jewish poets were also cantors. What was once spontaneous supplication often became a set part of the liturgy but, for the vast majority who were neither poets, improvisers, or able to rely on their memories, some form of prayer book was required.

Natronai, Amram's immediate predecessor, had sent a brief arrangement of the daily blessings to the community of Lucena in Southern Spain, but it was Amram himself who produced the authoritative siddur for Spanish Jewry. From Spain it reached communities in Portugal, Southern France, North Africa and elsewhere, becoming known as the Sephardi rite. The Jews of Europe who lived outside the Moslem world, and whose contact with the Babylonian academies was tenuous, used the Ashkenazi rite, which had its origin in the Land of Israel.

The scholars of the Holy Land were overshadowed by their Babylonian counterparts but attempted to reassert their independence when the occasion arose.

### *Saadiah Ben Joseph Gaon (882-942)*

Saadiah was the greatest Gaon and one of the most famous Jewish scholars of all time. His encyclopaedic knowledge enabled him to make vital contributions in such varied fields as biblical and Talmudic studies, jurisprudence, philosophy, lexicography, grammar, poetry, astronomy and liturgy. He was also a fearless polemicist, as the Karaites and others discovered to their cost.

Saadiah was born in Egypt to working-class parents and, when he was about 30 emigrated to Tiberias, where the study of Hebrew grammar and the *Masorah* (the vocalization and cantillation of the Hebrew text) was more advanced than in Babylon. The Karaites, who attached importance to the written word and none to its traditional interpretation, undoubtedly stimulated progress in these subjects. This in turn forced the Rabbanites, as they called their opponents, to re-examine the biblical text with emphasis on grammar and syntax. The influence of the Karaites was approaching its peak, and by fulfilling the precept of settling in the land, their major centers were Jerusalem, Tiberias and Ramle.

In an early polemical work Saadiah defined the Karaites as complete apostates, and not just members of a sect within Judaism. (In the 20th century, Karaites under Nazi occupation similarly argued that they were not Jews.) Saadiah went to the heart of the Karaite heresy by showing that without the Oral Tradition, the Written Law could neither survive or be understood.

During the tenth and eleventh centuries, academies in the Holy Land experienced a revival and, while falling short of those in Babylon, the heads were also called Geonim. The Geonim in the land of Israel were descended from Hillel, and one of them called Aaron Ben Meir wanted to restore his ancestors' prerogative of fixing the calendar. The practical result was that the communities in Babylon and the Holy Land celebrated Passover in the year 922 on different days. The Babylonian leaders found themselves fighting two battles simultaneously, one against the Karaites and the other against Ben Meir. At this point, Saadiah's knowledge of astronomy allowed him to intervene. His *Book of Seasons* was a successful refutation of Ben Meir's arguments, and immediately established his reputation as a scholar.

The fortunes of the academy in Sura were at a low ebb when Saadiah took over the leadership (928). The appointment was remarkable for its time, because for centuries the position had been the exclusive possession of just three families, two of which were of priestly descent. Always of independent spirit, Saadiah fell out with the Exilarch after two years in office and retired to Baghdad. By this time, the city was the capital of the empire and one of the richest and most splendid in the world. It also attracted one of the largest urban Jewish populations, which included the Exilarch (to be near the court) and the Gaon of Pumbeditha.

In Baghdad Saadiah composed two of his most important works, based on traditional scholarship and intellectual acumen above anything the Karaites could match. The first work was a translation of the Bible into Arabic, with a complete commentary on the first five books and a partial one on the others. Those who only understood Arabic were provided with an access to the sources and, among the Jews of Yemen, the translation was particularly popular. It contrasted favorably with the third century (B.C.E.) Septuagint, which was also a translation into the vernacular, but did little to help the Greek speaking Jews of Egypt retain their faith.

Saadiah's second major literary undertaking, also written in Arabic, was called *Emunot Ve'Deot* (*Beliefs and Opinions*). It was a philosophical treatise, in which he argued that true scientific inquiry and religious belief were complementary rather than contradictory. He was the first Jewish philosopher since Philo to combine faith and reason, to be followed three centuries later by Maimonides. Saadiah confirmed his scholarly reputation by writing an introduction to the Talmud and systematically presenting its laws, while his prayer book for the Jews of Egypt contained original compositions. In the field of polemics his writings proved the most effective means of checking Karaite influence, but his inability to compromise affected his private life. Saadiah's refusal to endorse a legal decision by the Exilarch, David Ben Zakkai, resulted in seven years of estrangement between the two, during which he was removed from office. After the reconciliation, neither lived long, and perhaps Saadiah's most fitting tribute was written some three centuries after his death by Maimonides; "He strengthened the wavering and spread knowledge of Judaism by his pen and words."

### The Holy Land During the Period of the Geonim

After the Arab conquest, the country was divided into two administrative districts (each called a Jund) governed from Tiberias and Ramle, while the country as a whole was ruled from Damascus, for "Falastin" was never an independent Arab state. Ramle was the only town built in the country by the Arabs, who allowed Jerusalem to become derelict.

Around the year 970 the Fatamides, a dynasty of Caliphs named after Mohammed's daughter Fatima, came to power. They and their followers were one of countless sects fathered by the Shiite Moslems that included Druses and Assassins. The method by which the latter disposed of their enemies added a new word to the English language, and Shiites in general bear much responsibility for the negative image given to Islam in western countries. Their reputation of bigotry and persecution was based on indiscriminate destruction of both churches and synagogues. This caused further destruction and desolation in the land, where local chieftains were already spreading anarchy in the absence of a central authority.

With Jerusalem a derelict city, Tiberias served as the country's spiritual center. It was there that the work of annotating the Bible was completed by a group of scholars known as Massorites. Without them, proper understanding of the Bible would not be possible, because to this day parchment scrolls contain no vowels or punctuation. Words containing the same consonants therefore can be read in ways that give different meanings, and sometimes the interpretation of the same word depends on whether the first or last syllable is accentuated.

The Massorites addressed themselves to all such questions and also devised musical symbols to determine how the words should be intoned, thereby grouping them into phrases and verses. Their name is derived from the word *masorah* which means tradition, because the correct reading of the scrolls is part of a tradition that goes back to Ezra and the Great Assembly.

There were two schools of Massorites, one in Tiberias and the other in Babylon, each with its own system of vocalization. The Tiberian system, developed by the family of Ben Asher proved to be superior and is the one in present use. Aaron Ben Asher (d. 930), who was a contemporary of Saadiah Gaon, was the family's last and most famous member, and one of his scrolls, noted for its accuracy, was copied centuries later by Maimonides. With modern technology, scrolls are checked against a computer, but the definitive text fed into the computer is still that of Ben Asher. In addition to the Masorah, the Holy Land produced composers of liturgical poetry during the period of the Geonim.

### Sherirah Gaon (d.1000) and Hai Gaon (d. 1038)

After Saadiah's death, the academy of Sura closed for 46 years, a sign in itself that the age of the Geonim was approaching its end. But before it did so, the academy of Pumbeditha produced two of its greatest figures in Sherira and Hai Gaon. They were father and son, who between them occupied the Geonate for 70 years (968-1038). Sherira is best known for a letter he wrote to the community of Kairouan in North Africa, describing the origins of the Mishnah and the Talmud, and their place in tradition to his own day. He traced his own ancestry to the Exilarch's family, noting that his forefathers shunned the office, because it was often exploited for personal ambition. They devoted themselves instead to studying and teaching in the academy of Pumbeditha.

Sherira enriched our knowledge of the entire period, earning him a leading place as an historian. He worked in conjunction with his son Hai, but both had enemies and were jailed after being maligned to the Caliph. Although friends intervened for their release, the incident left Sherira a broken man and, aged 98, he retired in favor of his son. He died two years later. Hai was the only Gaon to succeed his father and, for the next 40 years, attracted students from throughout the Diaspora. His many responsa dealt with such subjects as Biblical commentary, grammar, philosophy and liturgy. He codified the civil laws of the Talmud, and established the principle that wherever the Babylonian and Palestinian Talmuds differed, preference be given to the former. Hai died childless, just one year short of his father's 100-year life span, and was mourned even in distant Spain, where eulogies in his honor were composed.

## Spain succeeds Mesopotamia

The Geonim continued to live in Baghdad until the late 13th century, but Hai's death marks the end of an era. His successor was Hezekiah Ben David, who simultaneously held the positions of Exilarch and Gaon, until he was jailed and died under torture in a time of general oppression. Hezekiah's two sons fled to Spain, where the last known descendant died in 1154. Thus the dynasty of Exilarchs that had its origins in biblical times came to an end in the middle ages 1500 years later.

As the Geonim and the Exilarch had benefited when the Baghdad Caliphate prospered, so their influence waned when it declined. The unity of the Moslem empire after the capital was transferred to Baghdad (750) proved to be short lived. Islamic Spain was the first country to establish its independence under the caliphate of Cordova (756) and Egypt followed suit under the Fatamides in the tenth century. From this period Egypt, and Cairo in particular, became a center of Islam instead of an outpost. In order to retain control of their disintegrating empire, the rulers in Baghdad became increasingly dependent on Seljuk Turkish mercenaries. Originally Asiatic nomads who accepted Islam, Seljuks changed their role from servants to masters. By degrees the Caliphs became their puppets and their court, which included the Exilarch, suffered accordingly.

The increase in Seljuk Turkish influence meant the end of Arab domination in the Islamic world, bringing to an end centuries of Arab achievement and prosperity. With the stagnation of Arab civilization the position of minorities worsened, as they learnt in practice what previously they had known mainly in theory, that non-Moslems held inferior status. At best, Jews and others were second-class citizens, at times without the right to defend themselves when attacked. Despair spread, just as it had done under despotic Persian kings, whom the Caliphs ultimately came to resemble.

The Geonim themselves may have contributed to the eclipse of their academies, by following the Exilarch's example of living in Baghdad. As the Babylonian center declined, others in the Diaspora took its place, aided, unexpectedly, by an act of piracy.

Around the year 974, four Rabbis from the Babylonian academies were captured in the Mediterranean Sea by pirates. Death or slavery might easily have been their fate, but instead they were ransomed in different ports. One settled in Alexandria in Egypt, a second in Karouan in Tunis, and a third, Moses ben Hanoch together with his son, was redeemed by the Jews of Cordova in Spain.

It is generally assumed that Jews arrived in Spain soon after the destruction of the Temple, although it is not until the second century that their presence is beyond dispute. Relations with the ruling power of Rome were generally good but changed when the empire adopted Christianity. After the fall of the Western Roman Empire (476) the situation improved under the Visigoths, who showed tolerance as long as they remained uninfluenced by the anti-Semitic clergy. Although Christians, they followed the teachings of Arias of Alexandria, who taught that Jesus was less than divine. But in 589 the Visigoths adopted Catholicism, and Jews were forcibly converted.

Relief came in 711 when an invading force of Arabs and Berbers crossed the Straits of Gibraltar under the command of Tarik. (He gave his name to the rock, for Gabel, Arabic for mountain, when combined with Tarik, forms Gibraltar.) The Jews openly welcomed the Muslims, and often garrisoned captured cities behind their advancing army. After most of Spain was conquered in a short space of time, the Jews were granted full religious freedom, and those who had been forcibly converted under the Visigoths were allowed to return to their faith.

When the Ummayad Caliphs of Damascus were massacred in a dynastic struggle (749), a surviving member fled to Spain where he established an independent regime. Cordova, a provincial capital in Southern Spain, became one of the greatest and wealthiest cities of Europe, rivaling Baghdad's commercial and intellectual activity. In common with Granada, Toledo and Seville, which were other provincial capitals, it attracted a large Jewish population. Spain encouraged its Jewish communities to break their cultural and financial ties with the academies in the rival Baghdad Caliphate, and so the arrival of Rabbi Moses ben Hanoch in Cordova was welcomed. The rabbi of Cordova resigned in his favor, just as the B'nei Betera had resigned in Hillel's favor a thousand years earlier, after his arrival in Jerusalem from Babylon. The academy established by Rabbi Moses ben Hanoch attracted students from Spain and North Africa and, after he died, his son succeeded him until his own death in 1014. Through them, the method of study characteristic of the Babylonian schools was transferred to the Iberian Peninsula.

### Hasdai Ibn Shaprut (915-70)

The development of Spanish Jewry will always be associated with Hasdai Ibn (son of) Shaprut, one its greatest figures. He was the Caliph's doctor and adviser, in addition to being well versed in the Bible and Talmud. His chief claim to fame, however, was as a patron of learning, for he brought to Cordova Jewish philosophers, poets and scientists. Under his auspices, the Hebrew grammarian Menahem Ben Seruk composed the first complete dictionary of biblical Hebrew and Aramaic. A pupil of Menahem showed for the first time that all Hebrew verbs are based on a three-letter root.

In his role of statesman, Hasdai made contact with the famous kingdom of the

Khazars, whose king and nobles had embraced Judaism. Their faith greatly impressed Hasdai, and Joseph, the Khazar King (known as the Khagan) invited him to become his adviser. Nothing transpired however, because a Russian army overran the kingdom in 969, and a year later Hasdai died. During its existence, the Khazar Empire reached a relatively high degree of civilization and religious tolerance.

Cordova's prosperity did not last much longer because in 1013 it was captured by the Berbers from North Africa, who killed many Jews during their military incursion. The Berbers also had a loose tribal organization, and divided Spain into a number of petty kingdoms. Nothing however could uproot the vibrant Jewish culture that had taken root.

## Jewish Life in Northern Europe

The Muslims never succeeded in extending their power beyond the Pyrenees into the rest of Europe. Charles the Great, or Charlemagne (742-814) united France, Germany and Northern Italy into a strong union called the Empire of the West, the forerunner of what would become in 962 the Holy Roman Empire. The Pope encouraged a strong western union to make the Church of Rome independent of Byzantium, which is why he himself crowned Charlemagne (800). Charlemagne proved to be an energetic king who put the interests of state above those of the clergy, and so he welcomed the Jews for their trading links and commercial ability. Jewish merchants travelled freely throughout the empire, with safety of life and possessions guaranteed by the state. In Lyons, the market day was changed from the Sabbath, to accommodate Jewish traders. Jews were also valued for their linguistic skills, and a delegation sent to the Caliph of Baghdad included a Jewish interpreter, who was the only member fortunate enough to return.

Charlemagne held general consultative assemblies at least once a year and cared for the welfare of the poor. In addition, numerous schools were established throughout the empire for children of all classes, and the preservation of classical literature was due almost entirely to his initiative. Mainz, on the Rhine, became a cultural center, the German equivalent of Muslim Cordova or Baghdad. It also became a cultural center for the Jews. Responding to an appeal by the Jewish community, Charlemagne invited a famous rabbi called Kalonymos from Northern Italy to serve as spiritual guide. Kalonymos, who brought with him the scholarship of the Holy Land, founded a dynasty of sages, and his academy or Yeshiva in Mainz was the first to be established in Germany. Mainz, Speyer and Worms contained German Jewry's major communities.

Louis the Pious (814-40) Charlemagne's son, continued to protect the rights of the Jews, but after his death the empire was partitioned twice. The kingdom of the

Western Franks became the kingdom of France (the name France is derived from Franks) and that of the Eastern Franks, who retained their Germanic speech, became Germany. The emperors exercised little authority until Otto the Great (962-73), who created the Holy Roman Empire, and gave full support to the Church, to the detriment of the Jews.

### Rabbenu Gershom (c. 960 - c. 1040)

Prior to the arrival of Rabbenu Gershom in Mainz, German Jews turned to the scholars in the Holy Land for guidance, just as those in Moslem countries turned to the heads of the Babylonian academies. After his arrival, German Jewry became spiritually self-sufficient because his authority was recognised throughout Europe. Gershom was also known as Light of the Exile, and given the title Rabbenu (our teacher).

The fame bestowed on Mainz by Kalonymos some two centuries earlier increased under Rabbenu Gershom, as students came from France and Italy as well as Germany, to study under him. Although only a few of his glosses on the Talmud have survived, his fame as a Talmudist is well established and his teaching methods had a profound effect on his own and future generations. These methods were continued through his academy which survived for almost a century.

Rabbenu Gershom issued enactments that gave legal sanction to established practice or reflected the contemporary situation. The best-known examples forbade polygamy and prohibited divorce against the wife's will. In the interests of privacy he banned opening letters addressed to a third party and, in an age when Jews were forced or enticed into apostasy, he forbade reminding those who returned to Judaism of their lapse. The matter touched Rabbenu Gershom personally because his own son was forcibly baptized, and died before he could recant. The father observed a double period of mourning, one for the body and the other for the soul of his dead son. When he expressed his people's grief in liturgical poetry, the personal element was inevitably present.

### The End of the Period

Around the year 1000 C.E., instability characterized Jewish existence. In 1012 they were expelled from Mainz, possibly about the same time that Rabbenu Gershom's son was forcibly baptized. Many were killed a year later in Spain, during the Berber invasion, while many others were forced to flee.

In other Moslem countries anarchy was also rife, as Baghdad, where Turkish mercenaries ruled in all but name, became the capital of a disintegrating empire. Mesopotamia, once a thriving metropolis, became a cultural backwater, inevitably affecting for the worse the fortunes of Sura and Pumbeditha.

Some 500 years previously, the two academies had entered a period of decline from which they eventually recovered. This time their eclipse was permanent, bringing to a close the period of the Geonim. Hai, the last effective Gaon of Pumbeditha, and Rabbenu Gershom in Germany, died within a few years of each other, creating a need not only for new spiritual leadership, but also for a new spiritual center.

The leading students of Rabbenu Gershom would in turn raise a disciple destined to fill the vacuum. Rashi, as he is known, would guarantee that Jewish learning, on which Jewish survival depends, would find a new home in France, after the demise of the Babylonian academies.

**2000 B.C.E.**

**1**

**ABRAHAM**

THE PATRIARCHS

Teachers of Monotheism

HAMMURABI'S LAWS

Hittite & Egyptian Empires

DECLINE OF EGYPTIAN POWER

**1500 B.C.E.**

**2**

**MOSES**

JUDGES

Earlier Prophets

BEGINNING OF PHILISTINE SETTLEMENTS

Spread of Mediterranean Civilization

**1000 B.C.E.**

**3**

**DAVID**

KINGS

Later Prophets

RISE OF PHOENICIAN TRADE

Mesopotamian Empires

END OF BIBLICAL PERIOD

**500 B.C.E.**

**4**

**EZRA**

ZUGOTH

Joint leaders of the Sanhedrin and the rule of the Wise

BEGINNING OF ROMAN REPUBLIC

Spread of Hellenism

END OF ROMAN REPUBLIC

**0**

**5**

**HILLEL**

TALMUDIC PERIOD

Compilation of the Oral Law

BEGINNING OF ROMAN EMPIRE

Spread of Christianity

END OF ROMAN EMPIRE

**500 C.E.**

**6**

**RAV ASHI**

THE GEONIM

Heads of the Babylonian Academies

BEGINNING OF MIDDLE AGES

Spread of Islam

DECLINE OF BAGHDAD CALIPHATE

**1000 C.E.**

**7**

**RASHI**

THE RISHONIM

Earlier Authorities: Commentators & Codifiers of Talmudic Law

HOLY ROMAN EMPIRE

Crusades

END OF MIDDLE AGES

**1500 C.E.**

**8**

**JOSEPH KARO**

THE AHARONIM

Later Authorities: Commentators & Compilers of the Halacha

RENAISSANCE & REFORMATION

Spread of Western Civilization

END OF OTTOMAN EMPIRE RETURN TO ZION

**2000 C.E.**

**1000 C.E.**

*Rashi*

**500 years**

*Rabbi Joseph Karo*

**1500 C.E.**

Due mainly to the influence of Rashi, (Rabbi Solomon ben Isaac, 1040-1105), Northern Europe succeeded Mesopotamia as the new center of Jewish life. His classical commentary on the Talmud prevented it from becoming a sealed book.

This commentary, together with the Talmud itself, became the subject of further discussion by seven generations of Rashi's descendents and disciples, called by the collective name of Tosaphists.

Apart from France and the Rhineland, Spain also served as a major center for the Rishonim (Earlier Authorities), who specialized in codifying Talmudic Law. The three great codifiers of the period were Isaac Alfasi, Maimonides and Asher ben Jehiel.

Their decisions were taken into account by Rabbi Joseph Karo, who as a child was one of the exiles from Spain when that center came to an end.

In addition to the Talmud, Rashi wrote a classical commentary on the Torah, in which he was aided by the work of the Masorites, whose authoritative text and system of vocalization had reached Europe from Galilee.

In 1071 the Seljuk Turks captured Jerusalem from the more tolerant Egyptian rulers, thereby provoking the Crusades. The Crusaders took the city in 1099, and established the Latin kingdom of Jerusalem, which suffered a heavy defeat at the hands of Saladin, the Sultan of Egypt in 1187.

In 1211, 300 rabbis from France and England arrived in the country.

Nachmanides, who was forced to flee Spain and settled in Jerusalem, mentions, in his commentary to the Torah, the general desolation of the land.

Pope Urban II preached the first Crusade in 1095, in an attempt to recover the Holy Land from Islam. Those who answered the call were motivated by a combination of religious devotion and the prospect of plunder, and so while on the journey to fight the infidels, the Crusaders annihilated entire Jewish communities, along the Rhine Valley.

Most Jews died as martyrs, but a few chose apostasy, and engaged rabbis in public debates in which the Church served as prosecutor, judge and jury. Following one such debate, 24 wagon loads of the Talmud were burnt in Paris in 1242. Almost 50 years later the Jews were expelled from England, as an excuse to confiscate their assets, and in 1306 they were expelled from France.

The Black Death of 1348 lead to the massacre of Jews throughout Europe.

It took Spanish Christians about 500 years to reconquer their country from the Moors, completing the task in 1492.

The occasion was celebrated by expelling all Jews from the country. A few days later, Columbus set sail on his famous voyage of discovery.

*Chapter   Seven*

# From Rashi to Rabbi Joseph Karo

The Period of the Rishonim (Earlier Authorities) c. 1000 – 1500 C.E.

## *Influence of the Holy Land*

Acommon feature of the beginning of each major period outlined in this book is the central role of the Holy Land. The detailed history of the land commences with its association with the Jewish people when Abraham, the first patriarch, left his birthplace to make it his permanent home. It was the intended destination for Moses and those he led from the Egyptian bondage, and David, who later broke the Philistine domination, made Jerusalem its eternal capital. Ezra and Hillel, in successive generations, retraced Abraham's journey from Mesopotamia in order to revive spiritual fortunes in the Promised Land, and they succeeded to the extent that Hillel was likened to Ezra and Ezra to Moses.

Around the years 500 and 1000 C.E. a change took place, in that the influence of the Holy Land on Jewish history is associated not so much with individuals, as with collective works of scholarship. The Talmud of Babylon, which provided a unifying code for the scattered Diaspora communities around the year 500, was based on the Mishnah of Eretz Yisrael and owes much to scholars who travelled frequently between the two centers. It was also from Eretz Yisrael that the Babylonian Talmud reached Italy and from there to other parts of Europe.

Throughout the period of the Geonim, the Babylonian academies of Sura and Pumbeditha continued to overshadow their counterparts in the Holy Land except in one field, that of the Masorah (see previous chapter).

At that time the country was under Moslem sovereignty for, when not under

159

Jewish control, it was never more than part of an empire, rather than an independent state. Yet no matter to which empire it belonged, or irrespective of the dominant culture of the dispersed communities, no boundaries or language barriers could prevent the scholarship of the Holy Land from reaching the Diaspora. In this way the Masorah, completed in Galilee, reached Northern Europe, where it enabled Rashi to make his own distinctive contribution to Jewish learning, and hence to Jewish survival.

## *Rashi (1040-1105)*

Rashi (an acronym of Rabbi Solomon Ben Isaac) was born in the French city of Troyes, capital of the Champagne region. (The city gave its name to the troy weight and the region to a special white wine.) Married at 18, he left wife and home to continue studying in Germany, first in Worms and then in Mainz, where he had access to texts of the Mishnah, Talmud and commentaries written by Rabbenu Gershom and his disciples. Prior to the invention of printing when copyist errors were frequent, authoritative manuscripts were essential—especially for someone like Rashi, contemplating a commentary.

To be precise, when Rashi returned to Troyes aged about 25 after a five- year absence, he undertook not one, but two major commentaries, one on the Bible, and the other on the Talmud. The preferred method of biblical exegesis in Northern France was to explain the *Peshat* or plain meaning, and for this the work of the Masorites was indispensable. When necessary, therefore, Rashi refers to their vocalisation and notation system, explaining and expounding what is, in effect, nothing but an arrangement of curves, dots and dashes added to the original non-vocalised text. Rashi also quotes the Spanish school of linguists and grammarians, who used the Massoretic text to establish rules of Hebrew grammar.

Dedicated to explaining the text's plain meaning did not prevent Rashi from referring to the aggadic or homiletic form of exegesis favored in the south of the country. Popular everywhere, technical competence alone was not sufficient to make Rashi's commentary so famous. It was the first Hebrew work ever to be printed (1475) and consulted by Christian exegetes, it influenced the Reform-ation.

Among Jews, knowledge of Rashi's commentary has long been a basic require-ment for the educated layman, molding alike thought and language. The following are some of Rashi's aphorisms, memorable even in translation: "judge your fellow man in the scale of merit"; "without peace, there is nothing"; "whatever you do, do it from love"; "give to charity and give again, even a hundred times"; "everything depends on the heart." Even the word Judaism originates with Rashi, and love of his religion extends to love of his people and the Promised Land. The very first

## Some leading authorities in the Period of the Rishonim (Former Authorities)

### ❶ Northern Europe

Rashi (1040-1105)
Rabbi Solomon b. Isaac

Rabbenu Tam (1100-1171)
Rabbi Jacob b. Meir

### ❷ Spain

Rif (1013-1103)
Rabbi Isaac Alfasi

Tur (1270-1341)
Rabbi Jacob b. Asher

Rambam (1135-1204)
Rabbi Moses b. Maimon

Ramban (1195-1270)
Rabbi Moses b. Nachman

(1250-1327)
Rabbi Asher b. Jehiel

words of his Bible commentary anticipate modern criticism that the Jews have no right to their own homeland.

## Commentary to the Talmud

While working on his two commentaries, he served as a member of the Beth Din (Rabbinical Court), and earned a livelihood from growing grapes. Aged about 35, he established his own *yeshiva* (as the institutes of Talmudic studies were called in the post-geonic period) where discussions with students highlighted the passages that needed clarification.

There are three main reasons why Rashi's Talmudic commentary is a masterpiece of exegesis, essential for student and savant alike. Firstly, he was able to refer to some 500 years of scholarship since the Talmud was compiled, and whatever was missing he made good. Secondly, it was a comprehensive commentary, covering every tractate except two that were completed after his death by his son-in-law and grandson. Thirdly, its clear concise style included no superfluous word nor omitted a key one.

To cover the wide range of subjects dealt with by the Talmud, Rashi himself needed comprehensive knowledge drawn in part from observation and experience. Difficult Aramaic terms are translated into French, which amount to over 3,000 expressions when combined with those in the biblical commentary. A unique source, they are invaluable for knowledge of Old French.

## Rashi's last years

The last decade of Rashi's life was marred by the First Crusade and its bloody aftermath, affecting his health. The events are reflected in his Responsa, for as the recognised authority of his generation, he received queries from the Diaspora regarding every aspect of law and custom. Thus he counselled tolerance towards those who wished to return to Judaism after being forcibly converted, and exhibited concern for anyone widowed during the massacres.

A large section of the Responsa literature in general deals with the arrangement and wording of the liturgy, and Rashi's contribution was to compose a prayer book for use in France and Germany. During the period of the Crusades he composed *Selichot*—special penitential prayers— in which he expressed his people's grief. The Jewish people then, as on so many other occasions were "as a lamb brought to the slaughter" (Is.53:7), a verse taken from Isaiah's description of the suffering servant whom Rashi identifies in his biblical commentary with Israel.

Towards the end, Rashi was confined to a sick bed, where from weakness he was obligated to dictate his writings. When dealing with the subject of ritual cleanliness in the commentary on the Talmud, one of the last words he pronounced before he died was "pure." His son-in-law, to whom he was dictating, thereupon wrote: "our master was pure in body, and his soul departed in purity... From now on the words are those of his pupil" (Makkot 19b). In a wider sense, Rashi's pupils are to be found whenever and wherever the Talmud is studied, for without him it would have remained a sealed book.

### Rashi's Descendants (The Tosaphists)

Scholars who lived between the 11th and 15th centuries are known as the *Rishonim* (Earlier Authorities), and in Northern Europe Rashi and his descendants provided an unbroken chain of leadership for approximately half the period. Rashi's dynasty was a spiritual one, comprising generations of scholars many of whom were also direct descendants and, together, they were given the collective name of Tosaphists.

Rashi had no sons, but each of his three daughters married a distinguished disciple, and from marriage between one, Jochebed, and Meir, four sons were born destined for scholastic fame. The eldest was called Samuel (1085-1185), better known as Rashbam (the acrostic of Rabbi Samuel Ben Meir) whose first 20 years overlapped the life of his grandfather. The two studied together and, when Rashbam came to write his own biblical commentary based on the rules of grammar, he stated: "Rabbi Solomon, my mother's father, admitted to me that if he had time he would be obliged to make other commentaries based on the plain meaning of the text" (Gen. 37:2). He also completed one of the Talmudic tractates his grandfather had left unfinished.

Jacob (1110-1171), the youngest and most renowned of the four sons, is better known as Rabbenu Tam, because he shared the same name as the biblical patriarch who was described as *Tam* (plain or straightforward). His saintly character was matched by a keen intellect, and both combined made him the acknowledged spiritual leader of France and Germany, from where students came to study under him.

For some 200 years after Rashi's death, in the Yeshivot of France and Germany, questions put by students to teachers, and the resulting answers and discussions were recorded until they formed a new genre of Talmudic literature. It came to be called *Tosaphot*, meaning Additions, and originally referred to the additional notes to Rashi's commentary on the Talmud. In the course of time the Tosaphists extended their comments to the Talmud itself, bringing into play the same methodology the Talmud had applied to the Mishnah. They analysed the text and, pointing to apparent contradictions in different tractates, often gave alternative explanations to those of Rashi, but always in a spirit of admiration and respect, referring to him as *Ha-Kuntres*—"the Commentator"—without peer. Sometimes the Tosaphists are referred to by name, but mostly they remain anonymous, and their commentary together with Rashi's has always formed an indispensable part of every printed edition of the Talmud. From the yeshivot of Rashi's sons-in-law and grandchildren, disciples graduated who in turn served as spiritual leaders throughout Europe, including England.

The main centers of Jewish life during this period were in Champagne and along the banks of the Rhine, which formed a major commercial route. At trade fairs, there was a general meeting of scholars and laymen, through whom biblical and Talmudic interpretations crossed borders and sometimes continents. Students also passed between different centers, recording different interpretations, and often the reputation of the academies depended on the number of collections in their possession.

The 200 year activity of the Tosaphists roughly corresponds to the period of the Crusades, which were a series of wars between Christianity and Islam, in which the Jews suffered losses comparable in proportion to the Holocaust in the twentieth century.

## *The Crusades*

In 1073 the Turks captured Jerusalem from Egypt, halting pilgrimage and threatening Constantinople, capital of the Byzantine Empire. Pope Urban II answered an appeal for help from the Byzantine emperor, hoping in the process to extend the influence of the Latin Church and at the same time to syphon off the excess of Europe's population explosion.

In 1096 thousands of crusaders assembled in France, prompted in varying degrees by religious fervor and an opportunity for murder and pillage. The message soon spread that even before travelling to Jerusalem to fight the enemies of Christendom, vengeance could be exacted on the Jews nearer home. The victims of mob violence could have saved their lives through baptism, but in almost every case they chose death. Rouen was one in a long list of communities to face the choice.

When the Crusaders reached Germany, the Jews appealed to the emperor for protection, and the resulting caution was sufficient to inhibit Godfrey of Bouillon, the Crusader leader, but not his followers.

Under the pretext of religious zeal, they left behind a trail of death and desolation. The period between Passover and Pentecost, which was already a period of mourning in the Jewish calendar, became more so as the Crusaders progressed along the Rhine. By the time they reached the city of Worms, marauding bands had joined them and the Jews either took refuge in the Bishop's palace or barricaded themselves in their own homes. As in Rouen and elsewhere, the mob broke into their homes and dragged those they found to the baptismal font, where only a few escaped death by changing their religion.

Those inside the Bishop's palace survived a week longer until he was unable to do more. Advised to accept baptism, the Jews were granted time to prepare an answer, but instead set about slaughtering each other. Fathers killed their families and then themselves, rather than abandon their faith, but even this supreme act of heroism failed to move the mob, and the dead were stripped of their clothing.

In Mainz, the bishop also allowed the Jews asylum in his palace, and locked the city gates, which were opened from within after two days. Not everyone committed suicide, for some chose to die fighting for their honor. It is estimated that some 800 martyrs met their end in Worms, and 1100 in Mainz, and even the few who were saved by baptism soon repented and committed suicide.

In Cologne, the Crusaders entered the city the day before Shavuot (Pentecost), but forewarned, the Jews had taken shelter with Christian neighbors, leaving the mob to plunder their abandoned homes and destroy synagogues. Herman, the Bishop of Cologne, fearing those who had offered protection would be punished, encouraged the Jews to flee to a nearby forest. There they were soon discovered and most perished at the hands of the Crusaders or by committing suicide.

Elsewhere along the Rhine entire families drowned themselves in the river to escape apostasy. Even in the annals of Jewish suffering, the supreme acts of heroism exhibited by the Rhine martyrs in 1096 has little equal.

By the time the Crusaders captured Jerusalem in 1099, four fifths of their numbers had died in combat or by disease. They suffered heavy losses in Hungary because their lawlessness invited opposition and, while besieging the Turks in Antioch, they were decimated by infection and scurvy. As a consequence, out of an original force of 300,000, only 60,000 remained to capture Jerusalem following a siege of little over a month.

The Crusaders felt doubly motivated in slaughtering Jerusalem's Jewish population. Firstly, the Jews had welcomed the Islamic invaders, and secondly, it was believed that in former times they had helped Roman pagan emperors persecute the early Christians. An eye-witness account of the massacre states: "The slaughter was terrible; the blood of the conquered ran down the streets until men splashed in blood as they rode. At midnight, sobbing for excess of joy, the Crusaders came to the Sepulchre from treading the wine press, and put their bloodstained hands together in prayer. So on that day in July, the First Crusade came to an end."

Under Godfrey of Bouillon, the kingdom of Jerusalem was established, which extended at its peak from Beirut in the north to Eilat in the south. Although most of the Crusaders were poor, those who remained in the Holy Land were especially so, because the better-off returned to Europe as soon as possible. The Latin kingdom was not self-sustaining, existing through new waves of Crusaders, and falling to the Moslems in stages.

## The Tosaphists and Conditions in Medieval Europe

The Second Crusade (1147-49) was meant to counter Turkish military gains, but ended in dismal failure. A band of Crusaders in France threatened the life of

Rabbenu Tam, but a knight and personal acquaintance intervened, perhaps on the pretext of converting him to Christianity. Aware of the torture associated with forced apostasy, R. Tam permitted suicide for anyone unable to bear the suffering. A disciple called Jacob of Orleans took advantage of the ruling during disturbances in London, at the time of King Richard's coronation in 1189.

In 1171, 31 members of the community of Blois were burnt at the stake with the unity of God on their lips, following a blood accusation. A few weeks before he died, Rabbenu Tam prescribed a fast day and composed a lament to commemorate the martyrdom. In blood libels, Jews were accused of using Christian blood for ritual purposes, and the disappearance of a child or the finding of a corpse, especially before the festival of Passover, was often sufficient evidence to convict them of murder. In the example of Blois not even a corpse was considered necessary. The earliest blood libel took place in the English city of Norwich (1144) and more soon followed on the other side of the channel. As a result, when any minor incident might lead to incitement or slander, the Tosaphists did not allow any side in a legal dispute to take its case to non-Jewish authorities.

Isaac the Elder, a nephew and disciple of Rabbenu Tam, succeeded him as the leading authority and head of his academy in the next generation. Isaac had 60 outstanding pupils, each of whom knew a tractate of the Talmud by heart, so between them any given passage could be quoted or analysed, with the purpose of arriving at practical conclusions. This emphasis on practical conclusions is one of the major differences between the Tosaphists and Rashi. A great-grandson of Rashi, Isaac's name is the most frequently mentioned among the Tosaphists after Rabbenu Tam, and his family life reflected the tragedy of the times, because Crusaders killed his son.

Crusaders in the city of York formed an unholy alliance with fanatical clergy and indebted barons to besiege the Jewish population in the city's castle (1190). Following the example of the Rhine martyrs, the majority committed suicide, and those who remained were slain by the mob. The incident claimed between 150 and 500 victims, and the records of all debts owing them were burnt. Philip II of France proclaimed debts owed to Jews automatically cancelled if the debtors followed him in the Third Crusade (1189-92) and about the same time he destroyed the entire Jewish community of a townlet in Champagne, except for children under 13.

Philip and Richard I were allies in the Third Crusade which the former soon abandoned, and then plotted with Richard's brother John how best to divide England. Philip also made treaties with his Barons, whereby the Jews became feudal property, punishable by confiscation if they changed domain without permission. Isaac the Elder ruled that no Jew be allowed to buy such confiscated property. If this ruling was violated, the purchaser had to make restitution.

### R. Yehudah he-Chasid (1150-1217)

In the 12th century a group of Jewish scholars from Germany became known as the *Chassidei Ashkenaz* - "the pious ones of Ashkenaz" ( a term embodying the Jews of France and Germany). They stressed the ethical aspects of Jewish law and also its mystical elements. The best known among them was R. Yehudah he-Chasid, who absorbed much of his knowledge from his father, R.Shmuel he-Chasid.

R. Yehudah's piety became legendary, especially his deep concentration during prayer and his custom of constantly fasting during the day-time. He is best known as the author of *Sefer Chassidim*, which covers the topics of prayer, penitence and the laws of Shabbat among others. The work's great popularity is due to R. Yehudah's method of teaching ethics – by giving examples from daily life rather than abstract rules. He also wrote several kabbalistic works and synagogue poetry, including the well-known *Shir ha-Kavod* – Song of Glory.

The strong faith of R.Yehudah and the Chassidei Ashkenaz helped to sustain the Jews of Germany through their ordeals and suffering.

### The Tosaphists and Eretz Yisrael

In 1211, 300 Tosaphists, the spiritual leaders of England and France, left behind the massacres and blood libels of Europe to live in the Holy Land following its conquest by Saladin.

Saladin, the founder of a new dynasty in Egypt, was Islam's principal warrior, whose conquests were widespread. He was also the great opponent of the Crusaders and preached a *Jihad* or Holy War against the infidel. Henceforth it was Moslem Crusader against Christian Crusader, and Saladin scored a brilliant victory near Tiberias, at the battle of Hattin (1187). In the same year he took Jerusalem and the Christian's cause never recovered. The Third Crusade was meant to restore the situation, but its only achievement was the capture of Acre (Acco) and, in an eventual peace agreement (1192), the Latin kingdom was left with a narrow coastal strip from Tyre to Jaffa. The final scene followed a century later when the Moslems recaptured Acre.

In addition to being a great warrior, Saladin was a man of culture, a patron of literature and a theological debater. Maimonides, the great Jewish philosopher, preferred remaining as Saladin's court physician than to return to England in the service of Richard. If Richard and his fellow Crusaders had recaptured Jerusalem from the Moslems, the Tosaphists from England and France would never have been allowed to settle in Jerusalem, as they did during Saladin's tolerant rule.

This *aliyah* (emigration) to the Holy Land, did much to encourage Jewish resettlement of the country. One of its leading figures was Jonathan ben David ha-Cohen from Lunel, a city in Southern France that served as a bridge between the Jewish communities of Spain and those further north. Another leading figure was

Samson ben Abraham of Sens, a disciple of Isaac the Elder and author of *Tosephoth Shantz* and commentaries on part of the Mishnah. He died at Acre, and was buried at the foot of Mt. Carmel.

On his way home from the Third Crusade, Richard was captured and subsequently released on the payment of a huge ransom to the king of Germany. His subjects raised the sum, but the Jews were forced to contribute more than others.

## Public Debates

In the Middle Ages, Jews suffered from legal discrimination in addition to mob violence. Pope Innocent III, at the fourth Lateran Council (1215), forbade them to own land or hold public office, and they were required to sew a mark of shame on their garments like their brothers in Moslem countries.

Jews not convinced of the truth of Christianity by legislation or the power of the sword, were to be persuaded by the power of the word. Pope Innocent created the Dominican (Black Friars) preaching order, with special charge to win over the Jews. Apostates with knowledge of the Talmud were welcomed into their ranks, to initiate or assist in public debates. Both sides produced guide books for such occasions, which occurred mainly in Germany, France and Spain, from the 13th to 15th centuries. Mostly, the Jewish representatives found themselves answering accusations against Judaism in general, and the Talmud in particular.

For reasons of prestige the churchmen always chose a prominent rabbi to answer their accusations. Once, Rabbenu Tam represented the Jews of France, and in a later generation the choice fell on Jehiel of Paris (d. 1268), whose comments and decisions are found throughout Talmudic literature. The debate in which he participated was instigated by Nicholas Donin and proved to be one the most famous ever held. Donin, an apostate Jew turned monk, had previously appealed to Pope Gregory IX to have the Talmud burnt on the grounds that it slandered Christianity. The Pope turned to Europe's monarchs to have it banned, but only Louis IX of France took any action. Later canonised, Louis was both Crusader and anti-Semite. He summoned four prominent rabbis, headed by Jehiel, to answer Donin's accusations.

The debate, which took place in Paris in 1240 before the king, queen and highest church dignitaries, was in effect a trial of the Talmud. In the light of Louis' statement that the best way to argue with a Jew was to stab him with a sword, the result of the debate was a foregone conclusion. Two years later, 24 wagon loads of the Talmud and accompanying literature, all hand-written manuscripts, were publicly burnt in Paris. Later still, the Dominicans would progress from burning Jewish books to burning Jews themselves, but from their point of view, suffered a setback when one Robert of Reading, an English Dominican friar in the 13th century, converted to Judaism.

Jehiel continued to teach his students by heart but clearly, without books the French center of learning had come to an end. Like the Tosaphists in the previous generation, he emigrated to the Holy Land accompanied by many of his pupils, and re-established his academy at Acre (1260). Eight years later, he died and was buried at the foot of Mt. Carmel.

## Meir of Rothenburg and German Jewry

The 200-year activity of the Tosaphists came to an end with Rabbi Meir b. Baruch (1215-1293). A disciple of Jehiel of Paris, he witnessed the debate with the apostate Donin and saw the Talmud consigned to the flames. The event inspired him to compose an elegy, for he was one of the great liturgical poets of the Middle Ages. After returning to Germany, Meir served as rabbi to several communities, finally settling in the Bavarian city of Rothenburg. He served there for 40 years, heading the yeshiva and recognised as the leading authority of European Jewry.

At this time the Hapsburgs (1273-1918) came to power with the election of Rudolf I to the German throne. Rudolf regarded his Jewish subjects and whatever they possessed as his private property, and so he taxed them over and above what they gave to local rulers. Among Meir of Rothenburg's Responsa, two deal with Rudolf's financial claims, which are described as illegal extortion.

Between 1283-86 there was a series of blood libels in Germany, particularly severe even for the Middle Ages. Many were killed and thousands fled including Meir, who perhaps wanted to follow his teacher's example and live in the Holy Land. Whatever his intentions, they were frustrated when he was recognised by an apostate and reported to the authorities. They placed him in jail, where he spent the last seven years of his life. A large ransom fee was paid on Meir's behalf, but he was not released because Rudolf regarded the sum as his by right, without having to give anything in return. Meir totally opposed such an attitude with its implied status of servility towards the Jews, and thereafter forbade any further ransom attempt.

During captivity, R. Meir was allowed to compose responsa, annotate the Talmud, and receive students. After he died, his bones were kept as a potential source of extortion, until they were released for burial 13 years later.

The sufferings of German Jewry continued. In 1298 the community of Rottingen was accused of stealing a holy wafer which, according to the Church doctrine of Transubstantiation, could relive the pain of the crucifixion if pierced. A nobleman called Rindfleisch incited a mob in the southern part of the country into a frenzy, and then led it from city to city, committing murder and mayhem. In the space of six months about 100,000 were murdered, including Hillel ben Mordechai, a leading Talmudist and disciple of Meir of Rothenburg. Other outrages followed, often instigated by monks, but mostly the victims refused to save themselves by baptism. The Jews who did so returned to Judaism at the first opportunity.

A new stage in the martyrdom of German Jewry began with the Black Death (1348), one of three pandemics in the past 1,500 years transmitted to man by the flea of a rat. Millions died throughout Europe and the Jews were immediately suspected of poisoning wells and rivers. It mattered little that they drank the same water and also fell victim to the plague, as Pope Clement VI vainly pointed out.

In the city of Berne in Switzerland some Jews "confessed" to the crime under torture and as a consequence everyone in the community was burnt alive. News of the so-called confession passed from city to city and crossed borders, decimating the Jews of Europe, but especially those of Germany. In Mainz and Cologne, the Jews opposed entry into their quarter, but when resistance became futile, they set fire to their homes. Only a few principalities offered protection, which is why thousands fled to neighboring Poland. German Jewry remained prostrate for centuries, but there was never a general expulsion, due to the division of the country into a patchwork of petty states. In England and France where there was a centralised monarchy, the situation was different.

### Expulsion from England and France

Three kings ruled England between the emigration of the Tosaphists in 1211 and the general expulsion of 1290. John, who was king when the rabbis left the country, had a reputation for cruelty and, to finance his war with France, extorted money from all classes. He is best known in history for being forced to sign the *Magna Carta*, recognising that the power of the king is not absolute.

Henry III (1216-76) succeeded his father to the throne while still young, and so regents ruled the country. During the period of the regency conditions improved for the Jews, but deteriorated again after Henry became king in his own right.

Discriminatory medieval church legislation was put into full effect in England, perhaps more so than in any country on the continent. This included the wearing of a special badge and the prohibition to build new synagogues or employ non-Jews. In 1255 there was a blood libel charge, centered on the death of a young boy in Lincoln. As a consequence, some Jews were executed and others sent to the Tower of London. Eight years later civil war broke out between the king and his barons, who identified the Jews with their enemies and killed them indiscriminately. Henry for his part was an absolutist, who sought to pay for the extravagances characteristic of his reign by exploiting the Jews. Their request to leave the kingdom was rejected, but in the next reign they were forced to do so.

Edward I (1272-1307) developed the law and constitution, earning him praise as the English Justinian. For Jews the comparison had a more sinister connotation, because, reminiscent of Byzantine times, they were impoverished until they became dispensable. Edward forbade them to lend money on interest, the main source of livelihood hitherto allowed by the Church. Commerce and handicrafts offered no real alternative because Jews were not accepted into the guilds, and tenure of agricultural land was restricted to ten years. Eventually, they were obliged to pay tithes to the Church and listen to Dominican conversion sermons.

The climax came on July 18th, 1290, corresponding to the fateful Ninth Day of Av in the Hebrew calendar. On that day, the Jews were ordered to leave the country in little over three months, partly in deference to popular demand and partly in accord with what was thought to be good economic policy. In this way, the community that dated from William the Conqueror (1066) came to an end, not be restored until some three and a half centuries later.

On the other side of the channel Philip IV (1285-1314), who fought Edward for territorial possessions in France, adopted the expulsion order 16 years later. Apart from the English, Philip was also hostile towards the Knights Templars, (much of whose wealth he diverted to the royal treasury), and the Italian bankers known as Lombards. He even came into conflict with the Papacy, which is why from 1309-1378 all the popes were French and lived in Avignon. When he added Champagne to his possessions, 13 Jews were burnt in Troyes, Rashi's birthplace, on a charge of ritual murder (1288). Two years later he expelled the Jews driven from England by Edward I and in 1306 issued a general expulsion order that took effect on the tenth of Av. About 100,000 Jews left France, forced to abandon everything to the king, including debts owed by Christians.

Thus, by the beginning of the 14th century, the centers of Jewish activity in France, Germany and England associated with Rashi, his descendants and their disciples, ceased to exist. Spanish Jewry, with its long and rich history, now came to the fore.

### The Spanish Center

The eighth-century Moslem conquest of Spain left a Christian enclave in the north. From this base powerful kingdoms such as Castille and Aragon emerged and, uniting together whenever necessary, fought for the re-conquest of Spain throughout the Middle Ages. When Toledo, in the center of the country, became the capital of Castille (1085), Jews were entrusted with important state and financial matters, which meant that papal declarations against them were largely ignored.

After Toledo's capture, Christian progress was checked by new waves of Moslem forces from North Africa, imposing unity through a more fanatical form of Islam. Contemporary Jewish literature refers to the north of the country as the Land of

Edom, and the south as the Land of Ishmael. When in the Land of Ishmael, the Jews were given the choice of conversion or exile, the majority fled, leaving only a few to outwardly profess Islam. It was now the turn of Christian countries to offer refuge from Moslem persecution, reversing the pattern of centuries.

When the Moslems attained a high degree of civilisation and prosperity, they lost their military zeal. This enabled the Christians to make important gains in the 13th century, and out of the confusion of the re-conquest, Portugal was born. For about two and a half centuries, only the kingdom of Granada in the south remained a stronghold for the Moors.

During centuries of campaigns and counter campaigns, alliances and counter alliances, Spain was a country that alternately offered sanctuary for Jews or expelled them. In one part they may have been persecuted, while in another they prospered. Thus it came about that the three great codifiers of the age found in Spain hospitality or hostility, a country to flee to, or a country to flee from. The three were Isaac Alfasi, Maimonides and Asher Ben Jehiel.

### Isaac Alfasi and Samuel HaNagid.

Isaac Alfasi, known as the *Rif* (1013-1103) was 25 years old when Hai, the last effective Gaon of Pumbeditha died, and thus bridges two periods in Jewish history. He was born in Algeria but moved to Fez, hence the name Alfasi (of Fez) where he taught until he was 75, and composed a compendium of Jewish Law on which his fame rests. In this work he both summarised Talmudic debates, thereby facilitating their study, and presented Talmudic Law for immediate and practical application. Following soon after the Geonim he was able to refer to the decisions of Sura and Pumbeditha. A few generations later, Maimonides advised a foremost pupil to make Alfasi's work the main object of his study, and later still Joseph Karo regarded him as one of the great codifiers on whom Jewish law rests.

In his time, Fez was a place of intrigue, and after being slandered to the authorities, the Rif escaped to Spain. He stayed some months in Cordova before settling in Lucena, both cities situated in the southern Moslem part of the country. Two centuries previously, Lucena had become a Jewish city, and now Alfasi was appointed head of its academy, which attracted students from all over Spain and North Africa. The communities of these countries also turned to him for guidance, and his responsa are numbered in the hundreds, resembling in style those of the Babylonian Geonim.

Alfasi died at 90 years of age, just two years before Rashi, yet the two never met, because contact between Spain and Northern France was strictly limited. In their respective centers, each left behind a rich literary heritage, and disciples to pass on their teachings.

An older contemporary of Alfasi was Samuel Ibn Nagdela (993-c.1063), who corresponded with Hai Gaon and composed a eulogy on his death. Like Alfasi, Samuel codified Talmudic Law and even wrote an introduction to the Talmud explaining its methodology, but neither work has completely survived. His other literary achievements include a Hebrew grammar and poetry in the style of the Psalms. Being a linguist, he could write and speak several languages, which enabled him to enter into public debate with experts of Islam. As a philanthropist and patron he supported poets and scholars, and paid scribes from his own purse to copy manuscripts that he distributed to others.

The list of Samuel's accomplishments is still not complete, for he established his own academy in Granada, where he represented the Jewish community to the Moslem court. As such he was given the title *Nagid*, meaning Ruler or Prince, and to this day he is known as Samuel Ha-Nagid. His career began as a spice seller, but a flair for literary composition and a gift for wise counsel brought him into the service of two consecutive viziers, who employed him as politician, statesman and general. In the last role, he personally conducted military operations close to the front lines. As soldier, scholar, statesman, philanthropist all combined, Samuel Ha-Nagid has few equals, if any.

His son Joseph automatically inherited the position of Nagid but, never having experienced hardship or poverty, lacked his father's sensitivity. Unaware that a Jew in high position in a Moslem country could arouse resentment, his indiscreet behaviour contributed to a massacre in Granada, in which he was one of the victims (1066).

### Solomon Ibn Gabirol and Judah Halevi

Ibn Gabirol (1021-51) became a protégé of Samuel HaNagid after being orphaned young. He wandered much during his brief life of 35 years, suffering from intermittent bouts of depression and ill health. Yet despite these handicaps, or perhaps because of them, he composed some of the most inspired poetry in the Hebrew language. His verse, written in a biblical style, served as a model for the Spanish school of poets, and much of what he wrote has been incorporated into the liturgy. Ibn Gabirol was also the author of a philosophical treatise written in Arabic called the "Fountain of Life." In its Spanish and Latin translations, it became a source of study for churchmen, who knew its author by the corrupted form of Avencebrol or Avicebron. He also wrote a book of ethics.

An important stage in the Christian reconquest of Spain was the capture of Toledo (1085), where Judah haLevi (1075-1141) was born. In the unstable period that followed, he wandered between Christian and Moslem held territory, depending on which regime showed the greater tolerance. In the Moslem-held south he studied under Isaac Alfasi and composed a eulogy on his teacher's death. In Christian Castille, he returned temporarily to Toledo, where he practiced medicine and engaged in commerce. Intolerant Christian rule drove him once more south and towards the end of his life the even more intolerant Muslims made him abandon Spain altogether. Perhaps influenced by a messianic longing then widespread, he left family and friends to live in Jerusalem. He certainly reached Egypt and, according to legend, Jerusalem itself, where an Arab horseman killed him.

During all this political instability, Judah ha-Levi succeeded in producing Hebrew poetry unequalled since biblical times. In his younger years he composed secular verse, but later devoted his talents to religious themes. His love of God, Israel and the Holy Land found expression not only in poetry, but also in a major philosophical work written in Arabic, called the *Kuzari*. The framework to the book is a dialogue between the king of the Khazars and a Jewish sage who converts him to Judaism. The sage begins his presentation with history, not theology and, as the dialogue proceeds, shows that religious truths are superior to philosophical speculation.

Towards the end of the book there is an autobiographical reference when the sage declares his intention to live in the Holy Land. Judah ha-Levi was realistic enough to know that whether Christians or Moslems won final control over Spain, the Jews would always lose. No matter in what part of the country they found shelter, it would only be temporary.

A fellow student of Judah HaLevi was lbn Migas (1077-1141), who succeeded Alfasi in the rabbinate of Lucena. Ibn Migas was in turn the teacher of Maimon, scion of a famous family of scholars, and father of one of the greatest figures in Jewish history.

### Maimonides or Moses ben Maimon (1135-1204)

Rabbi Moses Ben Maimon, (usually shortened to Rambam, an acronym) was the next great codifier after Alfasi, second in chronological order, but first in importance. He was born in Cordova, the center of Jewish culture that had also been home to Samuel Ha-Nagid, lbn Gabirol and Judah ha-Levi. The same intolerance that had caused Judah ha-Levi to leave Spain, forced Maimonides' family to move to the Christian north. There, only 16 years of age, he composed a minor philosophical work, based on mathematics, astronomy and metaphysics. By the same time he had gained a wide knowledge of the Talmud, under his father's tuition.

Before Maimonides was 30, he and his family left Spain for Fez in North Africa, where many Jews had outwardly accepted Islam. He wrote a book to strengthen their faith and encouraged them to find a more tolerant environment, where they could return to Judaism. When Fez in turn became a place of Moslem fanaticism, the family set out for the Holy Land, staying six months in Acre, the port of arrival. After two crusades, the Jews of the Holy Land were few and impoverished, but Maimon, the head of the family, now old and tired, decided to stay while the others moved on.

Biographical features in the lives of Jacob, Joseph and Moses resemble those of Maimonides. Like Jacob, he led his family into Egypt for sustenance, like Joseph he sustained them there and was favored by the ruler of the land, and like Moses, he gave his people a code of law. The comparison with Moses is expressed in the saying "From Moses until Moses (Ben Maimon), there has not risen in Israel one like Moses." The biblical Moses had commanded the Israelites never to return to Egypt, which is why Maimonides added to his letters after his signature: "Who transgresses every day three negative commandments."

Shortly after arriving in Egypt (1168) Maimonides' father, brother and wife died in quick succession, causing him anguish and ill health. It also caused impoverishment, because his brother David who drowned at sea had been the main provider. Maimonides took it upon himself to pay off his brother's debts and support his family, and he did so by practicing medicine. After 15 years' experience, he was appointed physician to Saladin's court, while serving simultaneously as the official leader of Egyptian Jewry.

His fame spread far beyond Egypt, for the Jews of Yemen turned to him for guidance when persecuted by fanatical Shi'ite Muslims. Apostates and false messiahs increased their plight and Maimonides answered the appeal by means of a letter, expressing compassion and understanding, that strengthened their faith. Stressing the immortality of the Jewish people, the letter transcends the period in which it was written and in gratitude, the Yemenite Jews added Maimonides' name to the Kaddish prayer.

Maimonides major work was a systematic and comprehensive arrangement of Talmudic law, written for rabbi, judge and laymen alike. He called it the *Mishnah Torah*, meaning copy or repetition of the Torah, but the first word of the title is also a direct reference to the Mishnah of Rabbi Judah the Prince, in the third century. Although the Mishnah is divided into six main sections and the Mishnah Torah into 14, both works are written in pure Hebrew, used in a masterly, concise style. The Mishnah Torah would have done credit to an academy of scholars, yet it was completed by one man in ten years (1180).

Maimonides' second major work was also written over a ten year period. It was begun in Spain, continued in Fez and finished after having resided three years in Egypt, where medical and communal duties also claimed the author's time. The work was a commentary to the Mishnah, and in the introduction to the tenth chapter of Sanhedrin, Maimonides enumerated the Thirteen Principles of Judaism, later incorporated into the liturgy in poetic form (*Yigdal*). The commentary was composed in Arabic, like the *Guide to the Perplexed*, which was his third major work. The Guide was written for a specific disciple, but in general it was a reference work for anyone troubled by doubts in matters of faith. It deals with free will, providence, prophecy and biblical anthropomorphism and became a subject of study for both Moslem and Catholic theologians.

Maimonides' lesser-known writings are a collection of discourses, a treatise on the calendar and several medical books. He died in 1204, just three months short of his seventieth birthday, and was mourned in Cairo for three days by Jews and Moslems alike. Abraham, Maimonides' son and a scholar in his own right, succeeded as leader of Egyptian Jewry and the position passed from father to son until David, the last of the line, died in 1410. The head of the Jewish community in Moslem countries was called *Nagid*, although Maimonides himself never used the title. The first Nagid was a member of the Exilarch's family, and as such was descended from David. He arrived from Babylonia in 985, and the title came to its effective end in 1517, when the Turks took control of the country.

After Maimonides' death, two opposing schools of thought arose that either accepted or rejected his writings, known respectively as Maimunists and anti-Maimunists. In Spain and Southern France, the opponents objected to the philosophical elements, arguing that they might lead to misunderstanding and confusion. The main centers of opposition, however, were in Northern France, and in Baghdad, where efforts were being made to revive the glories of an earlier age, it was argued that the study of the Code would lead to the neglect of the Talmud.

Extreme critics even complained to the Dominicans that the *Guide to the Perplexed* was a danger to Christians as well as Jews, and on this pretext the monks publicly burnt copies in Montpelier and Paris (1233). Both sides were shocked by the level to which the dispute had sunk and when the Talmud was burnt in Paris nine years later, many regarded it as a punishment. One penitent was Rabbi Jonah of Gerona in Castille, who went from city to city in Spain preaching repentance and confessing his sin against Maimonides. He also wrote a book called *Gates of Repentance*, generally regarded as a classic on the subject. Before being able to fulfil a pledge and seek forgiveness at Maimonides' grave in the Holy Land, Rabbi Jonah became ill and died in Toledo (1263).

Foremost among the Maimunists was Rabbi David Kimchi (1160-1235) better known as Redak (from the initial letters of his full name). He came from Narbonne in Southern France, where the Maimunists were stronger than in the north, and gained his reputation as a biblical commentator and grammarian. Advanced in years, he travelled to Spain in an attempt to modify the anti-Maimunists objection to philosophy. He was not completely successful and died two years after Maimonides' books were burnt in Paris.

### *Nachmanides (1194-1270)*

The most famous of Maimonides supporters was Ramban or Nachmanides, whose full name was Rabbi Moses Ben Nachman. In Spain, where he lived, the Talmud was studied with his comments alongside those of Rashi, and his biblical commentary served as a model for later generations. He was also a linguist, mystic, doctor, and the recognised spiritual leader of his day, far beyond the borders of Spain. Acknowledging the full range of his accomplishments, many referred to him simply as Master. It was inevitable in the dispute between Maimonides' supporters and opponents, that both sides would seek his support. He decided in favor of the Maimunists, with the proviso that the *Guide for the Perplexed* should not be taught in public, since its author had written it for select individuals.

Nachmanides was obliged to travel to Barcelona to participate in a public debate with an apostate called Pablo Christiani (many Jewish converts adopted the name Paul). This took place in the royal palace of Aragon in 1263 with the king and queen among the distinguished audience. Nachmanides himself wrote one account of the event and a second was made in Latin. He countered the claim that the messiah had come and therefore Judaism had been superseded, by pointing out that in a true messianic age the world would not witness so much war and violence. Moreover Christians, he added, had shed more blood than anyone else.

After four days, the king brought the debate to a sudden end, rewarded Nachmanides and allowed him to return home. The Dominicans, for their part, asked the king to punish him after reading his account of the debate, and Nachmanides was obliged to flee from Spain. In 1267 he arrived in Jerusalem, and in a letter he described the desolation caused by a Tartar invasion seven years earlier. (In 1260 the Egyptians prevented a Mongol army from entering Africa by defeating it in the Holy Land.)

When in Jerusalem, Nachmanides established a synagogue that is still in use, and afterwards moved to Acre where he established a yeshiva.

During the last three years of his life when he lived in the Holy Land, Nachmanides completed his biblical commentary in which he wrote from personal observation: "Since our departure (from the Land) it has not absorbed any other people. Many have tried to inhabit it, but none have been successful" (Comment to Gen. 26:32). In his commentary to Maimonides' Book of Commandments, he criticizes its author for not enumerating dwelling in Eretz Yisrael as a positive commandment. In his own view, the precept to dwell in the Land was of special importance, just as he held that it should not be allowed to remain desolate or relinquished to any other people.

After doing all he could to strengthen religious life in the country, Nachmanides died in Acre in 1270, two years after Jehiel of Paris. According to tradition, their adjacent graves are at the foot of Mt. Carmel.

### Asher ben Yehiel and Jacob ben Asher

Rabbi Asher ben Yehiel (1250-1328), known as Rosh (another acronym) was the period's other great codifier. He escaped to Spain from the persecutions of Germany and stayed for a short time in Barcelona where he was welcomed by Rabbi Solomon Ibn Adret (1235-1310). Ibn Adret was a disciple of Nachmanides and recognised throughout the country as its spiritual leader. When he died, Rosh, who was serving as Rabbi of Toledo on his recommendation, took his place.

His compendium follows the order of the Babylonian Talmud, while taking into account the rulings of the Tosaphists in Northern Europe and of Alfasi and Maimonides. When he disagreed with the latter, his views were regarded as authoritative among Castilian Jewry. The method of combining European and Spanish teachings was also introduced into Asher's academy in Toledo, where for more than 20 years he taught students from throughout Europe.

Asher Ben Jehiel died a poor man, but although unable to leave his sons material possessions, bequeathed them an ethical will, containing advice and guidance on spiritual matters. Such wills were common in the second half of the Middle Ages, and were motivated by a father's wish that his children remain steadfast in their faith and lead useful lives. Many of the wills were written long before death, and were rich in aphorisms, as when Nachmanides counselled to speak gently to all men at all times, and Rosh warned his sons that even one enemy was one too many.

The best known of Asher's sons was Jacob (1270-1343), who fled to Spain from Germany with his father. He too wrote a code, called the *Four Rows* (*Turim*), in which he arranged the commandments according to subject matter, and not their order in the Talmud. As the name of the work implies, the laws are arranged under four main headings and include only those of post-Temple application. Some two centuries later, Rabbi Joseph Karo wrote a commentary on the *Four Rows*, and based his own code on its arrangement.

Jacob arrived in Toledo from Barcelona after his father's death and served on one of the city's rabbinical councils. The Jews of Castille and Aragon in his day enjoyed a large measure of autonomy that extended to levying taxes and imposing the death penalty. Jacob himself signed the death warrant of an informer because calumny constituted a threat to the entire community. Some Jews held important positions as courtiers and financiers, and their enemies were willing to strike at all Jews if given the opportunity. While Jacob was in Toledo, the king's treasurer was Joseph Benveniste, who was accused of enriching himself at the expense of the state. Benveniste died in jail and the minister of state who brought the accusation attempted to have all Jews robbed and expelled. There were no serious consequences, because the minister himself was executed for treason.

Jacob's son died of the Black Plague shortly after his own death. Spanish Jewry did not suffer from the repercussions of the Black Plague of 1348 to the same extent as communities on the other side of the Pyrenees, but its own period of suffering was soon to come.

### The Decline of Spanish Jewry

On June 6th 1391, the archdeacon of Seville preached an inflammatory sermon that set the mob on the Jewish quarter. Four thousand were slain, many baptised against their will, while women and children were sold to Arab slave traders. From Seville, the conflagration spread first to more than 70 other cities in Castille until finally it affected the entire country. In Aragon 250 Jews were killed in the city of Valencia despite royal protection, and in Barcelona they took refuge in the citadel. Some managed to escape, but others committed suicide, died fighting, or were forcibly baptised. Within the space of a year, communities that had existed for centuries were destroyed, and the position of those that remained was at best precarious.

Vincent Ferrer (later canonised) was a Dominican preacher who advocated that the Jewish problem could be solved in a more efficient way if the church and government took it out of the hands of the mob. Geronimo de Sante Fe was another monk with a special interest in the Jewish question. Known as Joshua Lorski before he became an apostate, he advised the anti pope Benedict XIII to hold a public debate, as part of a plan to encourage mass conversion. The result proved to be the last great debate of its kind in the Middle Ages.

In 1413 about 16 rabbis were summoned to Tortosa, a city in North East Spain, to represent the Jewish case. Benedict made it clear, in his opening speech, that the truth of Christianity was a foregone conclusion. The sole task of the rabbis therefore, was to answer Geronimo's claim that the sages of the Talmud were aware that Jesus was the messiah. Joseph Albo (d.1444), a noted philosopher and the leading representative discounted the proposition.

The debate lasted 69 sessions, over a period of 21 months. During this time, when the rabbis were away from home, friars moved among the leaderless communities freely making converts. The converts were then paraded before the rabbis in Tortosa, in order to dishearten them. When Geronimo could not prove the truth of Christianity from the Talmud, he condemned it as an immoral work. The result of the debate was that Benedict accepted the accusation, banned Talmudic studies and made it obligatory for the Jews to listen to sermons of conversion three times a year.

Fortunately Benedict's reign was brought to an end by a church council (1417), convened to end a schism to which he was a party, and his successor abolished the decrees.

### The Marranos

Jews unwilling to accept Christianity through persuasion were to be punished through legislation. Its aim was to increase poverty by restricting means of livelihood, and by prescribing clothes of coarse material to humiliate the wearer. As a result mass conversions took place motivated not by sincerity, but in order to escape the humiliating restrictions. Outwardly Christian, most of the converts observed some tenets of Judaism in secret in order to impart a measure of Jewish identity to their children and to maintain some link with the past.

Such converts were looked upon as a threat to Catholicism, especially when they came to hold important positions in government, commerce, army and the church itself. The jealousy, animosity and bigotry formerly reserved for the Jews was now transferred to them, especially when they performed such unpopular tasks as tax-collecting. The general populace called them by the derogatory term of *Marrano*, which means swine.

The fate of Spanish Jewry including the Marranos, was sealed when Isabella of Castille married Ferdinand of Aragon, joining Christian Spain in political unity. The royal couple's ambition was to conquer the last remaining Moslem enclave of Granada in the south and give Jews and Moslems the choice of baptism or exile. Purification of the country began with the Marranos, and in 1480 the Inquisition was introduced, with papal authority to try anyone suspected of being a secret Jew. Those suspected were not told the identity of their accusers, trials were held in secret, and torture was used to gain confessions. Their possessions were used to finance the war against Granada but part went to the informers, through whom the fires of the Inquisition were kept burning.

On February 6th 1481, the first Marranos were burnt alive. The procession to the stake was led by priests bearing crosses, followed by representatives of the secular authorities, and finally came the victims dressed in sackcloth. In Seville, 300 Marranos were burnt in the space of a year, and because so many profited from their confiscated wealth, no one was too concerned if the evidence was unsubstantiated. The Marranos appealed to the pope against the judicial murders, claiming that Ferdinand was not motivated by religious zeal, but from love of gain. The pope thereupon requested that a church representative be present at each trial, yet even this stipulation eventually fell into neglect. (The last Marrano was burnt in 1755, and by the time the Inquisition was abolished in 1834, it had claimed an estimated 340,000 victims.)

Matters became worse when a Dominican priest, possibly of Jewish extraction, became inquisitor general of Castile and Aragon in 1483. He was Tomas de Torquemada, confessor to Ferdinand and Isabella, whose harsh rules of procedure and the rigor with which they were enforced won him a reputation for cruelty.

While Marranos were being burnt at the stake, many with the unity of God on their lips, observant Jews were left in relative peace. So it came about that during the Inquisition, a professing Jew managed Ferdinand's financial affairs.

### The Final Catastrophe

The last great figure of Spanish Jewry, who did everything in his power to avert the final catastrophe, was Don Isaac Abrabanel (1437-1508), scholar, courtier and diplomat. His reputation as a scholar, whose interests included philosophy and the sciences, was gained while still young in Lisbon, the capital of Portugal and the city of his birth. He succeeded his father as royal financial adviser, and used both his authority and private wealth to redeem captive Jews from Morocco. Obliged to flee to Spain, he settled in Toledo, where he started a biblical commentary. Ferdinand invited him to administer Spain's financial affairs, and an important part of his task was to fund the war against Granada. In January 1492 the city fell, and the last vestige of Moslem rule in the country was eliminated. Ferdinand and Isabella used the re-conquest of Spain for Christendom as a suitable opportunity to expel their Jewish subjects. Abraham Senior, the rabbi of Castille, was also a courtier like Abrabanel, and in a joint audience with the monarchs, they attempted to have the expulsion order rescinded. It is said that at a critical moment, Torquemada stepped forward, and throwing a crucifix before Ferdinand and Isabella exclaimed: "Judas sold his master for 30 pieces of silver, now you would sell him again?"

Torquemada had hoped the Jews would prefer baptism to exile (Moslems were offered the same choice) but only comparatively few did so, in order to remain in the country or retain wealth and position. Abraham Senior was among their number. The original expulsion date of July 31st was changed to August 2nd, which fell in the same week as the fateful Ninth of Av. Of Spain's original Jewish population, some 50,000 remained by accepting baptism, 20,000 died seeking a new home, and 160,000 found refuge elsewhere. Thus, a continuous settlement of over 1,000 years came to an end. The islands of Sicily and Sardinia, part of Spain's possessions, were included in the edict.

Abrabanel was among the exiles, and in Naples he once again found employment as financial adviser to a king. After two years Naples fell to the French, and so he went to Sicily, Corfu, and back again to Naples, before settling in Venice, where he died. During all these wanderings and political changes, he managed to complete the biblical commentary and other literary compositions.

### Expulsion from Portugal

Manuel I, king of Portugal, wished to marry the daughter of Ferdinand and

Isabella of Spain, who gave their consent on condition that he follow their example by expelling the Jews. Previously he had been tolerant towards his Jewish subjects, but the prospect of a son who might one day rule over the entire Peninsula was paramount. Despite his promise that no investigation would be made into the faith of any New Christian, the majority chose exile.

The Jews were banished from Portugal in 1497, including 600 families from the Spanish exile, who had been granted refuge. There were not sufficient ships to take everyone assembled on Lisbon's quay, and so about 200,000 were left behind. Herded together in intolerable conditions, without food or water, priests moved among them to make converts. When persuasion failed, the king ordered his soldiers to take the Jews in carts to churches, where they were forcibly baptised. Some openly blasphemed the tenets of Christianity in the hope of dying as Jews, but the soldiers had orders to harm no one.

Most of those forcibly converted in Spain soon lost their Jewish identity, but in Portugal a minority succeeded in escaping to Moslem countries and other parts of Europe or even America, where they returned to their faith. Among those who remained and their descendants, thousands continued to observe some form of Jewish practice in secret, even up to the 20th century, when a few openly embraced Judaism.

The sufferings of the exiles did not end with actual expulsion, for treacherous captains extracted exorbitant sums from their passengers, and then abandoned them on desolate shores, exposed to hunger and diseases. Others, captured by pirates, were sold into slavery, and if suspected of swallowing jewels, had their bodies cut open. Solomon Ibn Verga was an exile and author of a book called *The Rod of Judah* in which he traced the sufferings of his people from Second Temple times to his own day. In some passages, he expresses feelings of helplessness and inadequacy, while in others a love of his people and religion that transcends everything. He illustrates this second train of thought with the story of an exile who in spite of being abandoned and bereaved cried out: "Master of the Universe, you have done everything to make me abandon my faith. Yet know of a surety that I am a Jew and a Jew I will remain."

## *The End of the Period*

Around the year 1000 C.E., the direction of Jewish life shifted from Mesopotamia westwards, in particular to Northern Europe and Spain. Under the influence of Rashi and his disciples (the Tosaphists) France and Germany succeeded the academies of Sura and Pumbeditha as the main centers of Jewish learning, while for some three centuries (c.900-1200), the Jews of Spain enjoyed a golden age, shared also by the Jews of Egypt, exemplified by Maimonides, who lived in both countries.

Yet a knowledge of the times shows that, in terms of understatement, conditions were not always conducive to study. In a sense, the nine Crusades that began in

1096 and ended in 1291 comprised a single Holy War that lasted 195 years. During the intermittent conflict, major Jewish centers, especially along the Crusader route of the Rhine Valley, were decimated, and Jews refused baptism at the cost of their lives.

What is surprising is not that the period produced apostates, but that their numbers were so small. Some of those engaged famous rabbis in public theological debates, sponsored by a Church that acted as prosecuting counsel and judge. The public burning of the Talmud in Paris (1242) following one such debate, marked the end of the French center.

The end of the Spanish center came with the re-conquest of the country by the Christians, after another intermittent conflict with Moslems that spanned most of the Middle Ages. During that conflict the Moslems were reinforced by fanatical tribes from North Africa, who introduced intolerance into the country, while Christian princes engaged in internecine struggle. And so while Christians and Moslems fought against or with each other in ever changing alliances, Spanish Jewry produced codifiers, philosophers, poets and commentators never since equalled.

But in a sense, between the years 1000-1500, the Jews were living on borrowed time, because in addition to the massacres and discrimination, in that period they suffered no less than 15 mass expulsions. The one from Spain was merely the culminating disaster that served as a watershed, because afterwards the major centers of Jewish life returned to the east. The exiles mainly found refuge in countries bordering the Mediterranean, although some expelled from Portugal in 1497 reached Holland and the New World. Yet for the immediate future, it was in the Turkish Empire and Poland that Jewish life would be rebuilt.

In 1492, however, those places were not yet fully developed. Whether in Christian or Moslem countries, Jewish life was generally at a low ebb, following one of the greatest tragedies in Jewish history. Once again Jewish survival hung in the balance, and once again salvation would come from the Holy Land.

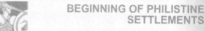

## 2000 B.C.E.

### ABRAHAM

**THE PATRIARCHS**

Teachers of Monotheism

**HAMMURABI'S LAWS**

Hittite & Egyptian Empires

**DECLINE OF EGYPTIAN POWER**

**1**

## 1500 B.C.E.

### MOSES

JUDGES

Earlier Prophets

**BEGINNING OF PHILISTINE SETTLEMENTS**

Spread of Mediterranean Civilization

**2**

## 1000 B.C.E.

### DAVID

KINGS

Later Prophets

**RISE OF PHOENICIAN TRADE**

Mesopotamian Empires

**END OF BIBLICAL PERIOD**

**3**

## 500 B.C.E.

### EZRA

ZUGOTH

Joint leaders of the Sanhedrin and the rule of the Wise

**BEGINNING OF ROMAN REPUBLIC**

Spread of Hellenism

**END OF ROMAN REPUBLIC**

**4**

## 0

### HILLEL

**TALMUDIC PERIOD**

Compilation of the Oral Law

**BEGINNING OF ROMAN EMPIRE**

Spread of Christianity

**END OF ROMAN EMPIRE**

**5**

## 500 C.E.

### RAV ASHI

**THE GEONIM**

Heads of the Babylonian Academies

**BEGINNING OF MIDDLE AGES**

Spread of Islam

**DECLINE OF BAGHDAD CALIPHATE**

**6**

## 1000 C.E.

### RASHI

**THE RISHONIM**

Earlier Authorities: Commentators & Codifiers of Talmudic Law

**HOLY ROMAN EMPIRE**

Crusades

**END OF MIDDLE AGES**

**7**

## 1500 C.E.

### JOSEPH KARO

**THE AHARONIM**

Later Authorities: Commentators & Compilers of the Halacha

**RENAISSANCE & REFORMATION**

Spread of Western Civilization

**END OF OTTOMAN EMPIRE RETURN TO ZION**

**8**

## 2000 C.E.

**1500 C.E.**

*Rabbi Joseph Karo*

**500 years**

**2000 C.E.**

Rabbi Joseph Karo's compendium of Jewish Law, the Shulchan Aruch, reached the Diaspora and united it with an authoritative code of conduct.

The scholars who followed are known as the Acharonim, or Later Authorities, whose main sphere of activity was Eastern Europe, especially Poland.

Foremost of the Acharonim was Rabbi Moses Isserles, a younger contemporary of Karo whose glosses on the Shulchan Aruch made it acceptable among Ashkenazi communities.

Elijah, the Gaon of Vilna, lived in the middle of the period, and used his immense influence to strengthen observance of the Shulchan Aruch. His contemporary was Israel ben Eleazar, better known as the Baal Shem Tov, who founded the largest revivalist movement in Judaism known as Hasidism.

After the destruction of European Jewry, in World War II, the center of the Jewish world returned to the Land of Israel.

The Shulchan Aruch was completed in Safed in the Galilee, which for a short period in the 16th century became the spiritual center of the Jewish world.

The disciples of the Baal Shem Tov and the Gaon of Vilna immigrated in the 18th century, to begin the resettlement of the land in modern times.

The main task of land reclamation began after 1882, with waves of immigration from Russia that were interrupted by World War I.

In the 20th century the British consistently reneged on the mandatory obligation to establish a Jewish National Home. Even so, in 1948 the State of Israel was established, providing the only historical example of a people returning to its land after almost 2000 years of exile.

In 1453 the Ottoman Turks brought the Byzantine empire to an end, and provided a haven for Jews soon to be exiled from Spain.

In 1517, they conquered the Holy Land, the same year that marks the beginning of the Reformation by Luther.

During the subsequent religious wars the Jews suffered in Germany, but remained unscathed in Poland. After 1648, and the end of the Thirty Years War, the situation was reversed, as Polish Jewry was decimated during the Chmielnicki uprising.

When Poland was partitioned out of existence between 1772-95, reactionary Russia inherited the largest concentration of Jews in the world.

The Balfour Declaration issued during World War I (1914-18) promised the Jews a National Home. The Holocaust during World War II (1939-45) made it a necessity for the survivors.

*Chapter Eight*

# From Rabbi Joseph Karo to the Present Day

## The Period of the Later Authorities (c.1500-2000)

Before describing the life and work of R. Joseph Karo, who stands at the head of this chapter, it is pertinent to observe that a major difference between recording events of a bygone age and those more recent, is that for the latter there is much more documentation. Therefore, the present chaper, which covers the modern period, is inevitably longer than the preceding ones, but nevertheless, many prominent events and personalities are still mentioned only briefly, if at all. This is an unavoidable consequence when history is presented in outline form, placing the emphasis on those who have contributed most to Jewish survival.

### R. Joseph Karo - (1488-1575)

Exiles who left Spain from the southern port of Palos would have seen the three ships of Columbus' expedition waiting to set sail on August 3rd 1492, a date that marks the beginning of American history. The time would come when masses fleeing persecution and pogroms would find refuge and opportunity in the New World, but in the time under discussion, only a small minority of the exiles would reach its shores. For the majority (some 90,000 out of 160,000) refuge meant the Turkish Empire, of which the territory occupied by modern Turkey formed only a part.

(As for Columbus himself, there are many biographical details that point to a Jewish descent. For example, Colon, which is how he often signed himself—never using Columbus—is also a Jewish name, shared by some who were burnt at the stake. In addition, he welcomed the company of Jews, whether professing, such as Abarbanel, or Marranos. Leading members of his crew, such as Louis de Torres, were of Jewish descent.)

Among the Spanish exiles was a four-year old child named Joseph Karo, but whether his father took him directly to Turkey or first of all to Portugal is not clear. What is both certain and providential, is that shortly before, in 1453, the Byzantine Empire had fallen to the Ottoman Turks, and the Sultan openly welcomed the Jews for their skills.

Joseph first studied under his father. He composed a commentary to the Code of Maimonides, removing the main objection to the work by quoting its sources. Moving between different cities, he served as chief rabbi in Adrianople, where he began a commentary to another code, the *Arba Turim* (*Four Rows*) of Jacob ben Asher. Called *Beit Yosef* (*the House of Joseph*) it was completed twenty years later in Safed.

In 1517 the Turks conquered Egypt and the Holy Land, opening up the Galilee for settlement, and allowing Safed, for a brief period, to become the spiritual center of the Jewish world.

When Karo arrived there in 1536, figures such as Moses Cordovero, author of a work on the Kabbalah called *Pardes Rimonim* (*Orchard of Pomegranates*), Moses Alschich, author of a popular Torah commentary—*Torat Moshe*, Moses Galante, who wrote a commentary on Ecclesiastes and many responsa, and Solomon Alkabetz, best known for the poem *Lechah Dodi*, which is sung in the synagogue on Friday night, had already established the city's fame. Safed's leading scholar was Jacob Berab, who wanted to renew the chain of ordination as a preliminary stage in the restoration of the Sanhedrin, but due to lack of unanimity, the idea never materialized. In 1542, the year following Berab's death, Karo completed his commentary, and then devoted a further 12 years to revising it. Simultaneously, he had succeeded Berab as Safed's chief rabbi, and taught some 200 students who attended his academy.

Caro's work was not so much a commentary as an independent source of Jewish Law. A supreme work of scholarship, he broadened its application for laymen by making a summary called the *Shulchan Aruch* (*the Prepared Table*). Following the Tur Code, the Shulchan Aruch is divided into four parts, which together regulate the daily life of the Jew and cover every major event from birth to death. This daily life is not divided into separate spheres of holy and profane, for even the simplest acts are elevated to a means of serving God.

Just as the debates of the Talmud are centered on the Mishnah, so successive generations added commentaries and super commentaries to the Shulchan Aruch, that together constitute present day Jewish Law. The Mishnah, Talmud and Shulchan Aruch are thus decisive stages in the development of the Oral Law, described as the greatest collective achievement of the Jewish people. The new stage in its history that began with Karo is called the period of the Acharonim, or Later Authorities.

Like other scholarly works produced in the Holy Land, the Shulchan Aruch reached the Diaspora via Italy. It was first printed in Venice in 1565 by Daniel Bomberg, a non-Jew who had previously published the Hebrew Bible and Talmud. Following the exile from Spain, the Jews were in more need than ever of the Shulchan Aruch's unifying force. Yet, despite its success, to this day many who observe its precepts are ignorant of its author's identity, for Karo somehow remains a semi-anonymous figure. There are even editions of the code in which his name does not occur on the front page. (Similarly, in general history, there was a period when Columbus was hardly known, which is why the New World he discovered is named after Amerigo Vespucci, a contemporary navigator.)

The Shulchan Aruch's orderly presentation and clear style belie the fact that Joseph Karo was also a mystic, which is obvious from a diary he kept. In an age when non-Jewish academics studied Kabbalah, this was clearly an era when rationalism and mysticism often went hand in hand, especially in Safed.

### Isaac Luria and Joseph Nasi

If Safed was noted for its Kabbalists, Isaac Luria (1534 - 72) was the leading proponent. He was born in Jerusalem, but after his father's death his mother took him to live with her brother in Egypt. Although he studied Talmud and engaged in commerce, his main interest lay in hidden wisdom, synonymous with the Kabbalah. Aged 35, he moved to Safed about the time the *Zohar* (meaning "splendor," a commentary on the five books of Moses, written in Aramaic) had appeared in print, and came under its influence. Luria's reputation as Safed's leading Kabbalist however was short lived, because he died of a plague, three years before Joseph Karo but less then half his age. He left no writings, but later generations inherited his teachings from a leading disciple called Hayyim Vital (d. 1620) in a book called *Etz Chayyim* (*the Tree of Life*).

Kabbalah was studied by the chosen few, until Luria pointed out that everyone possessed the potential to affect cosmic events. This brought it to the attention of a wider audience, especially those who saw in the expulsion from Spain messianic birth pangs. Isaac Luria is also known as ha'Ari, from the initial letters of *Adonenu* (our Master) Rabbi Isaac. The name itself indicates the esteem in which Luria was held, by virtue of his asceticism and saintliness.

Just south of Safed, situated on the Sea of Kinneret, is Tiberias, the seat of the last Nasi or Patriarch and now the focus of hope for national restoration. In contrast to the spiritual revival of Safed, Tiberias witnessed a political experiment, based on the principle of a land without a people, for a people without a land. The moving force was Joseph Nasi (d. 1579) a Spanish exile who settled in Constantinople. His talents enabled him to serve successive sultans with distinction, earning him the title Duke of Naxos. He was further rewarded with Tiberias and surrounding territory for an autonomous Jewish area. The city's walls were repaired by Suleiman the Magnificent, who previously rebuilt those of Jerusalem. (These are the walls that still encompass Jerusalem's Old City, described as a brilliant feat of military engineering and an architectural masterpiece.)

The self-sustaining colony Joseph established was based on wool trade and silk weaving. When conditions for Jews in the Papal States worsened, he sent ships to bring additional settlers, many of whom, however, were captured by pirates and sold into slavery. Setbacks and constant harassment by Arabs prevented the experiment from succeeding, despite Joseph's efforts and the generosity of his aunt Donna Gracia, a historical figure in her own right. After his death much wealth was confiscated, but the remainder still enabled his widow to support scholars and print Hebrew books. (Safed's printing press, in operation by 1563, may have been the first to be set up in Asia Minor.)

During Suleiman's reign, the Christians scored their first important victory over the Turks and, as the Empire entered into decline, so too did the Jewish community in the Holy Land. Ultimately, the political settlement of Tiberias failed, whereas the teachings of Safed were passed on to the Diaspora, especially Poland, the next major home for the Jews.

### The Golden Period of Polish Jewry (c. 1500 - c. 1650)

Cycles of disaster and recovery, settlement and expulsion, are common phenomena in Jewish history. Centuries before exiles from Spain settled in the Turkish Empire, Poland served as a haven for refugees from neighboring countries, but in particular from Germany. Successive disasters that befell Jews in Germany began with the Crusades, after which they were periodically attacked, massacred or expelled. Among the more infamous incidents were the Rindfleish persecutions of 1298 and the Armleder persecutions of 1336-38, following false accusations of ritual murder and desecration of the host. But even these episodes did not compare with the massacres at the time of the Black Death in 1348, which did not stop at national boundaries. In Poland the Jews were protected as much as possible by Casimir III, one of the country's most enlightened rulers, who limited the power of the nobles and clergy.

## Some leading authorities in the period of the Acharonim
### (A complete list of which would in itself require volumes)

**1 Eretz Yisrael**

Joseph Karo
(1488-1575)
Author of the
Shulchan Aruch

Isaac Luria
Ari
(1514-1572)
Kabalist

Rabbi Kook
(1865-1935)

Avraham Y. Karelitz
Hazon Ish
(1878-1953)

**2 Czechoslovakia**      **4 Lithuania**

Judah Loew
Maharal of Prague
(1525-1609)

Elijah b. Solomon
The Gaon of Vilna
(1720-1797)

**3 Poland**

Moses Isserles
Rama
(1530-1572)

David Halevy
Taz
(1586-1667)

Israel b. Eleazar
Baal Shem Tov
(1700-1760)

Yisrael Meir HaCohen
Hafetz Hayim
(1839-1933)

By the year 1500, Poland was a leading power enjoying a golden age. Safe from religious wars, its Jewish community formed the largest ingathering in the Diaspora. Economic and social factors were involved, because in the absence of a middle class, Jews acted as intermediaries between nobles and peasants.

Polish Jewry was encouraged to practise self-rule, creating in the process an organisational system known as the Council of the Four Lands (depending on when and into how many parts Poland was divided, it was also called the Council of the Three or Five Lands.) Its delegates were spiritual and lay leaders from the major communities, and its prime duty towards the government was to raise taxes. Internally, it decided on such matters as education, and maintained contact with Jewish communities in other countries. It met twice a year, with the spring fair in Lublin and the autumnal fair in Jaraslow, reminiscent of the bi-annual assemblies of the great academies in ancient Babylonia. There was also a similarity to the ancient Sanhedrin, because any council decision had the authority of law.

The educational system established by the Council set new standards, making learning compulsory between the ages of six and thirteen, while children of poor families were exempt from fees. Post-school tuition was provided by the yeshivot, whose reputation was unequalled throughout the Diaspora. In 1503 Rabbi Jacob Pollack founded a yeshivah in Cracow and his foremost disciple, Solomon Shakna, established another in Lublin. Neither left any books but the teaching method they used, known as *pilpul*, was designed to develop the acumen. By way of their students, their influence spread throughout Poland. Moses Isserles, Shakna's foremost disciple, also became his son-in-law.

## Rabbi Moses Isserles (c. 1525 - 1572)

Moses Isserles, Poland's leading spiritual authority, was also proficient in astronomy, philosophy and history, but he is best remembered for making Caro's code acceptable to Ashkenazi Jewry. The Hebrew word Ashkenaz means Germany, and accordingly Jews whose ancestors lived in that country in the Middle Ages are called *Ashkenazim*. In contrast, Jews whose ancestors lived during the Middle Ages in Spain (Sepharad in Hebrew) are called *Sephardim*. Both groups preserved their own languages, known respectively as Yiddish and Ladino, but different religious customs and ritual formed the greatest distinction between the two communities.

Joseph Karo was a Sephardi, whose code reflects the rulings of the community into which he was born. When the Shulchan Aruch reached Poland from Safed, Isserles annotated it by taking into account the decisions of Ashkenazi authorities. Jews from Spain living in Turkey and others from Germany living in Poland, as two examples, were thus united by the same code of conduct. (In addition to

Sephardim and Ashkenazim, Oriental Jews constitute the third major division of the Jewish people. Their ancestors settled mainly in the Middle East and North Africa, and their mother tongue was either Arabic, Persian or Neo-Aramaic.)

If Karo had not preceded him, Isserles would have published his own Code of Law, based on Ashkenazi practice. As it was, he subordinated his role by adding glosses to the Shulchan Aruch, thereby making it, in effect, a portable form of religious legislature for the entire people.

Students came from beyond Poland to study under Moses Isserles, just as he answered queries from other parts of the Diaspora. A synagogue he built in Cracow in his wife's memory still stands, while his most fitting tribute is that he was compared to his great namesake, Moses Maimonides.

Another figure who contributed to Polish Jewry's golden age was Rabbi Solomon Luria (1510-73), a friend and colleague of Moses Isserles. Of independent mind and consummate scholarship, Luria objected to the then fashionable pilpulistic or over-astute method of study, despite being criticised for his stand. He was also opposed to over-reliance on codes, advocating a return to the Talmud as the source of Jewish Law.

Isserles and Luria are best known as Rema and Maharshal, initial letters of their full names. Others known either by acronyms or by the titles of their works include Mordechai Jaffe (*Levush*), Joshua Falk (*Sema—Book of Enlightenment*), Meir of Lublin (Maharam), Samuel Edels (Maharsha) and Joel Sorkes (*Bayit Chadash - New House*). Their reputations were gained as commentators on the Talmud or Codes, heads of yeshivot, judges or communal rabbis, often in combination, and all lived during the first half of the 17th century.

### The Prague Center and Rabbi Judah Loew

A city renowned for Jewish scholarship during the period of the Later Authorities was Prague, then the capital of Bohemia, and later of Czechoslovakia (after it became a republic in 1919). Bohemia was part of the Holy Roman Empire, and even though its emperor protected the Jews at the time of the Black Death, a massacre in Prague in 1389 proved that they were not immune from mob violence. From the beginning, Prague's Jewish Quarter was an integral part of the city, and its famed Altneuschul is the only extant synagogue from the medieval period. It was also the first community from the same period to exhibit the symbol of the Magen David, the six pointed Star of David.

Bohemia's common border with Germany encouraged a large German population and ethnic problem long before this was exploited in the 20th century. Differences between Catholics and Hussites was another cause of friction, for Prague was the home of John Huss (d. 1415) who followed Wyclif and preceded Luther in preaching religious reform. The result was the Hussite Wars of 1419-36.

After 1526 Bohemia was ruled by the Habsburgs, who attempted to restore the kingdom to Catholicism, and twice expelled the Jews (1542 and 1561), only to readmit them. Rudolph II (d. 1612), the third Habsburg king, showed a keen interest in science, which brought him into contact with Rabbi Judah Loew (1525-1609), an expert in mathematics and astronomy, in addition to being an outstanding spiritual guide for his own and succeeding generations.

During his long career Judah Loew, also known as Maharal, studied in Poland where he was born, served as chief rabbi in Moravia, established a study hall in Prague where he taught, returned to Poland where he served as rabbi, and finally returned to Prague, where he was chief rabbi for the last 11 years of his life.

He advocated the traditional educational curriculum: "Five years old for scripture, ten years for Mishnah... fifteen years for Talmud" (Ethics 5:26), because in his day study of the Prophets and the Mishnah was neglected. He also took the education of adults into account. In other matters, his writings show Kabbalistic influence with an intellectual-philosophical emphasis, affecting the thinking, in later generations, of the Gaon of Vilna and Abraham Kook. The latter was the Holy Land's first chief rabbi, and a direct descendant of Maharal. A statue of Maharal on the main elevation of Prague's town hall survived German occupation in World War II, and is evidence of the esteem in which the city still holds him, some four centuries after his death.

If the institutes for Jewish learning in ancient Babylon were known as academies and in Poland Yeshivot, then the one established by Maharal in Prague was called a *klaus* (study-hall). Whatever the name, their purpose was to perpetuate Jewish knowledge and practice, without which the Jews themselves could not long survive. (A main purpose of this book is to trace the successive centers where that learning thrived best, and what internal or external pressures influenced their development or decline—see introduction.)

### *Yom Tov Lipman Heller*

No life story better reflects events in Central Europe in the first half of the 17th century than that of Yom Tov Lipman Heller (1579-1654), who was appointed *Dayan* (religious judge) in Prague at the age of 18. He was an important link in the transmission of Jewish learning, for in Prague he studied under Rabbi Judah Loew, who in turn had studied under Rabbi Solomon Luria. The scholarly dynasty continued when Heller attracted his own students. His writings exhibit a wide range of knowledge, in addition to expertise in Jewish law, but his most influential work is a commentary to the Mishnah found (at least in abbreviated form) in most printed editions.

When a revolution broke out in Prague in 1618 and Jews felt threatened, Heller composed two penitential prayers expressing the fears of the community. The revolt took place when Protestant Bohemian nobles felt their liberties threatened by the Catholic emperor, and the venting of their dissatisfaction initiated the Thirty Years War. For most of the time the conflict took place beyond Bohemia, because basically it was a struggle between German princes with foreign help, against the unity and authority of the Holy Roman Empire, represented by the Habsburgs.

To finance the war, the Jews were especially heavily taxed, and Heller was one of a committee that evaluated how the burden should be shared. Some who thought the evaluation unfair, accused him of maligning the king and Christianity. He was taken to Vienna, tried and sentenced to death, but Prague's Jewry interceded on his behalf and he was released on the payment of a large ransom. Forbidden to act as rabbi in Prague, he served in other countries, including Poland at the time of the Chmielnicki massacres.

Two contemporaries of Heller who helped give Prague its high reputation in the Jewish world were David Gans (1541-1613) and Isaiah Horowitz (1560-1630). The former had studied under Moses Isserles in Cracow before moving to Prague, where he came to know the famous astrologers Kepler and Tycho Brahe, both of whom worked at Rudolph's court. At Brahe's request he translated some planetary tables from Hebrew into German. His own work, called Tzemach David (The Shoot of David) covers general and Jewish history in two parts. Its main purpose is to highlight divine providence in Jewish survival.

Isaiah Horowitz studied in his youth in Prague and Poland and then served in several communities, including Frankfurt, before returning in middle age to Prague. There he combined rabbinical duties with teaching, always stressing the text's plain meaning and avoiding the pilpul method of mental gymnastics. In the last few years of his life, after his wife's death, he moved to the Holy Land, where his experiences reflect the harsh and corrupt conditions of Turkish rule. In Tiberias he completed his major work on Jewish laws and customs called Shnei Luchot ha-Brit - (Two Tablets of the Covenant) which he sent to his sons in Prague. He is sometimes identified with this work through use of its Hebrew acronym – Shelah.

## Reformation and Counter Reformation

In 1648, when the Thirty Years War came to an end, the Holy Roman Empire was reduced to a mere facade and, in general, there was religious decline. Germany had suffered most, with its population decreased, its commerce and industry in ruins and its agriculture destroyed. Throughout all the turmoil that characterised the Reformation in Germany, its peasant class was among the hardest hit, but at no time more than at the beginning of the period, when it was betrayed by Martin

Luther himself. This point is worth noting, because if he disappointed his own supporters, the Jews had far more cause for complaint.

When Luther openly attacked abuses within the church, he hoped that his reformed version of Christianity would attract the Jews. He even condemned their ill-treatment and wrote a series of articles stressing the Jewish origins of Christianity. But the attitude changed to virulent anti-Semitism after his overtures failed. The Jews, he now declared, were in league with the Turks, the avowed enemies of Christendom, and deserved to suffer because of their obstinacy. To increase their afflictions, Luther advocated the destruction of synagogues, the confiscation of property and the imposition of humiliating occupations. Failing all these measures to break their obstinacy, they should be driven out or annihilated. Luther disseminated anti-Semitism through both the written and spoken word, for he was a forceful preacher, capable of arousing mob violence.

Rome could not countenance any church reform that denied the authority of the pope, and so a movement known as the Counter Reformation emerged to fight Protestantism. Despite the vilification Jews suffered from Luther and his disciples, they were still accused of supporting the Protestants and were punished accordingly. In 1516, the Jews of Venice were confined to the "Ghetto Nuovo" or New Foundry, and in 1555, Paul IV issued an edict that extended the ghetto system to all cities in the Papal States (generally justified as protecting believers from the presence of Jews).

Among other repressive measures, Jews were confined to degrading occupations, forbidden to own property, heal Christians or employ Christian servants and, as a mark of shame, they were to wear a yellow hat. In 1569, when Pius V ruled the Papal States with particular severity, some Jewish communities in existence from antiquity were expelled. During the Counter Revolution in Spain, where the Inquisition was most free with the death penalty, most of the Protestants burnt were of Jewish descent. 16th century anti-Semitic legislation and practice set a precedent for 20th century National Socialism in Germany.

### Shtadlan and False Messiahs

*Shtadlan* is defined as a representative of the Jewish community who interceded with high dignitaries and legislative bodies on behalf of his people. No one lived up to this definition better than Rabbi Joseph (Joselman) of Rosheim (c. 1478-1554.) Rosheim is situated in Alsace, today part of France but then part of Germany, and at one stage in their war against the princes (1524-26) it was besieged by German peasants. The war had witnessed atrocities by both sides, which Joseph helped to limit, because, accompanied by the mayor of Rosheim, he entered the rebel camp and successfully pleaded for the city to be spared.

He knew how to speak not only before peasants but also before princes because when the Jews of Austria were threatened with expulsion, he appealed to the Emperor Charles V and the order was rescinded. After another expulsion order, when the Jews had been driven from Prague in 1542, he was instrumental in gaining their re-admittance. His achievements are all the more noteworthy, because the peasants were Protestants and the emperor Catholic, with neither side friendly towards the Jews.

To improve relations between Jew and Gentile, Joseph convened a rabbinic assembly whose resolutions he put before the princes, together with an appeal for toleration. A meeting with Luther, however, was not granted. Luther's anti-Semitism was carried on by his disciples, who resorted to the medieval practice of public debate. An expert in polemics, Joseph wrote a guide book for those forced into such disputes.

At one stage in his career he came into contact with two pseudo- messiahs.

David Reubeni, short and of swarthy complexion, came to public attention in Venice in 1524, where he claimed to represent the tribes of Reuben (hence his name) and half of Manasseh. He maintained they still existed somewhere in Asia, and his brother Joseph was their king. In an audience with Clement II, he asked the pope to make peace between Charles V of Germany and Francis I of France so that their combined forces might help his brother drive out the Turks from the Holy Land. The pope gave him a letter of recommendation to John III of Portugal, who was sufficiently credulous to promise ships for the venture.

Reubeni's mere presence in Portugal was sufficient to inspire a Marrano in the king's service to return to Judaism. Adopting the name of Solomon Molko, the former Marrano had himself circumcised and fled to Salonica, a prelude to an incredible series of adventures that have formed the subject of a novel. The pope himself became involved, by conniving to save Molko from the Inquisition as a relapsed heretic.

In the final scene of the drama, with the aura of messianic pretensions, he and Reubeni appeared before Charles V, against the advice of Joseph of Rosheim, and after refusing their appeal to fight the Turks, the emperor had them both arrested. Molko chose to die a Jew rather than live as an apostate and among the many deeply affected by his martyrdom was Joseph Karo. Reubeni was imprisoned in Spain, and whether he was a charlatan, merely self-deluded, or perhaps a combination of both, remains an unanswered question.

## Court Jews

Unlike Joseph of Rosheim, who appeared on behalf of his people in different principalities, Court Jews, or *Hofjuden*, served one specific ruler, and although they often intervened on behalf of fellow Jews, their main concern was finance. Marcus Meisel (d. 1601) a Prague financier, enabled Rudolph II to wage war against Turkey, but this did not prevent the emperor from seizing his wealth when he died. Although childless, Meisel did leave behind an unequalled reputation for generosity that extended beyond Prague to Poland and the Holy Land. Jacob Bassevi (d. 1634), another Prague financier and communal leader, served the Habsburgs during the Thirty Year War. He formed a consortium that leased imperial money, and was the first European Jew outside Italy to be ennobled. His property nevertheless was confiscated, and after his death his privileges abrogated.

It was during the Thirty Years War that Court Jews came into their own. As the conflict spread from Prague to Germany and other countries, Jews were found in Courts throughout Europe, responsible for the maintenance of large armies. They were active throughout the seventeenth and eighteenth centuries in peace time too, when their duties might include the funding of palaces or cities.

Court Jews lived in style and enjoyed special rights, but occasionally met a tragic end, as exemplified by Joseph Suss Oppenheim, who was executed in 1738, when his patron suddenly died. His career, which was depicted in both a novel (*Jew Suss*) and a Nazi propaganda film, illustrates how the life of any Jew was vulnerable, irrespective of influence or status.

The year 1648 marked a reversal of fortunes for the countries of western and eastern Europe. In that year, in the west, emphasis was laid on toleration instead of conflict, with the end of the Thirty Years War. But in Poland in the same year, the peace was disrupted when the violence and bloodshed from which it had been spared overtook it sevenfold.

### The Chmielnicki Massacres

Some 80 years before the fatal year of 1648, a large part of the Ukraine came under Polish rule. Polish nobles reduced the Cossack peasant population to serfdom and increased resentment by outlawing the Russian Orthodox Church, the majority faith. The inevitable revolt was led by Bohdan Chmielnicki, hetman (military commander) of the Ukraine. The Cossacks, masters of the art of mounted warfare, formed an alliance with the Tartars, and their joint forces scored an easy victory over the Polish army. For some time the Polish throne had ceased to be hereditary, and when the king died at this critical period, the nobles could not agree on a successor. A leaderless and weak Poland lay open to the invading hordes, which included Russian bands that participated in indiscriminate slaughter.

Jews were unpopular because Polish nobles employed them to collect taxes from the Ukrainian peasants. As the main objects of hate, they were killed without mercy, scrolls of the Law were desecrated and thousands of infants were thrown into wells or buried alive. Young women were often forcibly baptised and then taken as wives, but many chose suicide as the alternative. Even fortified cities, like isolated islands in a sea of rebellion, were not always safe, for whenever the Cossacks gained entry by subterfuge, Jews and Poles were slaughtered together. The citizens of Lvov, however, succeeded in buying off the besiegers with a large ransom, and those sold into slavery by the Tartars were ransomed by the Jewish communities if ever they reached as far as Turkey.

After several months John II (John Casimir, 1648-68) gained some respite for his stricken country by bribing the Tartars to withdraw and so Chmielnicki, left alone, was obliged to make peace. As a Catholic, John did not regard the Orthodoxy of the Cossacks as true Christianity, and allowed those whom they had forcibly converted to return to Judaism.

But the peace he made did not last, and what followed caused his reign to be known in Polish history as the Deluge. Chmielnicki persuaded Russia to annex the Ukraine and when the fighting was renewed, it was by combined Russian and Cossack forces. The cup of bitterness passed to Lithuania, where 25,000 Jews were massacred with the fall of Vilna, its capital city. In the same year (1655) that the Russians attacked Lithuania on Poland's northern border, Charles X, king of Protestant Sweden, attacked from the west. The Poles, suspecting the Jews of paying the Swedes to come to their rescue, joined the alliance of Tartars, Cossacks and Russians in decimating Polish Jewry. Thus, while the Cossacks were destroying the community of Lublin, the Poles committed atrocities in Kalish.

Mercifully, Chmielnicki died in 1657. His ambition of an independent Ukraine remained unfulfilled, and ten years later, a truce was made between Poland and Russia. If the wars ended, so too did the illustrious age of Polish Jewry. There are no accurate figures, but estimates speak of 250,000 slain, 3000 communities destroyed and thousands of refugees who fled to Germany, Holland, Italy and other countries. No statistics could measure the anguish of the survivors. The Council of Four Lands introduced an annual fast on the twentieth of Sivan to commemorate the 6,000 Jews of Nemirov, massacred in one day at the beginning of the Chmielnicki uprising, after refusing baptism. The Jewish authorities in Lithuania proclaimed a general three-year period of mourning.

Contemporaries of the massacres moved to compose lamentations were Sabbatai Cohen (1621-62) and David Halevi (1586-1667). The former managed to escape from Vilna prior to its capture by the Russians, and then lived in Lublin, Prague and other cities before he died aged 41. During his short life he wrote a commentary on two parts of the Shulchan Aruch, sometimes disagreeing with its author. From the beginning, the commentary established the *Shach* (an acronym of *Siftei Cohen*) as a leading figure among the Later Authorities.

David Halevi was his friend and academic rival, who is said to have mastered three of the more difficult tractates of the Talmud by the age of seven. He served as rabbi in different cities of his native Poland, and while in Ostrog, where he established a Yeshivah, he composed the first part of his famous commentary on the Shulchan Aruch. Called *the Rows of Gold* (*Turei Zahav*—abbreviated to *Taz* in Hebrew) the commentary eventually covered all four sections, and when necessary it upheld the authority of the Shulchan Aruch against other codes. After 1674 the commentaries of Shach and Taz appeared in all printed editions of the Shulchan Aruch, to become an essential reference for all matters of observance.

During the period of massacres, David HaLevi lost two sons and was himself forced to wander. Living to be an octogenarian, towards the end of his life he sent a son and stepson to Constantinople, to check the credibility of one Sabbetai Zevi, who was making messianic claims.

### Jewish Resettlement of Northern Europe

While Poland was being ravaged from without, England was passing through an internal religious, economic and constitutional crisis that led to civil war and the beheading of its king. Not a few Englishmen, therefore, and Jews everywhere, yearned for peace and a messianic era. It was believed that the goal might be hastened by the completion of the Diaspora, which meant the readmission of the Jews into England. No one espoused the idea more than Rabbi Menasseh ben Israel (1604-1657). Of Marrano descent, he lived in Holland where he started the first Hebrew press. A master of five languages, one of which was English, the rabbi entered into a dialogue with Oliver Cromwell, Lord Protector of England, who invited him to discuss the issue at a special meeting in Whitehall (1655).

Despite the intolerance with which Cromwell consolidated victory in the civil war, his attitude towards the Jews was one of understanding. When he realised that the result of the Whitehall Conference would be unsatisfactory, he brought its deliberations to an end. Denied a formal declaration, he connived at the readmission of the Jews, and with his tacit approval London's Marrano community reverted openly to Judaism.

By the time of the Whitehall conference, Marranos were living in certain German cities, but nowhere were they more tolerated than in Amsterdam. Ever since 1597, when Protestant Holland (as the country was later called) gained independence from Catholic Spain, Amsterdam served as the principal refuge in Northern Europe for Marranos. One descendant of Portuguese Marranos who lived there was a philosopher called Baruch Spinoza (d. 1677), whose heretical views led to his excommunication. We know what some members of Amsterdam Jewry looked like, including Menasseh ben Israel, because they are immortalised in portraits by Rembrandt van Rijn. He lived in the Jewish quarter for more than twenty years, and when painting biblical or other scenes, often used his neighbors as models.

## Sabbetai Zevi (1626-76)

Among those who came to Amsterdam in order to return to Judaism was a young orphaned Jewess, who had survived the Chmielnicki massacres by taking refuge in a convent. While in Amsterdam, she imagined herself to be the intended wife of the messiah, and her claim reached Sabbetai Zevi in far away Cairo, who sent for her to become his bride. Either a fraud, or else deluded by mystic studies into thinking that he was indeed the messiah, Sabbetai pretentious claims had brought about his expulsion from various communities in his native Turkey. In Egypt, he married Sarah, the refugee from Poland.

The year 1665 was a turning point in Sabbetai's career, for that is when Nathan of Gaza became his pseudo-prophet, encouraging his messianic pretensions and publicising them as much as possible. When Sabbetai returned to Smyrna, where he was born on the Ninth of Av 39 years earlier (the fast day would later be turned by him into a major feast), he was openly proclaimed the messiah.

He declared the following year as the one of redemption, in common with some non-Jews who also expected 1666 to mark the millenium, and who may not have been too surprised when virtually all of London was destroyed by the great fire.

Drunk with success, Sabbetai travelled to Constantinople, where his opponents had warned the Turkish authorities about the arrival of a madman. He was duly imprisoned and immediately became a martyr in the eyes of his followers. Fame or infamy brought him before the Sultan as a political rebel and, when faced with death or apostasy, he chose the latter. Disillusionment spread quickly among his supporters, but a few nevertheless followed him into Islam. These converts remained faithful to the false messiah even after his death, and their descendants still form a separate Turkish sect know as the Donmeh (Dissidents), located mainly in Salonica. The Sabbatean movement survived like a malignant growth, difficult to eradicate in one operation, and its members often followed the precedent of apostasy.

After almost two decades of bloodshed in Poland, Sabbetai's legacy was to leave the Jewish world even more demoralised for, as high as the hopes he had raised, so were the depths of despair that followed. At the height of the euphoria some families actually sold their homes, anticipating the journey to the Holy Land, as the memoirs of Glueckel of Hamelin, who lived at the time, relate. Not only the credulous were deceived, for even Spinoza did not discount a Jewish restoration.

An example of how far Sabbetai's influence reached is illustrated by Judah he-Chasid (d. 1700 - not to be confused with the famous ethical writer of the same name, who was a contemporary of Maimonides.) After a journey of many vicissitudes, Judah arrived in Jerusalem from his native Poland at the head of a group of followers. Misfortune struck when Judah died shortly after his arrival, leaving his followers demoralised and destitute. Because they were suspected of Sabbatianism, they were refused assistance by the local community and eventually forced to disperse.

A synagogue established by the pilgrims was destroyed by the Arabs in 1720, and was long known as the Ruin (*Churba*) of Judah he-Chasid. The Ashkenazi synagogue subsequently erected in the same place still bears the name.

Back in Europe the disillusionment of Polish Jewry after Sabbetai was compounded by the fact that the country was moribund. Religious trials, associated with Western Europe in the Middle Ages were introduced, as Jews were accused of ritual murder or desecrating the host. Even fabricated evidence was not always necessary to incite mob violence. Due to abject poverty, most survivors of the recent massacres were too preoccupied with subsisting to study, widening the gap between the masses and the intelligentsia, which included the rabbis. The gulf was felt most noticeably in the synagogue, exacerbated by the fact that the poor and ignorant were looked upon as superstitious.

Sabbetai Zevi's mission was a false one, but the spiritual vacuum he presumed to fill was real enough. The remedy was eventually brought about by two figures, either of whom might be expected to appear only once in a time span of several centuries. One symbolised the heart and the other the intellect of the Jewish people. Such was their influence that it remains strong and vibrant to the present day.

### Israel ben Eleazar - Ba'al Shem Tov (c.1700 - 1760)

Israel ben Eleazar, or the Ba'al Shem Tov, represented the heart of the Jewish people because through compassion, he reached out to the Jewish people and in capturing their affection, revived the prostrate body of Eastern European Jewry. His life is one of paradoxes because he was never the head of an academy, yet his pupils and disciples numbered thousands in his lifetime and millions after his death. He wrote no book or commentary, yet his teachings spread far and wide. He mixed with the simplest and corresponded with the learned, and like the ladder of Jacob's dream, he was set firmly on earth, yet reached up to heaven. But perhaps the greatest paradox is that although what he said has been minutely chronicled, there is only scant biographical material about the man himself.

Israel was born in 1698 or 1700 in a small town in Podolia, in south-west Poland. Orphaned while still young, he inherited a love of nature and a genuine concern for his fellow man. His love of nature became apparent when he often ran away from school to be alone in the forest, and his love for his fellow beings first expressed itself in the care he showed towards the young children in his charge. Having to provide for himself from the age of 12, he assisted in supervising school children, bringing them to and from school. About the age of 14 he became a *shamash* (beadle) in a synagogue and later married the sister of a well-known and wealthy Kabbalist, who was apparently none too enthusiastic about the match. This may explain why the couple soon left Brody, the city in which they were married, to live in a small town in the Carpathian Mountains. During this period Israel earned a meagre livelihood by digging lime from the ground, but he also had ample opportunity for solitude and contemplation. In the course of time, he acquired knowledge of the healing properties of various herbs and as a consequence people came to him for medical advice.

After living seven years in the mountains close to nature, the couple eventually settled in a town near Brody in Podolia (1736). By this time Israel had become known as the *Ba'al Shem Tov* (Master of the Good Name) abbreviated to *Besht*. People may have come to him for physical cures, but he specialised most in spiritual remedies for troubled souls. When virtually everyone had some reason to be despondent, he taught a message of love and joy that made him famous throughout Poland. The Ba'al Shem Tov taught by anecdote, parable and metaphor, as when he explained God's omnipresence by pointing out that He revealed Himself to Moses in a lowly bush, as a sign that he is everywhere. And just as every part of the creation reflects the Creator, so every individual deed should reflect worship of the Creator. Even small acts, he explained, could reap great spiritual benefits. His followers included rich and poor, learned and ignorant, and after his death their numbers increased until a mass movement was born. Among the teachings and customs that the Besht inherited from Isaac Luria and passed on to his disciples was the Sephardic prayer rite. Prayer played an important part in his message, for it is based on the principle, he stressed, that what God requires is the heart. He discouraged mortification, because it contradicted the words of the Psalm that God should be served with gladness; and as for salvation, he told those who listened to him to first believe they were worth saving. Personal redemption was his message.

All the Ba'al Shem Tov's teachings were based on love: love of God, love of the Torah, love of the people of Israel and love of the land of Israel. He regretted living outside its borders, but plans to emigrate did not materialise. His love of his people expressed itself when he was one of three rabbis to participate in a public debate by order of the Bishop of Lemberg. His opponents were followers of Jacob Frank (d. 1791), a charlatan who claimed to be the reincarnation of Sabbetai Zevi, and who allowed his followers freedom from moral restraint. If the Frankists had won, the Talmud would have been burnt, but on losing, they were obliged to abandon their religion. Other rabbis rejoiced, because the Jewish community was finally rid of the Frankists, but the Besht mourned because now they were irretrievably lost, like an unhealthy limb severed from the body. The incident illustrates how the Ba'al Shem Tov saw a divine spark even in the reprobate, as he once told a friend: "I believe that I love the most sinful member of the House of Israel even more than you love your only son." If a son errs, then he should be loved all the more.

On the second day of the festival of Shavuot (Pentecost) in 1760, the Besht died, having laid the foundations for the greatest revivalist movement in Jewish history. Through him, the influence of Isaac Luria in 16th century Safed re-emerged two centuries later in Poland, where it brought hope and color to an otherwise dull existence. Kabbalistic teachings progressed from being obscure doctrines for the few into a popular movement for the many.

The new movement came to be called Hassidism and its adherents *Hassidim* (Pietists). Those who looked upon them as an aberrant sect were known as *Mitnagdim* (Opponents), whose main center was the Lithuanian city of Vilna.

### *Elijah ben Solomon Kramer - The Gaon of Vilna (1720-1797)*

In the period of the Later Authorities, Vilna was a city of outstanding scholars, of whom the most eminent was Elijah ben Solomon, known also as the Gaon of Vilna, or simply as the Gaon. Gaon means genius, which sometimes hides the fact that he was also of saintly character, and as a title of respect, it had last been bestowed on the principals of Sura and Pumbedita. Yet paradoxically, the Gaon never established an academy nor taught in one, neither did he ever hold any rabbinic position. This much he shared with the Ba'al Shem Tov. But whereas the Ba'al Shem Tov was the main proponent of Luria's Kabbalah, the Gaon personified Joseph Caro's Shulchan Aruch.

Of the many words of praise written about the Vilna Gaon, perhaps the most eloquent are events in his life. Aged only six and a half, he was confirmed as a child prodigy when he gave an abstruse Talmudic discourse in Vilna's Great Synagogue. Aged nine he was an expert in the Scriptures, the Mishnah, the Jerusalem and Babylonian Talmud and Rabbinic literature. By ten years of age he had mastered the Kabbalah and was obliged to study alone, have surpassed all his teachers.

After marrying at 18 he studied in Poland, Lithuania and Germany, trying to remain anonymous, but failing to do so because his fame always preceded him. Finally he returned to settle in Vilna, and by the age of 30 his reputation as a scholar of the stature of previous generations had spread throughout the Jewish world.

The Gaon received offers from many communities to be their spiritual leader, but he refused them all in order to concentrate on his studies. These he pursued to the ultimate degree for, according to his son's testimony, in 50 years he never slept more than two hours a day and, even then, never more than half an hour at a time. His knowledge was encyclopaedic, for he committed to memory every major work of Jewish religious literature, including the Talmud which he reviewed every 30 days. Because he considered all knowledge to be included in the Torah and necessary for its understanding, he mastered astronomy, algebra and geography and wrote a book on geometry.

Up to the age of 40 he lived as a recluse, studying and producing all his works. There is not a subject relevant to Judaism on which he did not produce a book, notes, or glosses, which could have amounted to complete books. By virtue of his photographic memory and encyclopaedic knowledge, he could comment on any passage or establish the correct reading of any text, using the method of cross-reference. After 40, the Gaon ceased to write, and emerged from seclusion to teach a select band of disciples (perhaps 20 in number) each one of whom possessed a brilliant mind and genuine piety. These disciples were to disseminate their master's teachings, by becoming living examples of the Shulchan Aruch.

The Gaon regarded the Shulchan Aruch as the quintessence of Judaism and Talmudic Law, which is why he attached to it his own commentary. Not least, he regarded it as the unifying force of the Jewish nation, binding together its dispersed elements. This was a task of utmost importance because in 1764 the Polish government abolished the Council of the Four Lands, leaving millions of Jews without a central authority. To add to the general confusion, during the Gaon's own lifetime, Poland was divided in stages between Russia, Prussia and Austria until it ceased to exist as an independent state. Lithuania, and its capital Vilna, which had been part of Poland for two centuries, passed to Russia. The Gaon's belief in the power of the Shulchan Aruch to unite the Jewish people, explains why he set his signature to a severe manifesto against the Hassidim. He was afraid they might deviate from traditional Judaism and become a divisive sect, and although two prominent representatives travelled to Vilna to assure him there was no such danger, they were refused an interview.

Some 1,000 years after the Karaite schism, Vilna was a main center of Karaite settlement and, in the tradition of the Babylonian Geonim, the Gaon of Vilna opposed their influence. Consistent with their opposition to the Oral Law, the Karaites complained in a letter to the last Polish king that the rabbis had corrupted Mosaic teachings. Following the Frankists, they wanted a public debate in which the main defendant would be the Talmud itself, but the threat did not materialise.

The Gaon did not openly debate with either Frankists or Karaites, but fought against both sects more effectively through his disciples. One of them, Chayyim of Volozhin, founded a yeshivah that soon became the most famous in Lithuania, spawning many other yeshivot in which the learned methodology of the master was continued. Another disciple, Abraham Danzig, composed the *Chayyei Adam*, a popular summary of the first section of the Shulchan Aruch, citing the Gaon's opinions.

Like the Ba'al Shem Tov, the Gaon wanted to live in the land of Israel and even set out on the journey, but for some reason turned back. The ambition of both would be achieved vicariously through their disciples. After the Gaon's death, his writings were collected and published with much material based on notes taken by his disciples. There is not a branch of Jewish knowledge that he did not elucidate, in a clear, precise and authoritative style that was the hallmark of his genius, often explaining difficult texts in a way that eluded his predecessors, and raising and reviving the standard of Torah study for subsequent generations.

The study hall in which the Gaon wrote and taught continued to function until it was destroyed in World War II, and in 1997, the Lithuanian parliament held a special commemorative ceremony on the 200th anniversary of his death.

### Conditions in Western Europe

While Poland witnessed the decline and demise of its monarchy, Frederick the Great made Prussia the greatest state in Germany, and Louis XIV of France was called the Sun King, because of the brilliance of his court. The Grand Monarchy, as it was called, was characterised by Louis' (apocryphal) remark "The State—that is me." The reign of Louis XV (d. 1774), his great-grandson, is known as the Age of Reason, or Enlightenment, because of the galaxy of philosophers and scientists who criticised the established order.

With the Enlightenment, a new attitude developed among some Protestant intellectuals, who argued that through assimilation Jews could become useful citizens. This change led the dramatist Lessing, to produce a one-act play in 1749, *Die Juden*, in which for almost the first time a Jew was presented as a refined, rational human being. The attitude of Jews towards the Enlightenment varied. In France, it was associated with secularism and loose morals, and therefore considered dangerous in itself and a first step towards assimilation. But in Germany, with its center in Berlin, the Enlightenment was more creative and took the religious spirit into account. This approach attracted many Jews, who believed it possible to embrace rationalism and remain observant at the same time. The most famous advocate of this view was Moses Mendelssohn, the model of Lessing's play, who emerged from the ghetto to become one of Prussia's most respected thinkers and one of Judaism's most controversial figures.

### Moses Mendelssohn (1729-1786)

Moses Mendelssohn was born in Dessau, the son of a Torah scribe. When his teacher was appointed chief rabbi of Berlin, the 14-year-old pupil followed him there, earning a living as a copyist and private tutor.

Assisted by friends, Mendelssohn learnt High German, Latin, Greek, French, English and Italian, as well as philosophy and mathematics. Turning to literature, he wrote a work called Phaedon, described as a metaphysical-psychological-aesthetic treatise. The German academy wanted to accept him as a member, but the nomination was vetoed by Frederick the Great. Another of Mendelssohn's works established him as a leading philosopher of the European enlightenment, while Lessing, his friend and admirer, encouraged further literary activity.

At first Mendelssohn's writings contained little Jewish material, until publicly challenged by a Lutheran theologian either to disprove the truth of Christianity or convert. Mendelssohn answered by proudly proclaiming his loyalty to Judaism, and thereafter turned to matters of specific Jewish interest. A rationale of Judaism called *Jerusalem* won the acclaim of Christian scholars, including the philosopher Immanuel Kant. Mixed reception, however, was given to his translation of the Pentateuch into German, accompanied by a commentary. Critics claimed that the true purpose of the translation was to spread knowledge of German and disseminate German culture, rather than knowledge of the Torah. The biblical commentary was censured whenever it contradicted the classical sources.

Mendelssohn deplored Yiddish and, despite using it extensively himself, regarded it as a vulgar dialect which he wanted replaced by German. A knowledge of German culture, he was convinced, would eventually gain for the Jews both civil and religious emancipation. Many saw in him the spiritual leader of German Jewry, even though he worked as a merchant without holding any rabbinical position. Literary activity was confined to his spare time, and he died at the comparatively young age of 57.

The conflicts that Mendelssohn experienced were shared by many Diaspora Jews, who simultaneously tried to integrate into society while retaining their Jewish identity. The dichotomy exposed him to the charge that he tried to be all things to all men, for representatives of contradictory views were able to quote his opinions. The observant pointed to Mendelssohn's punctilious fulfilment of the commandments while the less observant quoted his statement that their fulfilment was not a fundamental part of the faith. Perhaps the greatest contradiction lay in his claim to defend Judaism, while according to his critics he actually undermined it.

Instead of combining faith and general culture as he intended, the most Mendelssohn achieved was to have Judaism retained in the home. In this also his success is doubtful, for members of his own family and many disciples ceased to be Jews even in their private lives. Two of his daughters were so eager to adopt the dominant culture that ultimately they accepted the dominant religion (a third daughter inherited her father's curvature of the spine, and never married). The famous composer Felix Mendelssohn, who was a grandson, was baptised when a child together with other family members, and the example of Mendelssohn's own descendants was followed with no less alacrity by his disciples. Thus while there are many Jews today who trace their descent to the immediate disciples of the Ba'al Shem and the Gaon of Vilna, sooner rather than later, the descendants of Mendelssohn and his followers were all baptised.

## Hassidism

The Ba'al Shem Tov had founded Hassidism, but it was a foremost disciple and successor who turned it into a mass movement. Dov Baer of Mezeritch (1704-73) first visited the Besht for a cure from prolonged physical mortification, but stayed to discover that his true malaise was spiritual. The Besht taught him how to achieve harmony through body and soul living in coexistence, not in opposition. Dov Baer provided a different type of leadership from the one he inherited. Unlike the Besht, he did not travel to meet his followers, partly because he suffered from physical disabilities, but mainly because it was in any case impossible to be in all places and available to everyone. He therefore sent out chosen representatives, each of whom was allotted a specific district in which to teach Hassidism, until ultimately it spread throughout Eastern Europe. Menahem Mendel was sent to White Russia and when once asked what he had accomplished there, answered: "When I arrived I found torn clothes and whole hearts, now it is the opposite." It was Menahem Mendel who travelled in vain with a colleague to meet the Gaon of Vilna to have the ban of excommunication against his movement lifted. After the failure of the mission, he left with 300 Hassidim for the Holy Land where, first in Tiberias and later in Safed, he continued to serve as the Hassidic leader of White Russia. He was succeeded by Shneur Zalman, the colleague who accompanied him to Vilna. The mass emigration of 1777 marks the beginning of Jewish settlement in the Holy Land in modern times.

Shneur Zalman (1745-1813), established his own distinctive branch of the Hasidic movement called *Habad*, a Hebrew acronym of Wisdom, Understanding and Knowledge. He himself possessed these gifts in no small measure, for in addition to Talmud, he mastered mathematics and astronomy. Habad's ideology is summarised in a volume of his collected sayings, called *Tanya*, which from the beginning served as a guide for his followers. Previously, under the influence of his master Dov Baer, he had produced a compendium of religious law following the same layout as Karo's Shulchan Aruch, but taking into account Hassidic practice.

Liady, where Shneur Zalman lived in White Russia, automatically became a center for his followers. It was also home to his critics, and following a denunciation to the authorities, he was imprisoned in St. Petersburg (1798). The charges proved unfounded and his release on the 19th of Kislev has been celebrated ever since by the movement as a vindication of Hassidism.

The last months of his life were affected by the Napoleonic Wars and the French advance on Moscow in 1812. Shneur Zalman ordered his followers to support the Russians against the invaders and, to escape capture, fled with his family to the interior of the country. He died after five months of wandering. After the first of his names, Shneur, his descendants are known by the surname of Shneerson, and because his son, Dov Baer (1733-1827) lived in the town of Lubavitch, each successive leader has also been known as the Lubavitcher Rebbe. Hassidim use the term rebbe instead of rabbi, and from Shneur Zalman to the last Lubavitcher Rebbe (d. 1994), there were seven generations of leadership.

Among the other 39 emissaries sent out to spread the message of Hasidism, Zusa of Anipoli (d. 1800) and his brother Elimelech of Lyzhansk (d. 1787) went to Galicia. Both became heroes in hassidic lore, and the latter established the mores of the Zaddik. The Zaddik (righteous man) is a hassidic leader of saintly personality, with ultimate authority among his followers. A Zaddik in the third generation of the movement, and one of the most famous, was Levi Yitzchak of Berdichev (d. 1810), who had the distinction of being a spiritual leader for both Hassidim and their opponents.

Levi Yitzchak used straightforward language when pleading for fellow Jews as when he asked God: "You always make demands on your people - then why not help them in their troubles?"Another of his statements is that the amount of love shown to one's fellow man is the gauge of one's love of God.

By this third generation of leadership, there was a noticeable degree of decentralisation, aided by the three partitions of Poland in 1772, 1793 and 1795, and the vast distances between the dispersed communities. The emissaries became leaders and founders of dynasties in their own right, each with a distinctive style and interpretation of the Ba'al Shem's message.

At the end of this third generation the battle was mainly over, and from being a persecuted movement, Hassidism had become a way of life for the majority of Jews in countries like Ukraine and Galicia, with sizeable groups of followers in other countries such as Hungary and Belorussia. Success, however, can be a danger in itself, because once revolutionary movements achieve their goal, they tend to split into factions that have more to do with personalities and slogans than with ideology.

This state of affairs was criticised most of all by some of the more outspoken Hassidic leaders themselves, such as Menachem Mendel of Kotsk (1787-1859), who saw in the Hassidism of his day the same lethargy it had once set out to overcome. In this light he told his followers: "He who sins and forgives himself, who prays today merely because he prayed yesterday – a very scoundrel is better than him." Included in his list of sins were sham, pretence and conformity. Although Menachem Mendel did not found a dynasty, the Rebbe of Gur to a great extent carried on his approach. As Jewish life following the general pattern became increasingly secular, so Hassidism correspondingly shut itself in, concentrating on organisation and adopting a position of defence. But whatever the criticism, at one of the darkest periods of Jewish history, it brought light and hope to countless followers, and over 200 years later is still strong and vibrant.

## Mitnagdim and Maskilim

Long after the Gaon of Vilna, Lithuania continued to be the center of opposition to Hassidism, and also due to his influence, by the 19th century it was the center of scholarship for the entire Diaspora. While Hassidim stressed the efficacy of prayer and the emotional content of religion, the Lithuanian Jew, or Litvak as he is colloquially called, emphasised the intellect and importance of Talmudic study. In prayer, the Polish Ashkenazi rite was retained.

The reputation of yeshivot such as Mir, Telz and Slobodka extended far beyond Lithuania, and the latter in particular became associated with the *Musar* Movement founded by Israel Lipkin (1810-83). Israel Salanter (as he is best known) stressed that Judaism makes no distinction between ethical and religious laws, and that observance and learning should be accompanied by a lifelong process of self-improvement and service to man. These lessons were implemented by the study of ethical works and lectures on ethical subjects.

In 1808 there was a mass emigration of Mitnagdim to the Holy Land, where they settled in Tiberias, and seven years later established an Ashkenazi community in Jerusalem. Many others followed, and to this day descendants of the old Ashkenazi settlers in the Land trace their origins back to this period of mass immigration of Hassidim and Mitnagdim.

Emigration to the Holy Land was encouraged among the followers of the Ba'al Shem Tov and Vilna Gaon, but not among the followers of Moses Mendelssohn. Their neglect of many important principles of Judaism, such as the centrality of Eretz Yisrael, is one reason why a truce was called between Mitnagdim and Hasidim. In general terms, their common enemy was secularism but, more specifically, it was the Jewish version of the Enlightenment, known in Hebrew as the Haskalah.

## Maskilim

The proponents of the Haskalah were called *Maskilim*, and although many of their ideas predated Mendelssohn, he is regarded as the movement's founder. More than anyone, he advocated the supremacy of reason which was the motif of the Enlightenment. The Maskilim viewed the majority of their fellow Jews as backward and, to radically alter the image, advocated the widespread adoption of secular culture and foreign languages. They deprecated Yiddish and developed Hebrew, all the while considering emancipation to be the main goal. Towards this end, the Maskilim fully co-operated with the authorities in using the classroom to spread secular knowledge and abolish separatism, with Mendelssohn's own disciples often setting the curriculum.

No one was a greater advocate of achieving emancipation through assimilation than David Friedlander (d. 1834), a friend of Mendelssohn and the first Jew to be elected to the Berlin City Council. He openly requested to be accepted into the church on certain conditions that were inevitably refused. Denied the opportunity of forming a sect within Christianity, Friedlander gave his attention to reforming Judaism. Assisted by others, he contributed to the wholesale apostasy that characterised Berlin's Jewish population, half of which accepted baptism in the following 50 years.

By the Second World War, descendants of baptised Jews who were Germans by Nuremberg Law standards, were enlisted into the army and participated in the destruction of European Jewry, of which their ancestors were once part.

Efforts by Maskilim and others to achieve emancipation were overtaken by events, because two revolutions, the first in America and the second in France, achieved the same goal far more quickly.

## The American Revolution

When the first Jews arrived in New York in 1654, it was then called New Amsterdam, and belonged to the Dutch. The governor, Peter Stuyvesant, thought the newcomers part of a "deceitful race." A decade later, the British replaced the Dutch, until over a century later, they in turn lost all their possessions - the Thirteen Colonies - following the American Revolution (1775-83). By that time, the number of Jews had increased from a few score to some 2,500, but after 1720 Jews of Spanish and Portuguese origin were superseded by those from Germany.

Incessant warfare in Germany meant that Jews were merely part of a general emigration. When the State of Georgia was founded in 1733, to provide asylum for debtors and oppressed German Protestants, Jews also found refuge there, making Savannah the third Jewish community in America, after Newport in Rhode Island (1678) and New York (1682). It should be remembered that the Pilgrim Fathers who arrived in 1620 denied tolerance to other Protestant sects, let alone Jews, who consequently were not granted unrestricted settlement until the 18th century.

Whatever American colonists thought of Jewish immigrants, they identified themselves with the ancient Israelites and were strongly influenced by the Bible. Hebrew was taught in the universities and often inscribed, as in the case of Yale, on their coats of arms. The first seal adopted after the revolution depicted the overthrow of Pharaoh in the Red Sea, with the motto: "Rebellion to tyrants is obedience to God." Clearly the new revolutionaries saw King George III as Pharaoh and themselves as the Children of Israel, who sought freedom to establish the ideal of a theocracy.

And if George Washington was the American Joshua leading an army towards independence, then some descendants of the ancient Israelites either served under him or provided financial assistance. Hayyim Salomon (d. 1785) was a banker and philanthropist, who risked his own capital for the patriotic cause, in addition to helping Americans taken by the English to escape. After the war Washington served as the first American President (1789), and the exchange of letters between him and the Jewish communities to mark the occasion are indicative of the high level of mutual respect.

When the American Declaration of Independence was adopted in 1776, it was accepted by the ringing of Liberty Bell, which bore the Biblical inscription "Proclaim liberty throughout the land" (Lev. 25:10). Biblical influence is also apparent in the very wording of the Declaration, as in the evident truths that "all men are created equal, and are endowed by their Creator with inalienable rights." As the British historian William Lecky put it, it was Hebraic mortar that cemented the foundations of the Republic, thereby influencing the conception of constitutional government throughout the world.

### The French Revolution

Just as the American Declaration echoes Biblical teachings, so it in turn was echoed in the Declaration of the Rights of Man issued by the French Revolutionary Government in 1789. But as far as the Jews were concerned, if the language used in both declarations was similar, the way each was interpreted was different. For whereas Jews were included in the American declaration, in the French one they were clearly not, and Jewish emancipation, even in revolutionary France, had to be achieved in two stages. Firstly, in 1790, it was granted to Sephardi Jews (of Spanish and Portuguese origin) on the grounds that they were not considered aliens, and only in 1791 was it made all inclusive. One opponent quoted Voltaire, who held that Jews were intrinsically bad.

Outside France, emancipation was granted wherever French armies brought their revolutionary message. In chronological order, this included Papal Avignon, Nice and the western banks of the Rhine, followed by Holland and much of Northern and Central Italy, including the Papal territories. Italy was captured and ruled by Napoleon Bonaparte (d. 1821), who received unprecedented praise from Italian

Jewry for granting civil rights. He raised expectations even higher when he set out in 1799 to conquer the Holy Land, for it was generally believed that after the conquest, he might hand it over to Jewish rule and restore the monarchy.

Entering the country from Egypt in the south, he conquered Jaffa after a four-day siege and then took Haifa. Support by British warships helped Acre to withstand a protracted siege, and the French were obliged to retreat to Egypt, decimated and plague-ridden. There was no attempt to take Jerusalem, and any hopes for a Jewish national restoration were dissolved.

Soon after returning to Paris, Napoleon took command of the entire Revolution, and in 1804 was crowned (by himself) as Emperor. Prompted by accusations against the Jews, he took a second look at them and not seeing them as true Frenchmen, decided to refashion them in his own image. His tools were an Assembly of Notables, followed a year later, in 1807, by a "Sanhedrin." Both were presided over by David Sinzheim (d. 1812) the rabbi of Strasbourg and one of the few delegates noted for learning and piety. The Sanhedrin of 71 members, composed of rabbis, laymen and reformers, reflected something of Napoleon's taste for the theatrical, but after four weeks of debate failed to introduce into Judaism changes desired by the emperor.

What did change for French Jewry was the organisational structure of the community. From 1808, governing bodies of rabbis and laymen were set up to provide an organisational hierarchy that has lasted until the present day. Simultaneously, Napoleon issued an order known as the "Infamous Decree," whereby the economic activities and freedom of movement of Jews in the eastern provinces of the Empire were restricted for ten years. It is not surprising that among Jews and non-Jews alike, Napoleon aroused ambivalent feelings, both towards his policies and towards the man himself.

Whatever fears or hopes the "Little Corporal" aroused (so dubbed because of his short stature) came to an end with his crushing defeat in Russia (1812) and narrow defeat three years later at Waterloo. The Congress of Vienna (1814-15) was convened to reassemble the European jigsaw after the Napoleonic upheaval and, for the first time, the Jewish question became a subject for discussion in an international forum. Despite the delegates' achievements, they failed to take into account growing national aspirations and, by ignoring the memory of the Revolution and the spirit of the American and French declarations, reactionary governments laid the ground for later insurrections.

Emancipation for European Jewry would come mostly in stages, with the revolutionary year of 1848 a critical one. In the meantime, only in America, Holland and France itself, did the Jews enjoy full equality immediately following the Napoleonic wars.

## *Baptised and Estranged Jews*

It is not surprising that Paris, center of the French Revolution, attracted liberal thinkers of all shades during the revolutionary period. Two such figures, who became friends, were the poet Heinrich Heine (d. 1856) and Karl Heinrich Marx (d. 1883) the chief theorist of modern socialism. Apart from sharing the same name, both were apostate Jews born in Germany. Heine was baptised at 28, in order to qualify as a lawyer (it was then that he changed his name from Hayyim to Heinrich) whereas Marx was baptised at the age of six by his apostate father. Like Freud and Einstein in the 20th century, both represented assimilated Jews who changed conventional attitudes towards society and the universe.

It is generally true that such Jews, when young, received neither at home nor at school any religious or national identity. It is sometimes assumed that in a different period, or under different circumstances, they might have become rabbis or great Talmudic scholars, and it has even been suggested that part of the Jewish mission is to periodically relinquish to the world figures of genius. While such trains of thought remain conjectural, what is certain is that according to Judaism (and for many Gentiles as well), even a Jew who undergoes baptism remains a Jew. As individuals, many an estranged Jew has earned a place in history, but when assimilation is widespread, it becomes a cause of national concern.

According to Henri Bergson (d. 1941), a philosopher who contemplated but rejected apostasy, the past of every individual is a dominating part of the present, never absent from the subconscious. On this principle, studies have shown how a Jewish past influenced Freud's theories, and inspired Heine to compose some of the world's greatest poetry. Marx's writings contain vitriolic attacks against Judaism and Jews, including Ferdinand Lassalle, a founder of Germany's first workers' party, with whom he disagreed on certain socialist principles.

Marx's anti-Semitism may well have been an expression of self-hatred, a common phenomenon among estranged Jews. In stark contrast, Benjamin Disraeli (d. 1881), a British Prime Minister baptised when young, actually boasted about his Jewish past in the House of Commons, and praised the Jewish people in his novels. He also advocated the emancipation of Britain's Jews.

Jewish emancipation on the continent was far less smooth, and in Germany in particular, far less civilized. First, the gains of the revolutionary years were nullified and then the Jews were subjected to physical violence. Motivated by hatred and fear of commercial rivalry, anti-Jewish riots broke out in Frankfurt and other cities, accompanied by the cry of "Hep! Hep!" revived from the period of the Crusades. (Hep is formed from the initials of *Hierosolyma est perdita*, Latin for "Jerusalem is destroyed.")

### Reform and the Science of Judaism

In 1819, the year of the Hep riots, the Science of Judaism (*Wissenschaft des Judentums*) was founded and the Hamburg Temple introduced a reformed prayer book. The three events are not disconnected. The riots proved to the Jews that their situation was at best tenuous, but even so they believed that if allowed to demonstrate that they were Germans first and Jews second, they would be accepted by the general population. And so they called themselves not Jews, but Germans of the Mosaic faith, and they prayed not in synagogues but in temples, which resembled churches, led by rabbis who resembled priests. Readings from the Torah were in abridged form without cantillation, while the congregation sat bare headed and prayed sometimes in Hebrew but mainly in German, accompanied by choir and organ. Churchgoers might feel at home, which is why Protestant pastors visited the Berlin Temple to listen to sermons. To pray for Zion was neither patriotic nor universal, and so the term Zion was deleted from the prayer book.

Among those who advocated changes in the synagogue service was Leopold Zunz (d. 1886) who as a university student played a leading role in establishing a society for Jewish culture and study. A principle aim of the society, in the years prior to emancipation, was to retain the loyalty of those considering baptism in order to pursue a career, but in the case of Heine and other prominent members, it failed. As an offshoot of the Jewish Enlightenment, the Society subordinated faith to reason, which is precisely why for many the Science of Judaism failed to inspire. In 1824 the society was dissolved, but the movement lived on, assuming different forms in different countries.

In Germany Abraham Geiger (d. 1874) helped establish and taught in a Wissenschaft seminary. He was also Reform rabbi in Breslau, Frankfurt and Berlin where he ministered to Germans of the Mosaic faith who simultaneously discarded the laws of Moses. Another enthusiastic reformer was Isaac Jost (d. 1860) who was also, like other Wissenschaft scholars, a devoted historiographer. His ten volume history made a distinction between the history of Israel and the history of the Jews, by ignoring the role of the sages as successors of the prophets. Gentile readers were meant to be persuaded that the Jews were sufficiently compliant to be worthy of emancipation. As Ze'ev Javetz (d. 1924) a later historian pointed out, no authoritative history of the Jews can be written without an understanding of Judaism, and this qualification was conspicuously lacking in the German school. Eastern European Jewry, where attachment to Judaism was strongest, was often maligned by German Maskilim, and largely ignored by the famous historian Heinrich Graetz (d. 1891). But it was in Galicia, once part of Poland before being annexed to Austria, that the Science of Judaism produced representatives more in line with Jewish tradition.

Foremost was Nachman Krochmal (d. 1840) who combined philosophy and history in his *Modern Guide of the Perplexed*, based on the principle of rise and decline of cultures, but with an upward progress. All thinkers at the time were aware of, if not influenced by, the German philosopher Hegel's theory of thesis, countered by antithesis to produce a synthesis. The theory (which was adopted by Marx and Lenin) implies historical progress, while for Krochmal progress implied increased spiritual awareness, with the Jewish people's spirit as eternal. His concept of history was clearly not secular. Solomon Rapoport (d. 1867) was influenced by Krochmal to take an interest in Wissenschaft methodology, and his many contributions to Jewish scholarship included bibliographical studies and a Talmudic encyclopaedia. At 50 years of age, Rapoport became chief rabbi of Prague, and together with other colleagues, was invited to condemn reformers in Frankfurt who declared circumcision optional. One of the colleagues was Samuel David Luzzato (d. 1865,) a biblical commentator who represented the new type of scholarship in Italy. His reputation added prestige to the "Instituto Rabbinico" in Padua, where he was principal professor. This seminary was the first of several established throughout Europe at the time (including Jews' College in London) whose purpose was to provide emancipated communities with a different style of spiritual leader, able when required, to act as representative to the non-Jewish world.

In the United States the Hebrew Union College had been founded by the Reform movement in Cincinnati in 1875, but its almost total abandonment of Jewish tradition shocked the more conservative elements, and led to the opening of the Jewish Theological Seminary in New York in 1886. Originally Orthodox in approach, this institution also gradually strayed from the ideals of its founders and eventually Yeshivah University (from 1886 onwards) also situated in New York, was founded to serve the needs of modern Orthodoxy.

A large proportion of graduates from the German theological seminaries served Reform congregations, and prepared them, through systematic abrogation of the law, to make the final break with Judaism. When Zunz, who was not adverse to change, observed the scene, he noted that it is ourselves we must change, not religion. Zunz was not Orthodox, but his statement soon became the watchword of those who were!

### Akiva Eger and Moses Sofer

*The Way of Life* is the name given to the first part of the Shulchan Aruch, and the term Orthodox applies to those who base their way of life on all four parts of the code and its commentaries. The word Orthodoxy itself was first used in connection with Judaism in 1795, and it soon became widespread, to distinguish its adherents from Reform, Haskalah and those who followed the general trend towards secularisation.

One of the first and most prominent rabbis who faced the challenge to Orthodoxy posed by Reform was Akiva Eger (1761-1837) who during the Napoleonic Wars had led a delegation of rabbis to negotiate Jewish rights with the French in the newly established Duchy of Warsaw. Like Warsaw, the city of Posen had once been part of Poland, after which it passed between different powers and, in 1814, Akiva Eger became its chief rabbi. The reformers had complained to the authorities against his appointment, which he held without remuneration to avoid material gain from sacred knowledge. High ethical standards and modest behavior earned him praise even from opponents. When aged 70 he received a letter of thanks from Frederick William III of Prussia, for aid to the sick during a cholera epidemic.

His yeshivah confirmed his reputation as a scholar, while his Responsa cover a wide range of subjects. Comments on the Talmud and related literature were published both during and after his lifetime, and are highly esteemed by scholars to the present day. R. Akiva Eger left behind distinguished descendants and disciples, but none more so than his son-in-law, Moses Sofer.

Chasam Sofer - R. Moses Sofer (1762-1839) - was rabbi in Pressburg, the most important community in Hungary, and his yeshiva was the largest since the Babylonian academies. He himself was the undisputed leader of European rabbis organised to confront the reformers, to which end he joined forces with the Hassidim and won the confidence of the government. Although not objecting to secular studies for a livelihood, he opposed the schools of the Maskilim, and condemned innovation for its own sake. Likewise, he was not a proponent of emancipation, because it implied a degree of assimilation. Instead he advocated a return to Zion, which his sons and disciples put into practice.

### Samson Raphael Hirsch and Azriel Hildesheimer

To describe the modern faction of German Orthodoxy, the term Neo-Orthodox came into fashion. Its forerunner was Isaac Bernays (1792-1849) the rabbi of Hamburg, where the prayer book introduced by the Reform Temple received his condemnation. It was a prayer book, he agreed, but not a Jewish one and, in protest against Reform rabbis who abandoned everything traditional except their title, he called himself *Haham*, as used by Sephardi Jews. Bernays (who was related to Heine, while a granddaughter married Sigmund Freud) was a forceful preacher and leading scholar, who influenced two younger contemporaries, Hirsch and Hildesheimer.

Although completely different in style, Samson (ben) Raphael Hirsch (1808-88) provided western Jews with a standard of leadership comparable to that of the Ba'al

Shem Tov and the Vilna Gaon in Eastern Europe a century earlier. Simplified in one phrase, his philosophy was *Torah im Derech Eretz*, based on a statement in the Ethics of the Fathers (2:2) which he interpreted to mean: "The study of the Torah is excellent when combined with the best of worldly culture." To prepare a new generation of Jews able to take its place in the world while remaining strictly Orthodox, Hirsch established three schools (one a high school for girls) with secular studies as part of the curriculum. Through education, Hirsch countered the Reform demand for "progress." What was needed, he taught, was elevation, namely the elevation of Jews to the ideals of their faith.

In 1876, a law was passed that enabled individuals to cede from a church or community without changing religious affiliation. Regarding co-existence with the Reform leadership as impracticable, Hirsch applied the enactment to his own congregation in Frankfurt, by breaking away from the main community. The move was supported by the pious Mayer Amschel Rothschild of the famous family of financiers, but opposed by Seligman Bamberger, a rabbinical scholar and leader.

Use of the organ became a major issue that divided Orthodox from Reform congregations and, although banned by Hirsch, his synagogue did have a professionally conducted choir, and he preached in German. That was also the language in which he composed his commentary to the Pentateuch and other writings. He was a nationalist who did not regard statehood as an end in itself, a view that strongly influenced the Agudat Yisrael party founded after his death.

Second only to Hirsch as leader of Modern Orthodoxy, Israel (or Azriel) Hildesheimer (1820-89) spoke especially to the intelligentsia. While in Hungary, he became a controversial figure by founding a yeshivah in which he taught secular subjects, after which he established a Rabbinical Seminary in Berlin. He directed it for 16 years on the principle that Orthodoxy was compatible with the scientific study of Jewish sources, thereby fighting the Haskalah with its own weapon of enlightenment.

In 1878 a conference was held in Berlin to decide the fate of the Balkan countries in South East Europe, and Disraeli, representing Britain, was one delegate who helped attain rights for minority citizens. The Roumanian government, however, managed to evade its responsibility, and then condoned violent anti-Semitic excesses. Two decades prior to these events, but in the same reactionary atmosphere, the Malbim became chief rabbi in the Roumanian capital of Bucharest.

### The Malbim and Moses Montefiore

The Malbim, an acrostic for Meir Loeb ben Jehiel Michael (1809-79), was recognised as a prodigy even before marrying at 14 (although divorced shortly afterwards). No one was a greater critic of the Reform movement, especially after a synod in Brunswick (1844) that abrogated marital and dietary laws. The Malbim accused synod members of destroying their communities, while Hirsch abandoned all hope of a united Jewish community, by adopting a secessionist policy.

Matters reached a peak when, following Reform accusations, the Malbim was imprisoned by the Roumanian authorities, and only released on condition that he leave the country. The accusations were of disloyalty and of impeding assimilation by insisting on adherence to the dietary laws. He became somewhat of a wanderer, because his candour and uncompromising nature prevented him from staying long in any one community. Even Hassidim, who were numerous in Roumania, were numbered among his critics.

The Malbim's lasting fame and popularity rest mainly on his Biblical commentary, in which he proved that traditional explanations were merely the text's plain meaning. Using linguistic rules, the unity of the Written and Oral law was thereby vindicated. Because of his opposition to the Reform Movement, the Roumanian Prime Minister described the Malbim as ignorant and an opponent of progress. In England, by contrast, Sir Moses Montefiore (1784-1885), who was also Orthodox and a critic of the Reform, was knighted by Queen Victoria. He was the first Jew to be so honored.

Montefiore was recognised as both the outstanding leader of Anglo- Jewry and the representative of persecuted Jews throughout the world. Retiring from business at 40, he devoted the rest of his long life to philanthropy. He lived to be 101 and the first of his many travels was to Damascus where, in 1840, the medieval blood libel was revived. He also journeyed to Morocco and Moscow, and as a strong advocate of a Jewish settlement in the Holy Land, made the last of his seven visits there aged ninety. The first neighborhoods built outside the protective walls of Jerusalem bear his name, for he was the founder of the modern part of the city. He encouraged the expansion of housing facilities for residents of the "Old *Yishuv*" whose spiritual wealth he admired, while attempting to alleviate their material poverty.

It was Montefiore who successfully intervened for the Malbim's release from prison, but it was on behalf of oppressed Russian Jewry that his diplomacy was most needed.

### Russian Jewry - 1725 - 1825

The basis of the Russian empire was laid by Peter the Great, whose death in 1725 was followed by a period of decline that lasted almost four decades. During this period, among Peter's successors were his widow Catherine I (once a Lithuanian maidservant), his niece Anna (vindictive and unchaste) and daughter Elizabeth, under each of whom the Jews were expelled from the heart of the country. With Catherine II, Russia progressed from eclipse to become the chief continental power of Europe, but the empress herself became an outspoken reactionary after the French

Revolution. In foreign policy she was decidedly imperialistic, for when Poland was partitioned out of existence in 1772, 1793 and 1795, Russia took more territory than either Prussia or Austria, making it the country with the largest concentration of Jews in the world.

Catherine died in 1796 and was succeeded by her heir Paul I. When it became apparent that he was insane, he was murdered and followed by his son, Alexander I. But whoever wore the crown after the annexation of Polish territory, regarded the Jews as a problem that required a solution. When the accent was placed on assimilation, Jews were allowed to attend schools and universities, and to move from restricted areas to where they could serve as colonising elements. The situation changed dramatically when Alexander was succeeded by his brother Nicholas I in 1825, for whereas the former began as a liberal and ended as a reactionary, the latter was a reactionary throughout his reign. Because he was naturally intolerant, there was never a question of whether the Jews were to suffer, but merely to what degree.

## *The reigns of Nicholas I and Alexander II*

Prior to the 30-year reign of Nicholas I (1825-55), Jews had been excused national service in return for an annual sum, whereas in 1827 he ordained that they continue to pay, but serve in the army also. Jews were both conscripted and literally kidnapped from the street to become soldiers for 25 years in abject conditions. Boys aged 12 and younger were herded like cattle and sent to distant parts of Russia, to be raised by peasants until they could be distributed among different units. Many of these cantonists, as they were called, either died on the way or were killed resisting conversion.

Although Jews had always been restricted to the former Polish territory in an attempt to keep them out of Russia proper, the actual term Pale, as a designation of regions where they were allowed to live, was not used until the reign of Nicholas. He created colonies for Jews throughout the wilderness of Russia to reduce their numbers, but like the Israelites in ancient Egypt, the more they were afflicted, the more they multiplied. Nicholas uprooted Jewish communities and deported them by foot, sometimes from farms into cities, and sometimes from cities into rural areas. Matters reached a climax with the Expatriation Law of 1838, which deprived 50,000 families of homes and livelihood.

Protest meetings were held inside and outside Russia, attended by Jew and Gentile alike. When Sir Moses Montefiore travelled to Moscow to personally intercede with the Czar, he was told that Russian Jews were different from other Jews, because they were Orthodox and believed in the Talmud. Regarded as the source of backwardness, the Talmud came under attack by the government from without, aided by missionaries, and by Maskilim from within.

By this time, Russia had succeeded Germany as the center of the Jewish Enlightenment, and working in co-operation with the government, Maskilim were to be found in every city of the Pale. Even in Vilna, the center of Lithuanian Orthodoxy, they established a Reform synagogue (1847).

German-born Max Lilienthal (d. 1882) was invited by the Russian government to supervise schools that were in effect anti-Talmud establishments. He was unsuccessful because even he came to realise that the government's real intention was to lead the pupils to Christianity. Emigrating to America, he became a founder of the Reform movement there and served as rabbi in Cincinnati. To produce more rabbis like Lilienthal, Russian Maskilim set up special seminaries that were none too successful.

The last years of Nicholas' reign were particularly brutal, as full use was made of the dreaded secret police and blood libel allegations against the Jews were renewed. In foreign policy, Nicholas led Russia into the disastrous Crimean War (1853-56), the immediate cause of which was a dispute with France over holy places in Jerusalem. In a wider context, it involved Anglo-Russian rivalry for the spoils of a decaying Turkey, the "sick man" of Europe. The accession of Alexander II (1855-81) at a time of military setbacks led to negotiations and the end of the conflict.

Following the war, Alexander instituted a program of internal reforms, the most important of which was the emancipation of the serfs in 1861, while Jews benefited during his reign from the abolition of the cantonist system and opportunities for higher education.

There were some revolutionaries, however, for whom Alexander's reforms were not sufficient, and included in their ranks were nihilists dedicated to destroying social institutions. Assassination was one of their means, and Alexander was one of their victims. With him died any hope for a tolerant society.

## The Reigns of Alexander III and Nicholas II

Alexander III, who reigned between 1881-94, was limited both in education and outlook. Following his father's murder, he suppressed revolutionary activities and liberal thought, and subjected minorities to Russification. His encouragement of the persecution of the Jews led to their being murdered and robbed on a scale witnessed nowhere else. From this period, the word pogrom entered the English language, defined as an "organised persecution and massacre, especially of Jews in Russia."

The "Black Hundreds," the scourge of the affliction, were self-styled "Genuine Russians" dedicated to attacking the Constitution and the Jews, whom they saw as the natural supporters of constitutional reform. So well did they do their work of spreading terror that they sent a shudder throughout the civilised world, resulting in the organisation of mass protest meetings. In Paris one such meeting was presided over by the author Victor Hugo, and attended by representatives of the Protestant and Catholic clergy. In Russia itself, however, another great writer, Leo Tolstoy, remained silent.

Of particular infamy was Nicholas Ignatiev, the interior Minister responsible for promulgating, in May 1882, a set of "temporary measures" that remained in force until 1917. These "May Laws," as they became known, further restricted Jewish settlement. Jews living outside the Pale were driven back, the Pale was made smaller and within the Pale itself there were expulsions from villages. Official government anti-Semitic policy further expressed itself in such diverse ways as limiting the number of places to Jewish students in institutes of learning, offering generous inducements to apostates and publishing the *Protocols of the Learned Elders of Zion*. These forgeries spread the lie of an international Jewish conspiracy to rule the world and have since been translated into many languages, including Arabic. The Russians anticipated the concept of Judenrein and attempted to make their country free of Jews in the following way: one third to emigrate, one third to embrace Christianity and one third to die of starvation. In the following years, Russia did force millions of Jews to emigrate and many died of starvation, but the attempt at mass conversion failed.

In 1894 Nicholas II, the last Czar came to the throne. If anything, restrictions were even more rigorously enforced and mob incitement further increased. Blood libels were followed by riots, and the Black Hundreds, encouraged by the government, carried out massacres. Even by the barbarous standards of Russian pogroms, the one committed at Kishinev in 1903 stands out. The body of a dead Christian boy was found and the murder automatically attributed to the Jews, even though it was later proved that the murderers were the boy's own relatives. The pogrom began on the last day of Passover, which corresponded with Easter Sunday, and lasted for three days, during which time many Jews were dragged from their hiding places and put cruelly to death. Apart from the dead and the wounded, synagogues and Torah scrolls were desecrated and property was looted or destroyed. On the third day, the army was belatedly commanded to restore order.

In 1905, following an abortive revolutionary attempt, there was another bloody massacre, and in 1910 a Jewish laborer, Mendel Belis, was put on trial for ritual murder. He was acquitted after two years for lack of evidence, but suspicion and discredit remained on him and all Jews. Some of the worst pogroms were perpetrated in places where Jews were like their Russian neighbors in every respect, except in the eyes of the law. The pogroms were a catalyst in making Russia's Jews realise that their future lay elsewhere, and the desire to emigrate seized all sections of the community.

Between 1881, the year of the first pogrom, and World War I (1914) over two million Jews made America their new home, but even so, numbers in Russia and

Eastern Europe did not decline. The natural population increase was merely transferred.

## The American Scene

In 1861, two decades before the mass emigration, some 22 million Russian serfs were freed by decree of the Czar. In the same year, a civil war broke out in America, that would take four years to free some 6 million negro slaves. In that conflict, the Northern States (The Union) were led by Abraham Lincoln, whose Emancipation Proclamation, later ratified by the 13th amendment, brought slavery to an end. (Although if Lincoln could have preserved the Union without freeing the slaves, he would have done so.)

The Southern States (the Confederacy) were led by Jefferson Davis, who appointed a close friend to a succession of high posts. This was Judah P. Benjamin (d. 1884) who was the most prominent Jew in the Civil War, but unfortunately, also the most unpopular in the South, where he became a scapegoat for military setbacks. In the north, Uriah Phillips (d. 1862) was a one-time commodore in the U.S. Navy, and although too old to fight in the war, he deserves mention for his important role in the abolition of flogging. In lesser positions, whether on or off the field of battle, Jews were to be found on both sides.

During one stage in the conflict, Ulysses Grant, general of the Union army, issued an order expelling all Jews from the Department of the Tennessee, in an attempt to halt cotton speculation. Lincoln earned the gratitude of all American Jews by promptly rescinding the order.

After the war, the North experienced a financial boom that enabled many German Jews to establish commercial enterprises, including department stores founded by former peddlers, some of which developed into the largest in the world. German Jews were the most prominent section of the community, because of the estimated 400,000 Jews in America at the time of the Civil War, they formed the majority. But whatever the country of origin, assimilation and intermarriage posed the most serious threat to American Jewry, just as in the colonial period, Jewish identity seldom survived the third generation.

Typical of the times was the Gratz family in Philadelphia, noted for its philanthropy and communal leadership, but many of whose members had intermarried. Atypical of the times was Rebecca Gratz (d.1869) who refused to follow their example and remained a spinster all her life. She devoted that life to helping others, especially in the field of Jewish education, and such was her reputation that through a mutual friend it reached Sir Walter Scott in England, who it is commonly accepted, used her as the model for Rebecca in *Ivanhoe*.

As in Germany, so in America to where it was transplanted, the Reform

Movement aided rather than checked the defection from Judaism. Max Nordau, a follower of Herzl, referred to Reform temples as "churches without a cross."

But with the mass immigration from Eastern Europe, the entire structure of the community changed. If in 1880 over 90 per cent of the country's 200 synagogues were Reform, by 1890, some 60 per cent of 533 synagogues were Orthodox. Yet Americanization also affected Orthodoxy, because as successive generations moved up the social scale, their religious allegiance often weakened, making them potential recruits for the various dissident movements.

The situation improved with the introduction of Jewish day schools, but not until the years 1933-51, with the immigration of important rabbis and scholars, would American Jewry enjoy a new vitality.

At the time of the Eastern European influx, New York was the center of the garment industry, in which the majority of immigrants found employment. Conditions however were intolerable - a 16-hour day in small, dirty and unventilated "sweat-shops," often located in the employer's dwelling. Few maintained Sabbath observance in the face of such pressures. These were the so-called "Dark Ages" in American municipal history, when the worst slums in the country were to be found in New York. Many Jews took the lead in demanding improvement in working conditions, often as a first step to involvement in politics.

One who took the plight of the refugees to heart, doing her best to ameliorate their suffering, was the poetess Emma Lazarus (1849-87). In the process, her own Jewish consciousness was aroused, inspiring her to write in defence of Judaism. The invitation to all who are hungry and in need found in the Passover liturgy finds an echo in her sonnet inscribed on the pedestal of the Statue of Liberty: "Give me your tired and your poor."

However, if conditions for the refugees in the "Golden Land" were hard, they could be even harsher for those who were ideologically motivated to make the Holy Land their destination.

### The Return to Zion

Despite the fact that the first return to Zion in the modern period was a religious one, all religious Jews agreed that full national restoration should be a divine process. The first to openly proclaim that redemption might also depend on human effort were two rabbis, Judah Alkalai (1798-1878) who lived in Jerusalem, and Zevi Hirsch Kalischer (1795-1874) in Prussia. Both were criticised either on religious or security grounds, because the new settlements they advocated would be vulnerable to attack.

Kalischer influenced Moses Hess (1812-75) to become the first assimilated Jew to turn to Zion. A friend of Marx and Engels, his socialist views are reflected in his book *Rome and Jerusalem*. He wrote that in their own homeland, the Jews would serve not so much as a spiritual but more as a political light to the Gentiles. The writings of these three precursors of modern Zionism did not produce immediate results, because in their time there was a measure of optimism about integrating Jews into society. More notice was taken after the year 1881, when Russian liberals and revolutionaries who maintained silence in the ensuing pogroms, disillusioned many Jews. One such disillusioned intellectual was Leon Pinsker (1821-91) who had studied law but realised that because he was a Jew, he would never be allowed to practise. Consequently he engaged in medicine. In a pamphlet entitled *Auto Emancipation*, following the first pogrom, he wrote that anti-Semitism was a psycho-pathological phenomenon, and not a social one. He concluded that as long as Jews were everywhere guests and nowhere hosts, everywhere a minority and nowhere a majority, they would always be vulnerable, for no matter how much they tried to be like their Gentile neighbors, they would never gain acceptance. Pinsker called on western Jews to help their co-religionists in Eastern Europe find a suitable homeland, not necessarily in the land of Israel.

## *Hovevei Zion and Bilu*

In the same year that Auto Emancipation was published (1882) and, due to the same circumstances, the *Hovevei Zion* (Lovers of Zion) movement was born. Its members advocated emigration to the Land of Israel, where alone the abnormal life of the Diaspora could be brought to an end. Because they provided Pinsker with most of his support, he became their leader and made Eretz Yisrael the focus of his aspirations.

Putting ideals into practice, groups of Hovevei Zion made *Aliyah*. (The last word of the Hebrew Bible, "and let him go up" namely to Jerusalem, comes from the same root.) A like-minded organisation composed mainly of university students called Bilu (a Hebrew acronym of the biblical verse "House of Jacob, come and let us go up") emigrated about the same time. From the very beginning the newcomers encountered difficulties. The land was ravaged by centuries of neglect and many were struck down by malaria. Not surprisingly many left, but those who remained were supported by Baron Edmond de Rothschild (d. 1934) even though the bureaucracy associated with his patronage often aroused resentment.

In all there were five main waves of emigration that brought Jews into the country in modern times, the first two between Russian pogroms and World War I. The first Aliyah (1882-1903, consisting of some 25,000 immigrants) saw the establishment of several important settlements, such as Zichron Yaakov, Israel's foremost wine-producing center, Hadera, established in the midst of malaria ridden swamps but today a prosperous city, Atlit, founded in 1903, which later became an experimental agricultural station and Kfar Saba, today an important administrative and cultural center.

The best known settlement of the Second Aliya (1904-14, consisting of some 40,000 immigrants) is Tel Aviv, founded in 1909 as a garden suburb of Jaffa. Degania A, founded the same year, became the first Jewish settlement on the Jordan's east bank, and Beer Yaakov, on the coastal plain, is today a center for yeshivot and educational institutions.

The language used in the schools and public buildings that these early pioneers built was Hebrew and, consciously or not, they were laying the foundations of a future Jewish state. Whether they were going about the task the best way became a matter of fierce debate.

### Herzl and Zionism

The word Zionist was first coined in 1886 to describe anyone who supported a Jewish national home in Zion, an idea that aroused immediate support or opposition among Jews and Gentiles alike. Neither group was homogeneous, with the Zionists divided between those who adopted a practical or political viewpoint.

The practical Zionists, who were the majority, argued that building up the land should take priority over seeking international recognition, whereas political Zionists adopted the contrary view. For the political Zionists, the achievements of the early settlers were too limited, too slow and too dependent on corrupt Turkish officials. Their first objective was to obtain a legal document or charter, acknowledging Jewish rights to the land, and full scale immigration would follow. The leading figure of political Zionism and of the Zionist movement itself was Theodore Herzl. Herzl (1860-1904) is a prime example of an assimilated Jew shocked out of complacency. When young, he attended the liberal temple in his native Budapest, before moving with his family to Vienna. After obtaining a doctorate in law, he turned to journalism and play writing. From 1891-5 he served as the Paris correspondent of a leading Viennese newspaper, in which capacity he reported the trial of Alfred Dreyfus, a Jewish officer convicted of passing on army secrets to the Germans. In 1894 Dreyfus was sentenced to imprisonment on Devil's Island, and although the charge was fabricated, it took until 1906 and much public protest before he was reinstated. Herzl heard the crowd shout "Death to the Jews" when Dreyfus was publicly humiliated, but it is accepted that his conversion to Zionism began earlier, as a reaction to anti-Semitism in Germany. Even before the Dreyfus affair, he had rejected conversion, and the spectacle of anti-Semitism in Paris, the home of emancipation, only served to convince him that his people needed their own homeland.

Herzl returned to Vienna, where he put forward his views in a book called *Der*

*Judenstaat* (The Jewish State). Unwittingly, he reiterated many of Pinsker's arguments, but without distinguishing between Eastern and Western Jews. The book's warm reception encouraged Herzl to organise and preside over, in 1897, the first in a series of Zionist conferences. The conference even had its own flag, a blue Star of David between two blue stripes on a white background, inspired by the traditional color and design of the tallit or prayer shawl. Herzl received special acclaim from the masses in Eastern Europe, precisely because he was a "Western" Jew who had returned to his people, and was spoken of in royal and messianic terms that he did little to discourage. The image of royalty was enhanced when Herzl met the Pope, the Kaiser, the Sultan of Turkey and other leaders to win support for his scheme. 1903, the year of the Kishinev pogrom, made the need for a haven more urgent than ever and he would have accepted the British offer of Uganda, if not for violent opposition within the movement.

The controversy contributed to Herzl's early death at 44, and split the Zionist movement.

### Zionist Factions and Counter Factions

Zionism without Zion was a feasible concept for those prepared to accept Uganda as an immediate sanctuary for the Russian refugees. They were called Territorial Zionists, and were led by the English author Israel Zangwill (d. 1926). When the Uganda offer was rejected, he left the Zionist movement to found the Jewish Territorial Organisation, with the aim of creating a homeland wherever possible.

Another author known as Ahad HaAm, pen name for Asher Ginsberg (d. 1927) led the cultural Zionists. Living mostly in Odessa, he was the son of a Hassid, who rebelled against his Orthodox upbringing, to become a devotee of the enlightenment and an agnostic. Even so, he remained sufficiently attached to the ethical ideas of Judaism to recognise the identity crisis for his generation. For him and his followers, Uganda could never replace Zion, the spiritual center of world Jewry.

To illustrate the fragmentation of the Zionist movement, one of the strongest critics of Cultural Zionism was Max Nordau (d. 1927) a physician, philosopher and thinker, who was Herzl's right hand man and a key figure at Zionist congresses. But Nordau in turn was criticised for his estrangement from Judaism, a charge often levelled against the Zionist movement in general. (As two examples, Nordau himself married a Protestant, and Herzl's only son became an apostate.)

To provide the movement with religious content, the Mizrachi party was established in Vilna in 1902. An abbreviation of *merkaz ruhani*, meaning spiritual center, the Mizrachi's founders included Jacob Reines and Samuel Mohilever, among other rabbis. Despite criticism for associating with secular Zionism, the

Mizrachi quickly gained wide support in Eastern Europe and established an educational network during the period of the Mandate. (In 1956 the Mizrachi changed its name to Mafdal – an acronym short for National Religious Party - when it merged with a sister, religious-Labour orientated movement.)

### Agudat Yisroel and the Hafetz Hayyim

Far from being a faction of Zionism, the Agudat Yisroel party was established in Poland in 1912 to counter both Zionism and Reform. Its members were fully aware that Russian Jewry needed a haven, but thought a sovereign state premature, and looked on Herzl as the latest false messiah. Being pragmatists however, the Agudists would give the Zionist movement de facto recognition in the 1930's by working to obtain immigration certificates to the Holy Land. Later still, after the establishment of the state, it would participate in coalition governments.

To protest the Aguda's acknowledgement of Zionism, some of its members broke away in 1935 to form the *Neturei Karta* (an Aramaic expression meaning Guardians of the City.) Centered mainly in Jerusalem, to this day the Neturei Karta regards the establishment of a secular Jewish state in the Holy Land as a sin, undeserving of recognition.

Although a founder of Agudat Yisroel, the influence of Israel Meir HaCohen (1838-1933) was such that he transcends any single party or faction. Better known as the Hafetz Hayyim, after the name of a book he wrote on the laws of slander, his humility and integrity became legendary, even in his lifetime. His best known work is the *Mishnah Berurah*, a commentary on the first part of the Shulchan Aruch that established him as a leading authority. His concern for every Jew led him to compose a guide for Jewish soldiers, women and other specific groups.

Recognised as the undisputed spiritual leader of his generation, students were attracted to his hometown of Radin, in Lithuania from different countries, automatically establishing it as a center of learning. Aware of the universal importance of religious study, he established a central fund for all yeshivot.

The Hafetz Hayyim was 76 years when World War I broke out, and when he died 19 years later, in 1933, Germany was on the way to embroiling mankind in a second, and even greater carnage. The two major conflicts would dramatically effect the history of civilization.

### The First World War (1914-18)

In 1914 the heir to the Austro-Hungarian Empire was assassinated in Sarajevo (in present day Yugoslavia) by a Serbian nationalist. As a consequence of open alliances and secret pacts, the local conflict developed into a European war, but eventually it became a global one, involving 32 nations. In a wider context, the First World War had its origins in 19th century territorial and economic rivalry between imperialist powers, leading to Germany, Austria-Hungary and Turkey on one side, opposed by England, France and Russia on the other.

Germany declared war on Russia on the first of August, which in 1914 corresponded to the Ninth of Av, a day long associated with disasters and suffering. The German-Russian front included the densely populated Pale of Settlement, and as cities changed hands, both sides treated the Jews as enemies. Accusations were often brought by Poles, who were aware that if found guilty, after perfunctory trials, the accused faced the death penalty. The Russian government, regarding the Jews as a danger to national security, forced them deep into the interior.

On the Western Front, it was not long before fighting became bogged down in trench warfare, with appalling losses on both sides. On the initiative of Winston Churchill, in 1915, Britain attempted to open a new front by forcing the Dardanelles, a strait that separates the Black Sea from the Mediterranean, and take Constantinople. The attempt failed, and losses on the Gallipoli Peninsula were particularly heavy.

### The Zion Mule Corps and Nili

Taking part in the campaign were 650 men of a detachment known as the Zion Mule Corps. It was founded by Ze'ev Jabotinsky (d. 1940) and Joseph Trumpeldor (d. 1920) in Egypt, where many young Jews who had left Eretz Yisrael found refuge, and were willing to fight for the British. Both men wanted a Jewish legion, but the British limited the idea to a Jewish transport unit, which was disbanded after the Gallipoli campaign. A first step, however, had been taken in Anglo-Zionist co-operation, and the Jewish legion was formed in 1917, with some who had served in the Mule Corps.

A few Jews inside Eretz Yisroel co-operated with the British by forming a spy ring that supplied vital information about Ottoman troop movements. The group called itself Nili (a Hebrew acronym of the biblical verse "The eternal One of Israel will not lie") and its leader was an agronomist of genius called Aaron Aaronsohn. He was one of the few to escape when the organisation was discovered in 1917, but neither he nor other survivors received aid from the Yishuv, as the Jewish community prior to the state was called. Firstly, Aaronsohn was unpopular because of his antipathy towards Socialism, and secondly, the Yishuv feared collective punishment from the Turkish authorities, having in mind the fate of the Armenians.

The Armenians, like the Jews, were often persecuted and discriminated against by the Turks because of their religion, but nevertheless played an important economic role. There was a hostile policy against them prior to the war, but shortly

## PERSPECTIVE OF HISTORY - THE NINTH OF AV

**The Mishnah (Ta'anit 4:6) telescopes history by linking tragic events in different eras, such as the destruction of the First and the Second Temples, through a common date: the Ninth of Av (Tisha be'Av in Hebrew). The same date also provides an historical pattern for later periods.**

| YEAR | EVENTS THAT OCCURRED ON THE NINTH OF AV |
|------|------------------------------------------|
| 1290 | Corresponding in the Gregorian calendar to July 18, it was decreed that all Jews should leave England. Consequently, some 16,000 left a little over three months later. |
| 1306 | In 1306 the fast of Av was postponed from the Sabbath to the following day (July 22), when some 100,000 Jews were expelled from France. |
| 1492 | Some 200,000 Jews were expelled from Spain, one of the most successful Diaspora communities ever to exist. The diagram illustrates the main routes taken by the exiles in search of refuge. |

| YEAR | EVENTS THAT OCCURRED ON THE NINTH OF AV |
|------|------------------------------------------|
| 1555 | Corresponding to July 12, the Jews of Rome and environs were forced into a ghetto. (It was not abolished until 1870, then the last ghetto in Western Europe). |
| 1626 | On the Ninth of Av the false messiah Shabbatai Zevi was born. His fraudulant claims and act of apostosy had a detrimental effect, both during and after his life time. |
| 1648 | Massacre of 3,000 Jews in Constantine, Poland, during the Chmielnicki uprising. |
| 1670 | Some 4,000 Jews were expelled from Vienna. (Fifty of the richest were invited to settle in Berlin, forming the basis of its Jewish community). |
| 1914 | Germany declared war on Russia, leading to World War I. During the first global conflict, hundreds of Jewish communities were destroyed. |
| 1929 | Arab provocation against Jews praying at the Western Wall on the Ninth of Av, developed into a full scale pogrom that spread from Jerusalem to other cities. A total of 133 Jews were murdered and more than 300 wounded. |
| 1941 | On July 31, Heydrich was ordered to carry out the Final Solution and the next night, as his instructions were being put into effect, the Fast of Av began. Many German "Actions" were planned to coincide with the fast. |

The Book of Zachariah (8:19), prophecies that in the future, the fast of Av, together with other fast days, "Shall become times of joy and gladness."

after its outbreak, they suffered their greatest single disaster, when the Turks accused them of supporting the Russian enemy. The entire population was deported, and in the process an estimated 600,000 Armenians died, or were massacred en route. The Turkish example of attempting genocide during the confusion of conflict was not lost on its ally, Germany, in the next war.

During World War I, rumors of Berlin's support for a Jewish national home, although unfounded, were nevertheless then credible. In London, the government adopted the idea as official policy.

## Contradictory Promises

It was British policy to foment unrest among minorities in the Ottoman Empire and then win them over to its own cause, especially when control of the Suez Canal was at stake. And if, as a consequence, ambiguous or contradictory statements were issued, and promises made that were later regretted, everything was subordinate to the overriding objective of winning the war.

To win Arab support, Sir Henry McMahon, Britain's High Commissioner in Egypt wrote a letter to Hussein, the Sheriff of Mecca, promising support for future Arab independence in return for an Arab revolt against the Turks. It broke out in 1916, with T. E. Lawrence, better known as Lawrence of Arabia, serving as a British liaison officer. At the same time, Sir Mark Sykes and Georges-Picot, representing Britain and France, divided up post-war spheres of influence in the Arab world. Eretz Yisrael would be under Allied joint rule, but later Britain would want the country for itself, as a strategic buffer adjoining Egypt.

In 1916, when Lloyd George became Britain's Prime Minister, the war situation was critical and would get worse. On land, troop losses were disastrous, while at sea German submarines alone were capable of deciding the outcome of the conflict. It was, in fact, unrestricted German submarine warfare that determined America's entry into the war. By the time it did so, in April 1917, Britain had only a few weeks' supply of food left. In the same year, Russian armies collapsed and a revolution overthrew the Czar, strengthening popular demand to take the country out of the war.

## The Balfour Declaration

It was in Britain's interest to keep Russia fighting as long as possible and have America mobilise as quickly as possible. It was believed that Jews in both countries could play an important role. In America, for example, in addition to Jewish public opinion, Louis Brandeis was both Zionist leader and Supreme Court Judge. In Russia, there was no stronger consideration than to overthrow the hated Czarist regime.

On November 2nd 1917, shortly after forces under General Allenby began the invasion of the Holy Land from Egypt in the south, the British Foreign Secretary Arthur Balfour sent a letter to Lord Rothschild, reminiscent of the Cyrus declaration in biblical times. It stated: "His Majesty's Government views with favour the establishment in Palestine of a national home for the Jewish people."

Behind the declaration was more than political expediency, because in common with other devout Protestants, Balfour held the Hebrew Bible, the Children of Israel and the Holy Land in high esteem. He once described the Jews as "the most gifted race that mankind has seen since the Greeks of the fifth century. They have been exiled, scattered and oppressed. If we can find them an asylum, a safe home in their native land, then the full flowering of their genius will burst forth and propagate."

Lloyd George was another student of the Bible who sympathised with the national aspirations of what he called a great and suffering nation. He was also a Welsh patriot, who was told by Dr. Chaim Weizmann that the Holy Land was a little mountainous country, about the size of Wales. Weizmann would become Israel's first president, but at the time he was a chemistry instructor at Manchester University, able to help the British war effort, and also in a position to influence the Balfour Declaration. Ironically, the most vociferous opposition came from Edwin Montagu, the only Jew in the government, who was anxious to prove that he was a loyal Englishman.

### End of the War (1918)

Five days after the Balfour Declaration was issued, the Bolsheviks in Russia under Lenin replaced Kerensky's provisional government to take control of the revolution. In 1918, the last year of a war in which Russia sustained disastrous military defeats, the Bolsheviks signed a humiliating peace treaty at Brest-Litovsk, allowing the Germans to concentrate all their forces in the west.

In the Middle East, Allenby completed the conquest of Eretz Yisrael, and included in his forces were 5,000 troops of the Jewish legion. (This was approximately half the number of Arab irregulars helping Britain at the time.) Serving with the legion were volunteers from the United States, including David Ben Gurion and Yitzhak Ben Zvi, who found refuge there together with others exiled from the Holy Land by the Turks. With the establishment of the State of Israel, they would become respectively its first Prime Minister and second President.

Although American troops landed in France in 1917, they did not engage in important action until the following year, when they ensured success in the final allied advance. After German resources were exhausted, its morale broken and the country divided by revolution, it surrendered, even though no decisive battle had ever been fought, and German troops occupied territory from France to the Crimea. This paradox would enable nationalists to claim that the army had not been defeated, but stabbed in the back by Jews.

Thus at the 11th hour of the 11th day of the 11th month, the war meant to end all wars came to an end. There are differing opinions whether the Treaty of Versailles signed in the following year was too harsh, or not harsh enough on Germany. What we do know is that the following two decades were merely a prelude to a second conflict.

### The Post War Period

The territorial adjustments that followed the Versailles Treaty redrew the map of Europe, and the new or redefined states that emerged were all bound by agreement to protect their minorities. Czechoslovakia under Thomas Masaryk was faithful to its pledge, unlike other countries such as Roumania and particularly Poland. There the League of Nations, another creation of the Versailles Treaty, was unable to prevent abuses. Poland imposed an economic boycott against Jews to encourage them to migrate, and among other discriminatory acts, they were excluded from the civil service and refused bank loans. In the course of time pogroms claimed hundreds of lives and destruction of property.

Loss of Jewish life was heavier in Russia, where a two-year civil war followed the peace treaty with Germany. The Red Army was opposed by the White (counter revolutionary) Army, which, with allied encouragement, was joined by Poles and Ukrainians. During the fighting, Jews in the Ukraine were slaughtered in their thousands. The Red Army eventually emerged victorious, inspired by Leon Trotsky, the commissar for war. Trotsky's original name was Lev Bronstein, and he was just one of many leading Jewish insurgents at the time. Others, who like him were to meet a violent death, were Rosa Luxemburg in Germany, Kurt Eisner in Bavaria and Bela Kun in Hungary. A biographical detail common to these revolutionaries is their rejection of both their religion and people.

At no time in modern history in fact did a minority of Jews fill so many prominent roles, arousing fears of a Jewish conspiracy to dominate the world. This was the theme of the scurrilous *Protocols of the Elders of Zion*, written by an agent of the Russian secret police in the 1890's, and distributed in the west after World War I. (Later, it would be utilised by Nazi and Arab propagandists.)

So strong was the association of Jews with communism, as bolshevism came to be called, that in America two acts were passed (1921 and 1924) that brought a virtual end to mass Jewish immigration. Many Jews longed to make a new home in the Holy Land, as emigration from Europe became a matter of increasing urgency. In Arab opinion, they were potential usurpers who had to be kept out by all means.

### Jewish Immigration and Arab Reaction

In 1922 the League of Nations approved the mandate for the British government to establish a Jewish national home. One year later, however, the British reneged on their trust by amputating 91,000 square kilometres of the mandated territory and creating out of it the Emirate of Transjordan, with its capital in Amman. It was given to Abdullah for his help against the Turks in the war.

Into the remaining 20,000 square kilometres between the Mediterranean and Jordan River (to be further reduced at later dates) there were three waves of immigration in the inter war years).

### From the Third to the Fifth Aliyot

While the first two waves of immigration took place before World War I, the Third Aliyah followed immediately afterwards (1919-1923, consisting of some 35,000 immigrants). Its main impetus came from the Balfour Declaration and anti-Semitism in Eastern Europe, and among other places, resulted in the founding of Ramat Gan and Ra'ananah, today both part of the Tel Aviv conurbation. Ra'ananah was founded by American Jews as a *moshav*, or smallholder cooperative, and was one of many agricultural settlements established at the time.

The rapid urban and rural development increased prosperity, which in turn attracted hundreds of thousands of Arabs from the economically stagnant surrounding Arab countries.

Paradoxically, while enjoying the benefits of Jewish immigration, Arabs simultaneously opposed it with a series of riots beginning in 1920. The instigator was El Husseini, a cousin of Jordan's King Abdullah, who fled the country, but returned under an amnesty to become Grand Mufti of Jerusalem. The appointment was made by Sir Herbert Samuel, the country's first High Commissioner, who was also the first professing Jew to reach cabinet rank. In a memorable public career, he was looked upon as a conscientious and liberal administrator, whose greatest mistake lay in failing to assess Husseini's true character. Throughout his life, Husseini's hatred of Jews motivated him to stir up violence against them, even at the cost of fleeing from criminal prosecution on various occasions. Due to him, any possibility of co-existence between Jews and Arabs disappeared.

The end of mass emigration to America in 1924 meant that more refugees turned towards Eretz Yisrael, resulting in the Fourth Aliyah (1924-28, consisting of some 90,000 immigrants). The majority came from the Polish and Eastern European middle classes, concentrating mainly in the urban areas and establishing modest enterprises. Thus in two years (1923-25) Tel Aviv's population grew from 16,000 to 40,000, while religious Jews established nearby Bnei Braq, with its network of yeshivot, schools and seminaries. When the Lithuanian community of Ponevez was destroyed in World War II, its famous yeshivah would be re-established in Bnei Braq (1944) as the largest in the country.

The success of fascism in Europe in the 1930's, especially in Nazi Germany with its policy of annexation, led to ever larger numbers of refugees seeking safety in Eretz Yisrael. This in turn led to Arab protest riots, inevitably instigated by Husseini. Such was the background to the Fifth Aliyah (1929-39) and although 225,000 entered the country, 20,000 left due to the harsh conditions. Settlements damaged during the 1929 riots were renewed, and the cultural contribution of the German immigrants affected the character of the entire country.

However, not all refugees from Germany found safety in Eretz Yisrael. Many, including scientists, went to America, the best-known of whom was the physicist Albert Einstein (1879-1956) the father of the theory of relativity.

In 1929, Britain's second Labour government under Ramsay Macdonald came to power, with little sympathy for the Balfour Declaration and Jewish national aspirations. When the Arab riots spread from Jerusalem to Haifa, with massacres in Hebron and Safed, the new government reacted predictably with a new White Paper that suspended Jewish immigration and land purchase. The Jews responded with "illegal" immigration or "Aliyah *Beit*," increasing settlements with the overnight construction of stockades with watchtowers. They acted in the knowledge that not those who entered the country were breaking the law, but rather the authorities who had reneged on the League of Nations mandate.

### The Country's First Chief Rabbi

The country's chief rabbi at the time was Abraham Isaac HaCohen Kook (1865-1935) who was the first to fill the position when it was created in 1921. To the degree that he had welcomed the Balfour Declaration, so he was disappointed as the British went back on their commitments. He reminded British officials of their divine task, as he put it, to establish a Jewish homeland and stated in a public speech that Britain would cease to be a great power if it failed to do so. Seeing in the return to Zion the beginning of national redemption, he was nevertheless critical of the Zionist movement for its secularism.

The leader of religious nationalists, Rav Kook was also accepted as a man of saintly compassion and keen intellect by the non-religious, whose standard of observance he was continuously trying to raise. He was mostly criticised, in fact, by Agudat Yisroel and leaders of the "Old Yishuv" who refused to recognise the authority of the chief rabbinate. A yeshivah established by Rav Kook in Jerusalem stressed the centrality of the Holy Land in Judaism, but in 1936, a year after his death, that land witnessed a new and more violent wave of Arab rioting. As a consequence, a commission headed by Lord Peel visited the country and recommended that it be divided between the disputing parties.

Jewish reaction to the rioting was organised defence, but the Peel recommendations split the leadership.

## Defence and Dissention

The first attempts at organised Jewish defence were made in the early 1900's, by an association of watchmen known in Hebrew as *ha-Shomer*. They guarded new settlements, but after World War I were prevented by the British from bearing arms. Similarly, during the 1920 riots, Jabotinsky's attempt to organise defence was thwarted by the British, who jailed and released him following widespread protests, and then banished him from the country. The riots proved to the Jewish community that it could only rely on itself for protection, and so the *Haganah* (meaning defence) came into being. Under the auspices of the *Histadrut*, or Labour Federation, its activities were necessarily clandestine because the British were officially responsible for security.

Haganah members volunteered for Orde Wingate's special Night Squads during the 1936-39 riots. Wingate was a British officer raised on the Bible, which he believed to be the moral foundation of mankind. Known by the Jews as *ha-Yedid* (the Friend), his Night Squads used darkness and every other surprise tactic to inflict heavy casualties on the Mufti's rebels. Wingate's pro-Jewish sentiment, very much the exception among Mandatory officials, caused them no little embarrassment, and he was sent out of the country, never to return. He died in a plane crash over Burma in 1944.

Non-Socialist members of the Haganah, coming mainly from the Revisionist youth wing called Betar, broke away in 1931 to form their own defence organisation called Etzel, or the Irgun, both shortened forms of *Irgun Z'vai Leumi* (National Military Organisation.) At first, Etzel retaliated against Arab attacks, but later included British targets, to the embarrassment of Weizmann and others who were dedicated to placating Arab and British alike. The Haganah would not be above handing over Etzel members to the British, or dealing with them themselves.

Just as Etzel broke away from the Haganah so, in 1940, Abraham Stern and a group of followers left Etzel, in protest against a war-time truce with the British. The new organisation was called Lehi or the Stern Group, which fought until disbanded in 1948.

In 1935 the Zionist Organisation itself was weakened by dissension when Jabotinsky, foremost advocate of a maximalist approach to a Jewish homeland, rejected the softer approach of the Zionist Organisation and automatically rejected the Peel commission's recommendation of partition. In contrast, the Zionist Organisation that he abandoned approved the plan as a basis for further talks. Most Arabs rejected it out of hand.

## *The Rome-Berlin Axis*

On the principle of my enemy's enemy is my friend, the Arabs were a natural ally of the fascist Rome-Berlin Axis formed in 1936. If Great Britain was one common foe, then the arch enemy was the Jew, who according to the Arabs wanted to take away their land, and according to the Germans wanted to control the world. For this reason, both repudiated the partition plan, because it would provide the Jews with a power base from where they could either acquire more territory or spread their 'domination.' The Arabs looked upon the British, authors of the Balfour Declaration, as patrons of the Jews, which is why during the 1936 -39 fighting they attacked both. Many of their weapons, among other means of support, were provided by the Axis powers who took on the role of protector.

The background to the Rome-Berlin Axis began in the 1920's, when Mussolini became dictator of Italy. His methods included the use of secret police and fascist militia to eliminate opposition, control the press and suspend parliamentary government. Mussolini was greatly admired by Adolf Hitler, who copied the same methods to become dictator of Germany in 1933. Both were demagogues who sought to rectify the 'injustices' of the Versailles Peace Treaty, playing on the fear of communism and demanding living space for their expanding populations. Both also, as champions of the Arab cause, were hosts to the Grand Mufti of Jerusalem, who collaborated by broadcasting Nazi propaganda during the war, and enlisting Moslems for the German army.

The major difference between Hitler and Mussolini, is that whereas the former was anti-Semitic (in terms of gross understatement), the latter actually counted Jews among close friends and supporters. The situation changed with the Rome-Berlin alliance, when Mussolini ceased to be Hitler's mentor and instead became his subordinate. Consequently, Italy was forced to adopt German anti-Semitic legislation, including the infamous Nuremberg Laws. According to these laws, formulated at a Nazi party congress in 1935, German Jews were forbidden to marry non-Jews and were deprived of civil rights that were graded for those of mixed descent. For introducing the Nuremberg Laws, Hitler received praise from all parts of the Arab world and beyond.

Norway's fascist leader, Vidkun Quisling, actually helped Germany conquer and rule over his own country, hence the dictionary definition of the word "quisling" as traitor. But in truth, countries like Poland, Hungary, Roumania and even to a lesser degree England and America, all had their quislings, willing to accept Germany's policy of anti-Semitism. The situation was not without paradox because the Arabs applauded anti-Semitism although they themselves were Semites and even though it encouraged Jewish emigration to the Holy Land. At one stage, German and Zionist officials worked together for that emigration; one party to the negotiations did not want the Jews, whereas the other tried to save them. Arlosoroff, the chief Zionist negotiator, was murdered on the Tel Aviv beach by unidentified assassins in 1933.

## The Refugee Problem

During the 1930's, England and France adopted an appeasement policy towards German violations of the Versailles Peace Treaty, which in turn invited further aggression. Hitler's reoccupation of the Rhineland (1936) was followed by the annexation of Austria (1938) exposing that country's 200,000 Jews to German brutality. To focus the world's attention on the situation, Herschel Grynszpan, whose parents were among thousands of stateless Jews trapped between Germany and Poland, killed a German diplomat in Paris. The incident provided an excuse for widespread attacks throughout Germany and Austria against Jews, resulting in 30,000 being sent to concentration camps and hundreds of synagogues either destroyed or damaged. *Kristallnacht* (night of broken glass, Nov. 10 - 11) marked a turning point in Nazi treatment of Jews.

At Evian, a resort on Lake Geneva, United States President Roosevelt arranged an international conference on refugees. Naive (Evian spelt backwards) is the best adjective to describe anyone who expected a positive outcome, because none of the 31 countries represented, with the exception of Dominica, were prepared to raise their woefully inadequate immigration quotas. Hitler was thereby sent a clear message that he could deal with the Jews as he wished, simply because no one cared.

1938, the same year as the annexation of Austria, Kristallnacht and the Evian Conference, also witnessed the Munich Pact, which exposed the bankruptcy of British and French appeasement. Submitting to Hitler's demands without even consulting the Czechs to whom it belonged, Chamberlain and Daladier gave him the Sudetenland. This prompted Churchill to observe that Chamberlain had preferred dishonor to war, but would have both. War came a step closer when, in the following year, German troops entered Bohemia and Moravia, the remaining parts of Czechoslovakia, without resistance. With every new conquest, the refugee problem became more acute, but Britain was determined to appease the Arabs hardly less than the Germans. The 1939 White Paper was the final betrayal of the Balfour Declaration. At a time when millions of Jews needed to be saved, 75,000 would be allowed into the land of Israel over a period of five years, after which immigration would cease altogether. Land purchase was confined to the coastal plain, and so the Jews were to remain a permanent minority in their own land. Ben Gurion, the Jewish Agency Chairman declared: "We shall fight Hitler as though there were no White Paper, and fight the White Paper as though there were no Hitler."

***"Would thay my head was water, and my eyes a fount of tears, that I might weep day and night for the slain of ....my people"*** *(Jer. 8:23)*

The stages of the final Solution were well planned. The wearing of the yellow star, imposed by legislation, led in turn to humiliation, segregation, degradation, starvation,deportation and annihilation.

No one had more contempt for Chamberlain and his appeasement policy than Hitler himself, which led him to believe that an attack on Poland would also go unchallenged. He demanded the reunion of Danzig with Germany, thereby once again claiming to put right the injustices of the Versailles Treaty. Germany attacked Poland on September 1st, 1939. This time after initial hesitation England and France did not acquiesce, and two days later, the Second World War began.

## The Second World War and the Holocaust

During the six years of the war, some 70 nations became involved, of which, by 1942, the main antagonists were the axis forces of Germany, Italy and Japan, opposed by the allied armies of Britain, Russia and America. At one critical stage, after the fall of France in 1940, Britain stood alone, but fortunately for the civilised world, Winston Churchill came to office in the same year, and proved to be the greatest wartime Prime Minister in British history.

Only the English Channel saved England from the fate that overtook the rest of Europe, for in the first stage of the war no country could withstand the German *Blitzkrieg* (Lightning War). This new type of warfare relied on a deadly combination of air power and mobile armored units, and in 1941 it was used in a surprise attack against Russia. For the two previous years, a non-aggression pact between Germany and Russia had been observed, enabling the two powers to divide Poland among themselves. It had also allowed Germany to concentrate its forces on a single front in the west and enabled Russia to rearm on a large scale.

Hitler's enemies were graded. In the west, he would have preferred England to remain neutral. Eastern European countries, especially Poland and Russia, whose populations were anyway considered inferior, needed conquering to provide living space for Germans, to root out communism, and to kill Jews, who were mostly concentrated in the east. The war against the Jews, which was given first priority, was fought for no reason other than to destroy them. Genocide was not to be the means to an end, but an end in itself. It is true that Hitler used anti-Semitism to come to power, but it is more accurate to say he came to power to destroy the Jews.

Others in the past, such as Czarist Russia, had considered genocide, but lacked either the means or the will to carry it through. Hitler, more than anyone in history, had the will, 20th century technology gave him the means and the chaos of war provided the opportunity. He also gained the support of the German people, or at least their tacit approval, through intimidation and indoctrination. Conscience and morality were considered degrading fallacies and, to achieve racial purity, every cruel and violent act was justified. The practice of conscience and morality, by contrast, as well as peace and consideration, were integral parts of biblical teaching, making Hitler's war against the Jews no less a war against Judaism. Ranged against

## THE STATISTICS OF GENOCIDE (1939-45)

| Country | Initial population | Estimated number of victims: 5,860.000 | Estimated number of survivors: 3,937.000 |
|---|---|---|---|
| Chechos-lovakia | 207,260 | 149,150 (72%) | 58,110 (28%) |
| France | 359,000 | 77,320 (22%) | 559,500 (75%) |
| Germany Austria | 751,000 | 191,500 (25%) | 272,680 (78%) |
| Greece | 77,380 | 67,000 (87%) | 10,380 (13%) |
| Hungary | 825,000 | 569,000 (69%) | 256,000 (31%) |
| Italy | 44,500 | 7,680 (17%) | 36,820 (83%) |
| Lithuania | 168,000 | 191,500 (78%) | 272,680 (25%) |
| Belgium Netherlands Luxemburg | 209,200 | 130,850 (63%) | 78,350 (37%) |
| Poland | 3,300,000 | 3,000,000 (90%) | 300,000 (10%) |
| Romania | 609,000 | 287,500 (47%) | 322,000 (53%) |
| Russia Estonia Latvia (Not all Russia was occupied) | 3,116,000 | 1,173.500 (38%) | 1,942.500 (62%) |
| Yugoslavia | 78,000 | 63,000 (80%) | 15,680 (20%) |
| Bulgaria | 50,000 | No victims | |
| Denmark | 7,800 | 60 victims | |
| Finland | 2,000 | 7 victims | |
| Norway | 1,700 | 762 victims | |

**Legend**
♦ represents 10,000 Holocaust victim
♦ represents 10,000 Holocaust survivors

the prophetic ideal of a heaven on earth was the German threat of hell on earth, and there was no room for the co-existence of both teachings.

Genocide, an integral part of that earthly hell, was to be achieved by the segregation, degradation and annihilation of the Jewish people, in three distinct stages. In the first six years of the third Reich, between coming to power and going to war (1933-39), Jews were segregated and degraded by discriminatory legislation throughout Germany and its annexed territories. Emigration or suicide were the only means of escaping the nightmare of daily existence. The eight concentration camps set up in the first phase were increased to more than 30 principal ones in the second, between the outbreak of war and the invasion of Russia (1939-41). Segregation and degradation were extended to occupied countries and taken a stage further with the establishment of ghettos, where death by starvation and disease was common. Not frequent enough, however, for the Germans, who introduced mass killings in the third stage mainly by shootings and gas chambers.

### *The Ghetto*

Ghettos were established to crowd together the maximum number of Jews in the minimum amount of space for the sole purpose of weakening and demoralising them prior to deportation to the camps. They were therefore always close to means of rail transport. Approximately 50 ghettos were set up, of which the largest and most minutely chronicled was in Warsaw. Behind its walls some half million Jews lived in intolerable conditions, with a density of ten to a room common. Privacy was impossible, sanitation deplorable, winter cold unbearable (especially for those who lived in the street) and starvation ever present. With resistance to disease minimal, an epidemic in 1940 claimed 43,000 lives, proving that the ghetto itself was an efficient method of extermination.

Whenever possible, the Germans coerced the Jews themselves to participate in their own destruction, from managing the ghettos to working in the crematoria. Thus in each ghetto they appointed a special council or *Judenrat*, whose task at first was to supervise daily life, confiscate valuables, pay fines or ransoms and select manual workers. By degrees, in the final phase, they were expected to supply victims for the death camps, and it was during this stage that Adam Czerniakow, head of the Warsaw Judenrat, committed suicide. The councils worked in co-operation with the Germans, but not necessary in collaboration, for often they tried to delay or minimise the implementation of orders. By offering a twelve-hour day for a plate of soup, there was hope that ghetto inhabitants might be allowed to survive as slave labor.

To enforce their decisions, the Judenrat were assisted by Jewish Police armed with truncheons. Some of the police were apostates, and in Warsaw the police chief was a convert to Catholicism. To encourage enrollment, they were given a larger food ration and were exempt from forced labor, but when the ghettos were finally liquidated, the members of both the Judenrat and the Jewish police shared the general fate.

### *The Final Solution*

Even before the war, Hitler spoke in public speeches about the annihilation of European Jewry, which was later referred to by German officials as the "final solution." The final solution took on new proportions as German troops, advancing into Eastern Poland and Russia in 1941, were accompanied by *Einsatzgruppen*. These were four special killing squads, each composed of up to 1,000 members, attached to the four main invasion armies. Their victims numbered perhaps a million, killed mainly in forests near cities and towns like Babi Yar in Kiev, Ponary in Vilna and the Ninth Fort in Kovno. Sometimes the Jews had to dig their own graves, but often they were shot at the edge of anti-tank ditches, while children in orphanages, residents of old age homes and hospital patients were shot on the spot.

The Einsatzgruppen operated with the knowledge and sometimes the co-operation of the German army, yet in time their methods received official disapproval, because the continuous murder of men, women and children began to have a disturbing effect on the executioners. Gassing was therefore developed as an alternative and so, in Russia and the Ukraine, mobile gas units painted like ambulances, accounted for tens of thousands of victims. Even so progress was too slow, and thus in January 1942, a conference was held in the Berlin suburb of Wannsee to address the problem.

The conference of some 15 high officials was convened by Reinard Heydrich, known as the Hangman of Europe, and deputy chief of the secret police under Himmler. In a single afternoon, with time for lunch and cocktails, the bureaucratic machinery was set up for the annihilation of 11 million Jews, including those of Great Britain and the neutral countries of Spain, Switzerland and Ireland. Adolf Eichmann, soon to be promoted and personally supervise the deaths of millions, took notes of the conference. (He escaped to Argentina after the war, where he was captured by Israeli agents, brought to Jerusalem for trial and executed in 1962.) Heydrich was assassinated four months after the conference, and in retaliation, an entire Czech village was destroyed. In his memory, the destruction of Polish Jewry was called Operation Heydrich.

In December 1941, Japan attacked American and British possessions in the Pacific, thereby extending the conflict to the Far East. Germany had previously signed a military alliance with Japan, which it was now obliged to honor by declaring war on America and thereby ensuring its own defeat. Paradoxically, the liberation of Europe was hastened in the eastern theatre of war, during a five minute bombing spell in the Pacific (June 6th 1942). In those five minutes American dive bombers destroyed a large Japanese battle fleet, ending the threat of invasion in the Pacific and allowing America to concentrate all its might against Germany. In the same year, British and Russian forces began to turn the tide of war inexorably in favor of the allies, making the Germans all the more determined to destroy the Jews. To this end, extermination camps were exploited to the full.

### Extermination Camps

About the time of the Wannsee conference, six extermination camps were set up in Eastern Europe, where the greatest numbers of Jews were concentrated and local populations offered least protest. (By contrast, the Norwegians and Danes exhibited great courage and initiative in saving Jews, and the Dutch held a general strike as a mark of identification.) The six extermination camps were Chelmno, Belzec, Sobibor, Treblinka, Majdanek and Auschwitz. (Auschwitz was both a concentration and extermination camp, the latter being called Auschwitz II or Birkenau.) The victims were brought to the camps from all over Europe in freight or cattle cars, with as many as 200 crowded into one wagon, and sometimes complete deportations were killed on arrival.

At Auschwitz, 20,000 could be killed and burnt daily, by using Zyklon B gas, first developed to exterminate rats. The *Sonder-kommandos*, who worked the crematoria, eventually shared the general fate.

When selections were held on the arrival ramp, the younger and stronger were chosen to live a little longer. Henceforth they were not known by their names, but by a number tattooed on their arms. Aside from routine sadistic shootings and beatings, death might come from overwork, starvation or disease, and in winter from freezing, because the clogs and thin-stripped uniforms were completely inadequate against the cold. The overcrowded barracks contained three-tiered bunks covered with rotten straw, and so, without sanitation, typhus and dysentery were common. Even in this inferno there was a hierarchy of prisoners, distinguished by the color of the triangle sewn on their uniforms. The star worn by the Jews placed them on the bottom rung.

Block 24 in Auschwitz was where medical experiments were performed, involving sterilisation and the amputation of limbs, without anaesthetics and in the name of science. Among the many doctors involved, the most notorious was Josef Mengele, who specialised in experiments on twins.

### Revolt

When those remaining in the ghettos learnt that the deported were not taken to the east for resettlement as promised, but to extermination camps, they chose to rebel.

Warsaw was the first ghetto in which it was decided that to die fighting for honor was the best way to be remembered, and the decision was put into effect on the eve of Passover 1943, when the Germans attempted to deport the remaining 60,000 Jews.

Rabbi Menahem Zemba (1883-1943), one of Warsaw's leading scholars and a member of the city's rabbinical council was a foremost advocate of the uprising. His writings acquired great renown, and regarding Eretz Yisroel, he disapproved of any partition plan. His last ruling was to give full religious approval to armed resistance, and although Catholic circles offered him refuge, he chose to remain in the ghetto.

Mordechai Anieliwicz, who led the revolt, represented a younger leadership typical of the ghettos; in every one in which Jews resisted, they did so with few weapons and without significant support from non-Jewish organisations. Survivors of the uprisings, especially from the Cracow, Kovno and Vilna ghettos, formed partisan units that hampered the enemy by derailing trains and ambushing patrols.

After the liquidation of the ghettos there were fewer transports, and so prisoners employed in the concentration camp system realised that they themselves would be the next victims. This was a major factor behind the rebellions that took place in Treblinka (August 1943), Sobibor (October 1943), Auschwitz (October 1944) and Chelmno (January 1945). In Auschwitz, one of the crematoria was damaged and three guards killed, but 250 camp prisoners died in the reprisals. Following the uprisings in Sobibor and Treblinka there were mass escapes, but most were caught, and Sobibor was closed soon afterwards. By the autumn of 1944, Auschwitz was in the process of liquidation, as the last mass deportations it received were from Hungary.

### Hungarian Jewry and Gentile Reaction

By the beginning of 1944, air warfare had turned overwhelmingly in favor of the Allies, allowing an invasion force to cross the English Channel on June 6th and land in Northern France. Even before the Normandy invasion, when it became clear that Germany would lose the war, its satellite states did everything possible to loosen their ties. This applied not least to Hungary, and to forestall plans of independence, German troops entered the country in March 1944. Adolf Eichmann visited Budapest soon afterwards to implement the final solution, and consequently ghettos with Judenrats were established and deportations begun. In Central Hungary, Jews were forced to enter into ghettos on Passover (a year after the Warsaw Ghetto rebellion) with half an hour's notice and, by July 1944, 437,000 had been sent to Auschwitz. By October rail transportation was no longer available and Auschwitz was reaching its end, so the Germans marched 27,000 men women and children over 100 miles to Austria, inflicting a high death rate. Apart from the ghetto in Budapest, Hungary was *Judenrein*. Death marches, particularly from concentration camps in the wake of retreating German armies, became a common feature in the last stage of the war, resulting in a estimated quarter of a million deaths.

Whatever the exact figure, it would have been greater if not for Raoul Wallenberg, a young Swedish diplomat, who saved hundreds from the Hungarian death march by giving them improvised Swedish citizenship. He rescued 33,000 more by housing them in rented buildings that he made part of the Swedish legation, and when Eichmann ordered the liquidation of the Budapest ghetto, Wallenberg convinced the officer in command to disobey. Following his example, the Swiss, Spanish, Portuguese and Vatican legations performed acts of rescue, but no one saved Wallenberg from the Russians when they entered Budapest in 1945. He went to meet them, and was never heard from again.

The industrialist Oscar Schindler was another righteous gentile who saved Jews during the war. A factory he set up in Cracow employed thousands who would otherwise have perished, and later he transferred his Schindler Juden, as they were called, to Czechoslovakia, where they were eventually liberated. But the examples of Wallenberg and Schindler stand out as exceptions to the general rule of indifference. The Russians rewarded Wallenberg's humanitarianism by incarcerating him for the rest of his life, while the Catholic Schindler put to shame Pius XII, head of the Catholic Church. The only time the latter criticised Germany was after the war, when Hitler had committed suicide. Churchill alone supported Jewish appeals to destroy the Auschwitz crematoria, but even so they were bombed only once by mistake. The intended target was a nearby military installation that was attacked ten times. The question of where was God during the Holocaust conceals the more pertinent question of where was man?

### Eretz Yisrael During World War II

At the height of German military success, it seemed that the Jews in Eretz Yisrael might share the fate of their brothers and sisters in Europe. By the first half of 1941, the Germans were in Greece and Crete, while Rommel's Afrika Korps, having driven the British from Libya was threatening Egypt. To the north, Syria and Lebanon were under the control of the Vichy French government, a tool in the hands of the Germans whose planes used Syrian airfields. A Russian defeat also seemed imminent, and so Eretz Yisrael, threatened from north and south, was in the middle of a German pincers movement.

While plans were being made for a suicide stand on Mount Carmel, similar to the one on Masada during the Roman period, Isaac Herzog (1888-1959) the country's

## THE TWO MAIN CENTERS FOR JEWISH REFUGEES IN MODERN TIMES

Immigrants from Russia, about the turn of the twentieth century, pass the Statue of Liberty as they enter America where most Jews found refuge.

Holocaust survivors reach the shore of the Promised Land, despite official British policy.

second Chief Rabbi declared that there would be no third destruction. A former Chief Rabbi of Ireland, he moved to Jerusalem, where he argued the Jewish claim for a homeland before various commissions. He stated that the Jewish genius is essentially religious, and the Holy Land is where this genius finds true expression. During the war Herzog appealed to world leaders on behalf of his people, and after Germany's defeat, travelled to Europe, to retrieve orphans placed in convents, or with non-Jewish families.

Others from the Yishuv who assisted survivors in Europe were members of the Jewish Brigade. At first, the only British concession towards the Jews of the Yishuv who wanted to participate in the conflict was to train them in partisan warfare. But on Churchill's intervention, the Jewish Brigade was formed as part of the British army. With its own flag and insignia the Brigade served in North Africa, Italy and other parts of Europe.

The Jewish Brigade was formed in 1944, the same year in which 32 volunteers from the Yishuv were parachuted into occupied Europe, to collect information and bring out survivors. Six were captured and executed, including the writer Enzo Sereni and the poetess Hannah Szenes.

A year later the most costly war ever in human life and suffering came to an end. With six million, or a third of their number murdered, the Jews suffered proportionately more than any other people.

Hitler was dead, but his spirit lived on in different countries. In Poland, 350 camp survivors were murdered in pogroms because, like ghosts from the grave, they had returned to claim their homes. In the Arab world Hitler was criticised, not for attempting genocide, but for leaving the task unfinished. There were anti-Jewish riots in Egypt and Libya, while in Syria there were mass arrests and synagogues were destroyed. General Patton, the American military governor of Bavaria, showed more leniency towards conquered Nazis than liberated Jews. The latter lived in the same camps and wore the same clothes as when prisoners, and if necessary, Patton added barbed wire to keep them enclosed. Conditions improved when he was relieved of his position. Allied policy was based on the principle that Germany was needed by the western powers in the cold war against Russia, whereas the displaced persons were nowhere wanted. Even so, to confirm their faith in the future, those confined to the displaced persons camps produced the highest birth rate of any Jewish community.

## American Orthodoxy

With the Eastern European center irretrievably lost, and in 1945 a future Jewish state anything but inevitable, America assumed the role in the Jewish world that a millennium earlier had belonged to Babylon. Three personalities who helped

American Jewry to flourish were rabbis - Aharon Kotler (d. 1962), Moses Feinstein (d. 1986) and Menachem Mendel Schneerson (d. 1993).

The lives of the first two were remarkably similar, for Rabbis Kotler and Feinstein were both born in Russia and recognised early as child prodigies. In manhood, they emigrated to America, where R. Kotler established a yeshivah in Lakewood, New Jersey, and R. Feinstein taught in New York. Both were elected to positions of prominence in the Orthodox Jewish world, especially in the field of education, and in their writings both compiled responsa and elucidated Talmudic tractates.

But whereas R. Kotler is best remembered as a prominent yeshivah head, whose original teaching methods attracted students from all over the world, R. Feinstein became recognized as the leading halachic authority of his time. As such, he answered thousands of queries from all over the world, that included questions involving science and technology, and problems connected with Jewish life under communist rule. R. Kotler died in his 70th year, while R. Feinstein lived to become a nonagenarian. The ripple effect of the leadership and influence of such personalities revolutionized American Jewish higher education, reversing the trend towards assimilation

R. Schneerson provided a different style of leadership. Better known as the Lubavitcher Rebbe, he inherited the position of leader of the Chabad hassidic movement after his father-in-law died in 1950. To New York, the movement's center since 1939, came the prominent and the ordinary, many from other continents but all seeking guidance, assistance or encouragement, in every possible form.

In addition to the spoken and written word, addressed to both individuals and to large audiences, he sent emissaries world wide, to unite remote communities and reach out to isolated individuals.

## *Prelude to Rebirth*

Less than a month before Germany's unconditional surrender in May 1945, Roosevelt suddenly died and was succeeded in the presidency of the United States by Truman. In July of the same year Churchill lost the British general election to the Labour party, and Truman asked the new government to allow 100,000 displaced persons immediate entry into Eretz Yisrael. The request was flatly rejected by Ernest Bevin, Britain's Foreign Secretary, who had little sympathy for Jews and whose bankrupt country depended on Arab oil.

The Jews responded with illegal immigration, but most of the ships were intercepted and the passengers interred in Cyprus. In a vicious circle of events, the Jews demolished British radio and radar installations and in a single night in June 1946, destroyed 11 bridges that connected the country with neighboring states. On the last Sabbath of the same month, known as Black Sabbath, the British retaliated with thousands of arrests and confiscated a cache of arms. A few weeks later the Irgun blew up a wing of the King David Hotel in Jerusalem that housed the British administration. The casualty list of 86 (mainly British) could have been avoided if an earlier telephone warning had not been ignored.

Thereafter, the Mandate became increasingly unworkable. In April 1947 four members of the Irgun were hanged in Acco jail, and two other resistance fighters committed suicide while awaiting the death penalty in Jerusalem. In the following month, the Irgun freed 251 prisoners from the Acco jail in a daring raid, but three of those who carried it out were captured and hanged. The hanging in retaliation of two British sergeants (one of whom had a Jewish mother) was not the final act in a chain of violence, for some anti-Semitic policemen, calling themselves the British League, set off an explosive device in Jerusalem's city center, causing much damage to life and property.

In an atmosphere of near anarchy, the British placed barbed wire around their administrative buildings in Jerusalem, and the complex became known derisively as Bevingrad, recalling the heavy defence of Stalingrad in World War II. Bevin himself referred the problem to the United Nations, the successor of the League of Nations, which acting on the advice of a special committee, voted for partition (November 29th 1947). The Jews accepted the recommendation, because it offered an immediate haven for those still living in camps. Crowds danced in the streets of Tel Aviv and a day later the Jews of Rome danced under the Arch of Titus. The Arabs opposed the creation of a Jewish state whatever its size, because they felt they were being made to compensate for Hitler's crimes.

After the United Nations vote, the British declared that they would evacuate the country by the end of six months. During that period, Jewish and Arab irregular forces prepared for the inevitable war to follow by jockeying for position. Arabs destroyed two Jewish settlements, and in retaliation, combined Irgun and Lehi forces attacked the nearby Arab village of Deir Yassin, close to a suburb of Jerusalem. Subsequent fighting was heavy and according to accounts some Arab guerrillas disguised themselves as women, while others were killed after resistance ended. News of the incident, invariably referred to as a massacre, spread quickly to other Arab villages, encouraging many to flee.

To avenge Deir Yassin, the Arabs attacked a convoy on its way to the Hadassah Hospital, situated on the Mt. Scopus enclave in Jerusalem. Some 80 doctors, nurses and students were murdered, and although the British had a military post less than 200 yards from the ambush, they ignored repeated appeals to intervene.

The Irgun conquered Jaffa during the last stage of the mandate. The Arabs had used its port to bring reinforcements into the country, and from the minaret of its

## CHANGING BOUNDARIES

The country's boundaries have changed throughout history, but never so frequently as in the 20 th century, as illustrated by three examples.

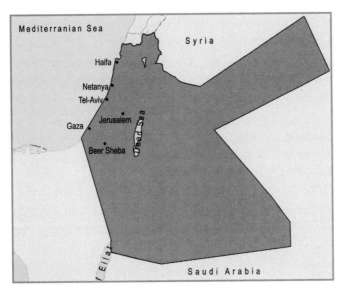

The borders entrusted by the League of Nations to the British, in 1921 within which the Jewish National Home was to be created.

Only one year later, however, the entire area east of the Jordan was detracted, in order to create the Emirate of Transjordan.

Map of the 1949 Armistice Agreement. It was accepted by the Arabs only because of their inability to destroy Israel.

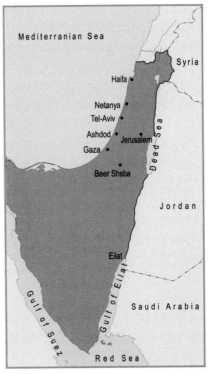

The borders after 1967 War. They correspond to natural features and are more defensible, but they have been in a stage of contraction ever since.

mosque had shot into adjacent Tel Aviv. After months of heavy fighting, Jaffa was eventually captured by literally burrowing from house to house.

Although the Jews gained Jaffa, they lost the agricultural complex of Gush Etzion, of strategic importance because it overlooked the Jerusalem-Hebron highway. The four religious settlements which it comprised fell to Jordan's Arab Legion, which took survivors into captivity. Some months previously, reinforcements of 35 fighters had tried to reach the settlement, but just short of their destination were surrounded and killed by hundreds of Arabs, who mutilated their bodies.

Two days after Gush Etzion fell, the mandate ended.

## The War of Independence (1948-49)

Following the Holocaust, the United Nations vote that gave the Jews their homeland was possibly one of the few examples of conscience deciding a resolution. The resolution was moreover supported both by Russia and America, engaged in a cold war when they could hardly agree about anything.

Above all it provided an unprecedented historical example of a people regaining statehood after almost two thousand years of exile. On May 15, 1948, the last British soldier left the country, and the State of Israel was born. Minutes afterwards, President Truman gave its provisional government de facto recognition, and a few days later, Russia recognised it de jure.

The Arabs attempted to destroy the new state as five armies (those of Jordan, Egypt, Syria, Lebanon and Iraq) attacked simultaneously. All were equipped with modern weapons and Saudi Arabian units were attached to the Egyptian army. Local guerrilla forces and German instructors, who were either invited or found their own way to the Middle East, also participated.

A British arms embargo had prevented Israel from being properly equipped for the first part of the war, and so it met the Arab invaders with a miscellany of weapons that contained virtually no artillery or armored vehicles. Its Air Force consisted of light, single engine planes. During this first stage of the war, the I.D.F. (Israel Defence Force) was in effect a partisan army, using Molotov Cocktails to fight tanks. Rearguard action was successful enough to allow arms and fighter planes purchased abroad to arrive and halt the Egyptian advance in the south on May 29th. Israel incurred its most serious loss the previous day, when the Arab legion captured Jerusalem's Jewish Quarter. The mainly Orthodox population was taken captive, synagogues were destroyed, and tombstones from the Mount of Olives were used by the Jordanians to build latrines. Abdullah, King of Jordan, then incorporated the Old City of Jerusalem and the entire West Bank into his own kingdom, contrary to a United Nations resolution.

## MODERN DESCENDANTS OF THE MACCABEES

A soldier of the Jewish Brigade in the African Desert during World War II.

Jewish soldiers after liberating the Western Wall in 1967.

A truce that began on June 11th allowed the Jews to receive vital arms from Czechoslovakia, whereas Britain, the Arab's main supplier, was prevented by the Security Council from exporting weapons into the area. Ten days into the truce, a ship commissioned by the Irgun, called the Altalena (Jabotinsky's pen name), containing arms and immigrants, was sunk off the shore of Tel Aviv in an operation led by Y. Rabin on Ben Gurion's orders. Efforts were being made to unite the different resistant movements into one army, and Ben Gurion considered the Irgun's claim to some of the arms a challenge to his authority. When fighting recommenced the following month, the Irgun no longer existed as a separate force.

With its new arms, the I.D.F. was transformed into a modern army forged in battle. Able to take the initiative, it captured Nazareth, Ramle and Lod with its international airport. Israel's three flying fortresses bombed Cairo and Damascus before a second truce took effect (July 19th-October 15th). By the end of the final round, Israel possessed the southern part of the country, apart from the Gaza Strip. Egypt was the first to sign an armistice agreement (February 29th 1949), followed in successive months by Lebanon, Jordan and Syria.

### Support for Israel

By the end of the War of Independence, Israel was almost bankrupt. Flooded with refugees and the need to feed and house them, the government increased taxation and issued public bonds. In 1951 Ben-Gurion flew to the United States to launch a drive for Israel bonds, and the response of American Jewry exceeded all expectations. Within six years, $250 million worth had been purchased.

The United Jewish Appeal (established in 1939) raised large sums annually to assist Israel, especially in absorbing Jewish refugees from Eastern Europe and the Arab countries. This continuous political and moral support for Israel from American Jewry has been a significant factor in the state's struggle for survival.

### Internal Debate

As far as the Arab nations were concerned, they had lost not so much a war as the first round in Israel's struggle for existence. In effect, Israel's true war of independence has lasted ever since, with intermittent periods of non-belligerency. During these periods, fundamental questions came to the fore, all part of the ongoing debate about a religious or secular state. After the War of Independence, the debate centered around education and the enlistment of female soldiers, creating the first crises for Ben Gurion's government.

Prior to invading Israel, Arab leaders had advised Palestinians to leave the country temporarily, in order to facilitate its conquest. In addition to those who followed the advice, others were either driven out or fled from fear. Some 800,000 were involved, approximately the same number of Jews forced to leave Arab countries, with the establishment of the state. But whereas the Jewish refugees were absorbed in a comparatively short space of time, mostly in Israel, the Arabs allowed their refugees to languish in squalid camps. The camps were essential in the Arab propaganda war against Israel (waged with no little success), and in providing recruits for various terrorist organisations. If not for these reasons, Arab governments themselves could have solved the refugee problem with only a small amount of their oil revenue, and with some good will, the population exchange could have been settled by peaceful negotiation.

A major difficulty faced by refugees from Arab countries in Israel was cultural. Even by comparison with the early years of the state, the countries of their origin were backward, and secular Zionists encouraged them to believe that acclimatisation to a modern state was incongruous with loyalty to ancient traditions. The Yemenites in particular were devout, and while the Aguda and Mizrachi wanted to provide their children with a religious education, Mapai, Ben Gurion's Zionist-Socialist party, thought otherwise. A government crisis developed, and following the 1951 elections, religious schools shared equal status with secular schools in the state education system, but not before a large proportion of Yemenite and Holocaust surviving immigrants were forcibly cut off from their religious heritage.

In the following year a bill was passed that required Orthodox girls to do national, instead of military, service. The Aguda party was foremost in opposing any form of female conscription, which led Ben-Gurion to discuss the matter with the Hazon Ish, the generation's recognised authority on Jewish Law and practice.

### The Hazon Ish (1878-1953)

Hazon Ish was the pen name of R. Avraham Yeshayahu Karelitz, and the fact that Israel's Prime Minister came to him, and not vice versa, as a gesture of respect, is the more remarkable because he held no official position. Neither had he ever been ordained as a rabbi, studied in yeshivah or established one. The number of his responsa was also limited, yet everyone from the learned to the layman came to him for ruling or advice, and thousands of students looked to him as their spiritual guide.

The Hazon Ish himself, by seeking the plain meaning of any text, was the spiritual disciple of the Gaon of Vilna, and as a younger colleague of the Hafetz Hayyim, left Lithuania for the Holy Land when the latter died in 1933. After his arrival his fame spread, even to the 25,000 Jews who comprised the World War II community of Shanghai. This number included students of the famous Mir Yeshivah who had escaped from Europe to China's largest city, from where they asked when they should observe the Day of Atonement (1941). The question involved intricacies concerning the International Date Line, and required knowledge of mathematics, astronomy and Jewish sources for an answer.

Although the Hazon Ish allowed the growing of plants in water (hydroponics) during the Sabbatical Year, he challenged the ruling of the Chief Rabbinate that permitted sale and cultivation of the land. He loved the very soil of the country, but was not a Zionist, and rejected the viewpoint of the religious nationalists who sought accommodation with a secular state. There is no record of his discussion with Ben Gurion, neither was there ever a second meeting, primarily because there was no shared ideology. Whereas the Hazon Ish is remembered for his saintliness and learning, having established the contemporary halachic practice in agricultural related matters, Israel's first Prime Minister is best remembered for his strong and pragmatic leadership.

Ben Gurion led the country in one more war before he finally retired in 1963, by which time he had served (except for a year's interval) as Prime Minister and Minister of Defence for fifteen years. The end of the century and the millennium were 37 years away, but in that period the premiership would change 12 times and Israel would fight six more wars.

### The Sinai Campaign and the Six Day War

The Sinai Campaign of 1956 was fought while Ben Gurion was still premier, and comprised a series of offensives that began on October 29 and lasted eight days. It was provoked by continuous *fedayeen* (terrorist) attacks and by economic warfare, led by Egypt's Gamal Nasser, who closed the Suez Canal and the Straits of Tiran (situated respectively in the north and south of the Sinai Peninsula) to Israel's shipping. His nationalisation of the Canal also threatened the British and French oil supply route, and so those two countries, in collusion with Israel, attacked Egypt on different fronts. Israel's capture of the Sinai Peninsula was swift and devastating (4 Israeli prisoners to 6,000 Egyptians) and resulted in the reopening of the Straits of Tiran.

However America, under President Eisenhower, ensured that Israel withdrew, together with the Anglo-French forces that had managed to seize the northern part of the Suez Canal. While Nasser remained in power with his reputation enhanced, Britain's was severely damaged, and United Nation troops were stationed in Sinai to guarantee international navigation.

In 1967 Nasser replaced those troops with his own, closed the Gulf of Eilat (or Aqaba) to Israeli shipping and created a united military front of Egyptian, Jordanian, Iraqi and Syrian forces with the express intention of overthrowing Israel. Also dedicated to destroying Israel, as its covenant makes abundantly clear, was the P.L.O. (Palestine Liberation Organisation) created at an Arab summit in Cairo in 1964. Despite all these threats, the international community remained indifferent, while at home Prime Minister Eshkol lacked charisma and Yitzhak Rabin, the Chief of Staff, was temporarily incapacitated following a collapse.

With Moshe Dayan enlisted as Minister of Defence and Menahem Begin serving in a national unity government, Israel launched a pre-emptive attack on June 5, destroying the Egyptian, Syrian and Jordanian air forces within a few hours, thereby ensuring victory in a war that lasted only six days. Israel's ground forces reoccupied the Sinai Peninsula and captured the Gaza Strip, the West Bank and the Golan Heights in brilliant military operations. It would have been willing to implement U. N. resolution 242 to withdraw from territories occupied in the war, if the Arabs, in turn, had accepted Israel's right "to live in peace within secure and recognised borders."

### The War of Attrition and the Yom Kippur War

The War of Attrition (1967-70), consisted mainly of artillery duels across the Suez Canal, following Arab inability to defeat Israel in conventional battle. In addition, there were terrorist incursions by the P.L.O. from Jordan, where they formed a state within a state. The Black September, another terrorist organisation, came into being in 1970, named after the month in which Jordan's King Hussein turned his guns on the Palestinians, who threatened both the stability of his kingdom and his own life.

Thereafter, the P.L.O. under Yasser Arafat moved to Lebanon, ending that country's period of peace and prosperity.

Three years after Nasser died and was succeeded by Anwar Sadat, Egyptian forces crossed the Suez Canal, beginning the Yom Kippur War (October 6th-25th 1973). Surprised, weakened by the fast and grossly undermanned, Israeli forces were attacked at the same time by the Syrians in the north and barely managed a holding action. After a general mobilisation, Israel counter-attacked on both fronts, giving rise, in Sinai, to one of the largest tank battles in history, and a turning point in the war. Under Ariel Sharon, Israeli forces crossed the canal into Egypt, thereby trapping the Egyptian Third Army, stranded on the eastern bank. To save its client state from a crushing defeat, Russia urged a United Nations cease-fire, which resulted in resolution 338 that called for "negotiations between the parties... aimed at establishing a just and durable peace." During the war, President Nixon and Secretary of State Kissinger approved a massive American airlift, to make good Israel's losses.

After the war, an Arab oil embargo created a worldwide shortage and heavily increased prices, for which Israel was held responsible. In Israel itself, Prime Minister Golda Meir and Defence Minister Moshe Dayan were forced to resign, as part of their responsibility for over 2,600 soldiers killed in the fighting. Yitzhak Rabin and Shimon Peres respectively, took their places.

A post-script to the Yom Kippur War took place in 1976, when Arab and German hijackers forced an Air France airliner, bound from Tel Aviv for Paris, to land in the Ugandan airport of Entebbe. After the non-Jews were freed, one hundred Israelis were retained as hostages for the release of convicted terrorists, held mostly in Israel. Despite the vast distance involved, Israeli commandos were flown to and from the heavily guarded airport, bringing back the hostages in one of the greatest ever rescue operations. The United Nations was asked to condemn the action, which simultaneously struck a blow against international terrorism and raised Israel's esteem at home and abroad.

## *Peace or a Piece of Paper*

In 1977, for the first time, a right wing government broke the long held Labor monopoly on political power and took office in Israel, led by the Polish born, Yiddish speaking Menahem Begin (1913-1991) who paradoxically, was most popular with Sephardic voters who held grievances for years of discrimination under Labour governments. Such was his standing in his own party (known since 1973 as Likud), that he remained for almost 30 years its undisputed leader, despite losing eight consecutive elections. In a series of dramatic moves, Begin invited Sadat to address Israel's parliament and in the following year, the two attended a summit meeting sponsored by Jimmy Carter, at the American presidential retreat of Camp David. In the year after that (1979), a detailed agreement between Egypt and Israel was signed on the White House Lawn, in which Israel agreed to relinquish the Sinai Peninsula, including its new settlements, in return for peace with the strongest of its neighbors.

Arab reaction was unequivocal. Egypt was successively expelled from various Arab and Islamic organisations, apart from suffering economic boycott and diplomatic ostracism. In 1981, Sadat himself was murdered by militant Muslims, without being publicly mourned by a single Arab head of state or without expressions of grief even from his own people. There were millions of others, however, throughout the world, including Israel, who admired Sadat for his personal courage. R. Menahem Mendel Schneersohn, leader of the Chabad movement in New York, expressed the wish that Israel's leaders would stand up for their own country's interests with the same determination; he nevertheless opposed the Camp David Agreement.

What he and others found particularly objectionable was provision for Palestinian autonomy, which in turn would lead to a Palestinian State. Quoting the halachah, he maintained that no individual or government had the authority to relinquish any part of the Holy Land. To those who claimed that everything is permissible for the sake of peace, there was the counter argument that withdrawing to indefensible borders only invites aggression. This was true even if the Arabs did not look upon concessions as a sign of weakness, or cease proclaiming that Israel was their sworn enemy.

Within Israel itself, Rabbi Zvi Yehuda Kook (d. 1982), spoke about the government's treachery when he heard about the Camp David agreement. Son of the country's first chief rabbi, he proclaimed that biblical and historical sanctions entitled Jews to settle in their own country, making him the natural leader of Gush Emunim (the Bloc of the Faithful) whose members put his teachings into practice.

Diametrically opposed to Gush Emunim was the Peace Now Movement, that believed West Bank settlements to be both illegal and an impediment to peace. Although supporting the Camp David Agreement, Peace Now opposed Begin's policy of settling the West Bank, and became exceptionally vociferous during his attempt to uproot the terrorist infrastructure in Lebanon.

## Operation Peace for Galilee and the Intifada

Having obtained a cold peace with Egypt, Israel became involved in a torrid war in Lebanon, where the P.L.O. was engaged in fighting that country's Maronite Christian community, while simultaneously attacking Jewish targets in Galilee. The P.L.O. was armed with Russian missiles and backed by Syria, whereas the Maronites were supported by Israel. In June 1982, Israel moved into Lebanon in an operation called Peace for Galilee, which as its name implies, was meant to bring peace to Israel's northern border.

Equipment captured on the ground confirmed that the P.LO. was evolving from a terror group into a fully equipped modern army. After besieging the P.L.O. in Beirut, where it was based, Israel succeeded in driving it from Lebanon altogether and, among the Arab nations where its members were dispersed, Tunisia became the new headquarters. After the P.L.O. expulsion, Maronite Christians entered the Moslem refugee camps of Sabra and Shatilla, where instead of searching out remaining terrorists, they carried out a general massacre. As the Maronite patron, Israel was condemned for the incident and domestic pressure from the political left forced Ariel Sharon to resign as Minister of Defence. The same source blamed Begin for the deaths of 600 soldiers in the war and, with his spirit broken, he retired from public life for the last nine years of his life.

Following the 1984 and 1988 elections, Israel was ruled by governments of National Unity, in which the premiership was shared, on a rotation basis, between Shimon Peres (Labour) and Yitzhak Shamir (Likud). During the first of these governments in 1987, with Shamir as Prime Minister, a new type of warfare, known as the *Intifada*, broke out, in which Arab youths armed with stones and slings attacked Israeli patrols. Ordinary citizens, especially West Bank settlers, were also the targets of stones and petrol bombs, but the many casualties did not attract the attention of the world's media, determined to portray Israel as the aggressor.

Because it is such a useful means of propaganda that cannot be defeated by conventional methods, and because it spreads fear among Israel's population by disrupting daily life, the Intifada is an indispensable tool in the hands of the P.L.O. Unlike other battles that Israel was able to conclude with an armistice, the Intifada has no end, but merely passes through different phases. If Israel takes no action, it fails to defend the security of its citizens; if it uses force to counter it, it is immediately condemned for its aggressive actions.

### *The Gulf War and the Madrid Conference*

When Begin was Prime Minister in 1981, Israeli planes destroyed a nuclear reactor that French technicians were helping to construct in Iraq. Inevitably condemned at the time, the wisdom of the operation became evident nine years later, when Iraq invaded Kuwait and sent long range missiles over Israel. The sadistic nature of Iraq's dictator, Saddam Hussein, had been proven in a previous war with Iran (1980-88), when he used poison gas to kill fellow Moslems.

A 28-nation coalition led by America opposed the invasion of Kuwait, including Arab countries that insisted on Israel's exclusion. Consequently although 39 long-range missiles fell on Israel, it was prevented from doing anything in response, but miraculously, many of the buildings destroyed were empty, and occupants of others emerged unscathed. The last missile fell on Tel Aviv only minutes before the Gulf War (1990-91) came to an end in an overwhelming defeat for Saddam Hussein, who wanted to link Iraq's withdrawal from Kuwait with Israel's withdrawal from the territories.

Other countries, especially Arab ones, thought likewise. Thus in the year the war ended, a conference was held in the Spanish capital of Madrid to resolve the Middle East problem. The era was a dramatic one, because the end of communist rule in Russia and East Europe the previous year marked the end of the Soviet Empire; and the reunification of Germany, divided since World War II, was symbolised by the demolition of the Berlin Wall. America and Russia were co-sponsors of the conference, which set a precedent, with bilateral talks between Israeli and Arab representatives, followed by multilateral talks in Moscow. Yet despite the fanfare with which the talks opened, they proved fruitless.

In Israel, right wing coalition members resigned from the government in fear of territorial concessions on ideological and security grounds, forcing a general election. In 1992, Rabin made a political comeback by returning to the Prime

Minister's office after a 15-year absence, and broke the eight year pattern of broad-based governments of national unity by forming a coalition with Meretz and Shas. Meretz was further to the left on the political spectrum, while Shas was an Orthodox Sephardi party with a wide educational and social program, which depended to a large extent on government backing.

Israel's left wing government was determined to come to an agreement with the Palestinians, even if it meant relying on the Arabs in the Knesset for a majority in matters that included national security, for the first time in the country's history. The agreement was eventually reached through secret talks in the Norwegian capital of Oslo.

### The Oslo Accord (1993)

Of necessity the talks were secret, because a Knesset law forbade direct contact with the P.L.O. and, away from the spotlight of the media, the results could be presented as a fait accompli, forestalling opposition. Beginning with Israeli withdrawal from the Gaza strip and Jericho area, a five year period would follow in which a Palestinian Council would work with Israel in building mutual trust, leading to a final settlement on such matters as borders, settlements and the status of Jerusalem.

Much fine print was attached to the Oslo Accord signed on the White House Lawn by Rabin, Arafat and American President Bill Clinton in 1993, but it mattered little, because even the large print was ignored. The P.L.O., for example, was required to amend its charter that calls unequivocally for Israel's destruction, but to date, despite protestations, no new version has ever been publicised. The Palestinian police force, allowed by the Accord, is in effect an army that exceeds by several thousand the number originally permitted.

Israel itself supplied the P.LO. with guns and training, in the naïve expectation that Arafat would use them to fight Hamas, another Islamic Resistance Movement. Instead, the arms were turned against the source that supplied them and so, in place of peace, Oslo ushered in a new and more violent phase of the Intifada.

It was in hope therefore and not on results that Arafat, together with Rabin and Foreign Minister Peres, was awarded that 1994 Nobel Peace Prize. The vitriolic anti-Jewish content of the Palestinian media should in itself have invalidated the prize, just as Hitler's anti-Semitism should have prevented his nomination for the same award in the 1930's. The two can be mentioned in the same breath, for both devoted their lives to fighting Jews and what one began, the other would have finished, if given the chance.

In signing the Oslo Accord, Arafat had before him the precedent of Mohammed, who made a ten year truce with the infidels of Mecca, and then broke it some two years later by taking over the city. He also had in mind the Trojan Horse tactic, because Oslo allowed him to direct terrorist operations within those borders that Arab armies had failed to penetrate from without. By regulating the intensity of the violence against Israel's citizens, Arafat was even able to topple successive governments, unwilling to deal with him effectively as the terrorist he really was, while bound by agreement to treat him as a partner for peace.

Rabin was the first Prime Minister to fall, due to an inability to curb the level of violence. After a series of anti-government demonstrations, he was in fact murdered after leaving a counter rally in Tel Aviv on November 4th 1995. Too many unanswered questions, and contradictory facts and statements, strengthen the claim that the young student convicted of the crime was merely a cover.

## The End of an Era

Rabin's funeral attracted world media coverage, but most of Israel's population, let alone the world at large, was ignorant of Rabbi Solomon Auerbach's funeral nine months earlier. Ignorant, that is, except for the estimated 300-400,000 from a broad spectrum of Jerusalem residents and others who followed the cortege and the countless more who revered his reputation and what he stood for. A scion of one of Jerusalem's great rabbinical families, Auerbach (1911-1995) was regarded as the leading halachic authority, despite the words on his headstone that speak of him only as a teacher.

His decisions reflect the latest developments in medicine and science, and are often quoted by other authors. He devoted much time to teaching, counselling, supporting orphans and visiting the sick, as well as his own writings. Apart from the individual loss, for many his death also marked the end of an era.

The end of an era for American Jewry occurred in 1993 with the passing of R. Joseph Soloveitchik, a great Talmudic scholar who was also a master of contemporary philosophy, theology and science. Heir to a great Eastern European dynasty, his great-grandfather, who bore the same name, was for a while joint head of the yeshivah of Volozhyn, while his grandfather, R. Chaim Soloveitchik ('The Brisker' 1853-1918), revolutionised Talmud study by his analytical method.

R. Soloveitchik, known affectionately as 'the Rav' in American modern Orthodox circles, of which he was the acknowledged spiritual leader, succeeded his father as head of the Talmud faculty at Yeshiva University in 1941. The prestige gained by this institution, a training-ground for potential American pulpit rabbis, which also provided an Orthodox environment for study of secular disciplines, was largely due to his influence. His writings, especially *The Lonely Man of Faith* have been constantly analysed and interpreted.

## The Turn of the Millennium

If Rabbi Soloveitchik spoke of a crisis of faith facing the individual, then by the turn of the millennium, the Jews were facing a crisis of faith on a national scale. The passing of many prominent religious leaders in a short space of time, created a vacuum that left all Jews, in a certain sense, spiritual orphans.

In addition to the spiritual crisis, at the turn of the millennium there were two other crises calling for immediate solutions. The first was demographic, because Jewish population figures are virtually the same as in 1967, meaning that for the past 40 years the natural increase has been cancelled by those who lost their Jewish identity through assimilation, a phenomenon of catastrophic proportions comparable to the Holocaust.

The other major crisis was centered around Israel's political leadership, indirectly effecting Jews throughout the world. In 1998, Israel celebrated its Jubilee Year, inviting comparison between Israel as a fledgling state and the contemporary situation. For most of the first fifteen years of statehood, David Ben-Gurion served as prime minister, and despite his faults and mistakes, which are recognized even by his admirers, he provided a strong and charismatic leadership, which is acknowledged even by his critics. These two virtues were conspicuously absent between 1995-2005, when Shimon Peres, Benjamin Netanyahu, Ehud Barak, and Ariel Sharon held the premiership in quick succession, with a shared genius of dividing the nation, instead of uniting it. In addition to failing to check the mounting number of terrorist incidents or lessen the severe economic hardships, they all lost public support because they proved at best to be mere politicians, not above involvement in public scandals, when the country needed statesmen. In particular, they lacked the ability to withstand pressure from successive American presidents, all of whom required Israel to make territorial concessions.

Another characteristic of the country's first premier, that none of his successors inherited, was his well-known zeal for biblical history. It was surely this that made him transfer the country's temporary capital of Tel Aviv to the eternal one of Jerusalem. Ehud Barak, by contrast, outdid any of his predecessors in concessions, by offering to divide Jerusalem and relinquish the Temple Mount. It should be added that whether dealing with the Palestinians or Syrians, all his offers were rejected, leading to the conclusion that the Arabs were unwilling to sign a peace treaty with Israel, irrespective of the conditions.

## September 11, 2002, and its Aftermath

Like the day when Japan attacked the American fleet at Pearl Harbor without warning in 1941, so the date 9.11.02 stands out in infamy. On that date, Muslim

## DEMOGRAPHIC CHANGES IN THE PAST ONE AND A HALF CENTURIES

| Year | 1850 | 1880 | 1900 | 1914 | 1930 | 1948 | 1967 | c. 2,000 |
|---|---|---|---|---|---|---|---|---|
| Number of Jews in the world (in millions) | 4.7 | 7.7 | 10.5 | 13.6 | 16 | 11.5 | 13.5 | 13.2 |

The diagram below shows the number of Jews c.2000 in the main population centers.

 represents 1,000,000

represents 10,000

**1 America** 5.600.000

**2 Israel** 4.700.000

**3 Canada** 600.000

**4 France** 600.000

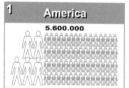
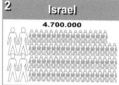
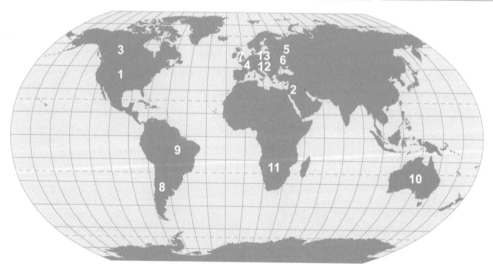

**5 Russia** 450.000

**6 Ukraine** 310.000

**7 Great Britain** 300.000

**8 Argentina** 230.000

**9 Brazil** 130.000

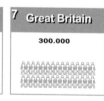

**10 Australia** 95.000

**11 South Africa** 92.000

**12 Hungary** 70.000

**13 Germany** 60.000

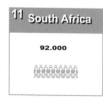

hijackers crashed two civilian jet liners into New York's multi story Twin Towers, and a third into the Pentagon, teaching the world that dealing with terrorism was not just Israel's problem. The thousands of innocent victims proved that the hijackers were not motivated by altruism, no matter how misguided, but by hate and jealousy. The Twin Towers symbolized America's technological and financial supremacy, and the Pentagon - its military might. The date was also symbolic, because it marked the eighth anniversary of the Oslo Accord, signed in Washington.

While the atrocities received world-wide condemnation, Palestinians cheered, just as they would later revere Sadam Hussein, when President George W. Bush sent American led coalition forces into Iraq, to eliminate weapons of mass destruction. Previously, Bush had sent American troops into Afghanistan, in an unsuccessful attempt to track down Osama Bin Laden, the Saudi-Arabian dissident, whose al-Qaeda terrorist organization was responsible for the Twin Tower atrocity.

Despite the fact that the Palestinians showed their contempt for both America and Israel by calling them the "big and little Satan," Bush continued the policy of his predecessors, in pressuring Israel to meet Palestinian demands, in a plan called the Road Map. The end result of the Road Map and Sharon's own Disengagement Plan was identical: Jewish settlers in the Gaza Strip and West Bank were to be forcibly evicted from their homes by Israeli troops, as a preparatory measure for the establishment of a Palestinian state to exist alongside Israel. Such a concept, however, conveniently ignores the fact that the Middle East is not Switzerland, where a canton system is viable. King Abdullah of Jordan and President Sadat of Egypt were the only two Arab leaders prepared to accept Israel's existence, and both were assassinated for their temerity. In addition, Abbu Mazzin, the new Palestinian leader after Arafat's death in 2004, is a revisionist historian who holds that the Holocaust is a myth invented to justify a Jewish state. His own intended state will leave Israel only nine miles wide at its narrowest point, at a time when Israel contains the largest number of Jews outside America.

Such is the volatile situation at the time of writing these lines, that any attempt to predict the future is not only well nigh impossible, but even foolhardy. Yet, it is clear even now, that the question of relinquishing territory is bound up with the nature of the state itself. In the Knesset, the most ardent supporters of disengagement were also the most vociferous advocates of secular legislation, an attitude reflected among the general population where in contrast, those who want a state with a Jewish content openly demonstrate against the uprooting of any settlement.

If admittedly we lack the perspective of time to judge events, in January 2003, one Israeli undoubtedly experienced the perspective of space. This was Ilan Ramon, the first Israeli astronaut, on board the ill-fated American space shuttle Columbia. Although not a particularly observant Jew on earth, in space he regarded himself

*Epilogue*

Because history is a continuous process, no final word can be written. But in order to anticipate the future, no less than to understand the past, an epilogue does enable the salient features of Jewish history to be reiterated and distinct patterns to be traced.

One outstanding feature is that in every period there are major centers of learning, where foremost scholars are looked upon as the nation's leaders. Their literary works ensure that Judaism remains at the heart of Jewish existence. More often than not, the rise and fall of empires and dynasties influence where new centers are located, and how long they survive.

It is only natural that Jewish culture flourished best in empires whose leaders were favorably disposed towards the Jews. In general, the reputation of any prominent leader can be gauged by his attitude towards the Jews. Cyrus the Great, Alexander the Great, Julius and Augustus Caesar, the first Antonine Emperors, Casimir the Great, Suleiman the Magnificent, down to Winston Churchill and religious freedom in America in modern times, are all remembered with esteem in both Jewish and world history.

Conversely, virulent anti-Semitism is a characteristic of the world's most notorious despots, including Antiochus Epiphanes, Ivan the Terrible, Joseph Stalin and Hitler. Because Jews are obliged by their religion to maintain a distinctive life style, they are the natural enemies of totalitarian regimes in every age.

In the period following Cyrus the Great, the Great Assembly brought the Bible and Prayer Book very much into their present form. Judah the Prince, who compiled the Mishnah, was a friend of Marcus Aurelius, one of Rome's noblest emperors, and Joseph Karo compiled the Shulchan Aruch during the memorable reign of Suleiman the Magnificent. All this literary output, and much more besides, is a product of the Holy Land. Even the Babylonian Talmud, although considered more authoritative than its Jerusalem counterpart, is based on the Mishnah of Eretz Yisrael, and quotes extensively the debates and rulings of its scholars.

As outlined in the body of this book, these compilations reached the Diaspora at times when Jewish existence was most threatened, thereby acting as a portable "state" which preserved and revived the dispersed communities. Thus the Jewish people, Judaism and the Holy Land share a symbiotic relationship which can be traced like a golden thread running through Jewish history.

Anti-Semitism is another recurring theme. Anti-Semites throughout the ages have been aware of what constitutes Jewish survival, and what they consequently need to undermine. Anti-Semitism follows no logical sequence - suffice to mention 20th century anti-Semitism, in which atheistic Communism, racist Nazism and fundamentalist Islam share little in common except an aversion to Jews. Communism, which denied the Jews their religion, and Nazism, which denied them their lives, both belong to the past. Not so Islamic fundamentalism, which is very much a present-day threat, and not just to Jews.

Theologically, anti-Semitism has been interpreted as a divine reminder that we are to be a nation apart. Thus Jews who negate their people, their religion or their homeland, are siding with their enemies, by substituting a gradual national demise inflicted from within for a traumatic one inflicted from without.

At the entrance to one of the blocks in the Auschwitz museum, prominence is given to the words of the American philosopher George Santayana: "The one who does not remember history is bound to live through it again." One of the many cogent lessons of Jewish history exhorts Jews to remember that their historical destiny is inextricably intertwined with their homeland. For a major part of their history, the land of Israel was their national home, where judges, priests and kings were their leaders, just as it was there that the prophets uttered their immortal words. It was there also, as we have seen, that they produced their major literary works, affecting the destiny of other nations, in addition to their own.

When not through choice, but persecution, the Jews became a minority in their own country, they nevertheless maintained a continuous presence until today, when they once more constitute a majority.

Following another discernible pattern, the ancient homeland provides once again a refuge after an overwhelming national disaster. History provides no other example of a people regaining independence after so many centuries of exile, in itself an example of the tenacity and conviction of the Jews in clinging to their faith.

If the past serves as a guide for the future, the Jews will continue to survive, despite their comparatively small numbers and their bitterly contested and coveted homeland, situated on a narrow strip of territory between the eastern Mediterranean and the desert. As observed by King Solomon long ago, "the race is not to the swift, nor the battle to the mighty," for intangible factors such as morale, motivation and above all, faith, determine who emerges victorious. From the beginning it was stressed that the Jews are not a numerically significant people, yet they still undertook their unparalleled journey into history. If they have survived until the present day, and continue to do so until the final redemption, their secret lies in their being the "People of the Book," which is the source of both the faith and precepts which have always accompanied and defined them, and which span time.

*Index*

**A**

Aaron 32, 34, 43
Abrabanel, Don Isaac 181
Abraham 11, 12, 17, 18, 20, 21 22, 23,
    24, 26, 27, 31 33, 37, 52, 55, 159,
    168
Acharonim (Later Authorities) 189
Agudat Yisrael 218
Ahab 60, 61, 62
Ahaz 64, 67
Alexander Jannai 96
Alexander the Great 86, 87, 102, 267
Alexandria 87, 88, 99, 112, 114, 151, 152
Alfasi 172, 173, 174, 178
aliyah 167, 225, 234, 235
American Orthodoxy 248
American Revolution 211
amidah 56, 85, 119
Amoraim 127, 129, 131, 132, 133, 134
Amos 59, 62, 63
Amram Gaon 147
anointing 62
anti-Semitism 76, 113, 139, 196, 197,
    214, 225, 226, 234, 237, 240, 261,
    267, 268

Antigonus 86, 87, 100
Antiochus Epiphanes 95, 267
Apocrypha 119, 127
apocrypha 206
apostasy 154, 165, 166, 201, 211, 213
appeasement 238, 240
Arab conquests 142, 145
Arafat, Yasser 144, 257, 261, 262, 265
Aramaic 20, 83, 92, 108, 113, 124,
    126, 133, 146, 147, 152, 162,
    189, 193, 228
Ark of the Covenant 33, 34, 52
Ashkenazim 192, 193
Assyrian empire 68
Av Beth Din 94

**B**

Ba'al Shem Tov 202, 203, 204, 208,
    210, 217
Babylonian academies 128, 129, 132,
    142, 147, 151, 154, 155, 159, 217
Babylonian exile 25, 71, 101
Babylonian Talmud 128, 132, 133, 159,
    268

271